'Hartman's very concise and easy-to-access book on sexuality and relationships moves its readers progressively through the issues surrounding Autism Spectrum Conditions (ASC) and associated social concepts. This book is essential reading for professionals and families alike, because it's the first if its kind to include the wider understanding of relationships, as well as sexuality. For so long those of us living with ASC have been marginalised in this regard with so little attention being given to our legitimate needs. Frankly, firmly and with sincere but gentle understanding, Hartman addresses the usual concerns of being a sexual human being (or not as the case may be) with consideration to gender and ASC. I highly recommend this book to all interested parties whose commitment to our best is their uppermost conviction.'

— Wendy Lawson, psychologist, counsellor, social worker and author of Sex, Sexuality and the Autism Spectrum

'Who knew there are so many things to consider when planning for sexuality and relationship instruction? Well, now we know. This book is an A to Z of what needs to be addressed and how to go about it in collaboration with parents. A great contribution to curricula for kids with ASD!'

— Rita Honan, PhD, RegPsychAFPsSI, BCBA-D, School of Psychology, Trinity College Dublin, Ireland

'Hartman demystifies the area of relationships and sexuality education with this clear, comprehensive and respectful "how to" manual. She maximises the potential for success by meeting every conceivable obstacle head on and providing detailed guidance and strategies that can be adapted to meet the individual person's needs. An excellent resource for teachers of pupils with ASD.'

— Mary McKenna, Special Class Teacher for children with ASD, Scoil Mhuire, Ballyboden, Ireland

'This book is gold. Anyone whose role it is to teach sexuality and relationship education to children and adolescents on the autism spectrum will find the answers to all their questions. Davida Hartman provides not only a convincing rationale for education in all aspects of sexuality, but also a wealth of straightforward and easy-to-apply teaching strategies. She includes references to the most up-to-date research in the area, and inspiring quotes from well-known ASD authors. She is reassuring, inclusive, positive and respectful. With this book on your shelf, you will be well equipped to teach a comprehensive, relevant and fun sexuality and relationship programme to this important population of young people.'

— Sarah Attwood, author of Making Sense of Sex: A Forthright Guide to Puberty, Sex *and* Relationships for People with Asperger's Syndrome

D1368374

Sexuality and Relationship Education for Children and Adolescents with Autism Spectrum Disorders

Making Sense of Sex
A Forthright Guide to Puberty, Sex and Relationships for People with Asperger's Syndrome
Sarah Attwood
Illustrated by Jonathon Powell
ISBN 978 1 84310 374 5
eISBN 978 1 84642 797 8

Asperger's Syndrome and Sexuality
From Adolescence through Adulthood
Isabelle Hénault
Foreword by Tony Attwood
ISBN 978 1 84310 189 5
eISBN 978 1 84642 235 5

Sexuality and Severe Autism
A Practical Guide for Parents, Caregivers and Health Educators
Kate E. Reynolds
ISBN 978 1 84905 327 3
eISBN 978 0 85700 666 0

Girls Growing Up on the Autism Spectrum
What Parents and Professionals Should Know About the Pre-Teen and Teenage Years
Shana Nichols
With Gina Marie Moravcik and Samara Pulver Tetenbaum
ISBN 978 1 84310 855 9
eISBN 978 1 84642 885 2

Personal Hygiene? What's That Got to Do with Me?
Pat Crissey
Illustrated by Noah Crissey
ISBN 978 1 84310 796 5
eISBN 978 1 84642 114 3

An Exceptional Children's Guide to Touch
Teaching Social and Physical Boundaries to Kids
Hunter Manasco
Illustrated by Katharine Manasco
ISBN 978 1 84905 871 1
eISBN 978 0 85700 659 2

Sexuality and Relationship Education for Children and Adolescents with Autism Spectrum Disorders

A Professional's Guide to Understanding, Preventing Issues, Supporting Sexuality and Responding to Inappropriate Behaviours

Davida Hartman

Illustrated by Kate Brangan

Jessica Kingsley *Publishers*
London and Philadelphia

First published in 2014
by Jessica Kingsley Publishers
73 Collier Street
London N1 9BE, UK
and
400 Market Street, Suite 400
Philadelphia, PA 19106, USA

www.jkp.com

Library of Congress Cataloging in Publication Data
Hartman, Davida.
 Sexuality and relationship education for children and adolescents with autism spectrum disorders : a professional's guide to understanding, preventing issues, supporting sexuality and responding to inappropriate behaviours / Davida Hartman ; illustrated by Kate Brangan.
    pages cm
Includes bibliographical references.
 ISBN 978-1-84905-385-3 (pbk. : alk. paper) -- ISBN 978-0-85700-755-1 (ebook) 1. Children with autism spectrum disorders. 2. Youth with autism spectrum disorders. 3. Sex instruction for people with mental disabilities. 4. Sex (Biology) I. Title.
 HQ54.3H37 2014
 306.7087'4--dc23
                        2013028697

British Library Cataloguing in Publication Data
A CIP catalogue record for this book is available from the British Library

ISBN 978 1 84905 385 3
eISBN 978 0 85700 755 1

Printed and bound in Great Britain

For A., M. and b.

Acknowledgements

I am grateful to the many people who have helped me with the ideas presented in this book. My deepest thanks to David Hingsburger for being so influential in both my writing and my professional practice. Thank you to Dermot Rafter for designing the UPR model for supporting challenging behaviour. Thank you also to my other colleagues in the Developmental and ASD Psychology Department (Lorraine Seery, Clodagh Power, Maeve Kavanagh, Deirdre Holden and Valerie Graham) for developing the UPR model and other behaviour management materials adapted for this book, and for being so enthusiastic and supportive of my efforts. Special thanks are due to Moira Kennedy, who provided not only expert proof-reading and advice but also kindness, generosity and support along the journey. Of course, this book couldn't have been written without my family or husband. But mostly I am grateful to the authors and advocates with ASD who share their thoughts and experiences and in doing so have contributed greatly to my understanding of both ASD and humanity, with special thanks to: Liane Holliday Willey, Wendy Lawson, Luke Jackson, Temple Grandin, Stephen Shore, Jim Sinclair, Andee Joyce, Lindsey A. Nebeker, Michael Higginbotham, Jerry Newport, Mary Newport, Elizabeth Boresow, Susan Golubock and Leah Jane Grantham.

Contents

Part III: Supporting

Part IV: Responding

Appendices

Author's Notes

The term ASD (i.e. autism spectrum disorder) is used throughout this book to cover the broad spectrum of autism spectrum disorders, including autism, Asperger's syndrome (AS) and pervasive developmental disorder (PDD). At times, the term AS is used to refer to someone who has been previously diagnosed specifically with AS.

The term 'intellectual disability' is used in this book, as opposed to 'learning difficulty' or 'learning disability', although it references the same construct.

This book is written for professionals working with children and adolescents up to 18 years of age. For ease of reading, the term 'child' or 'children' will be used throughout the book to refer to any child under the age of 18, unless they are specially referred to as an older child, adolescent, teenager or pre-teen.

Following are acronyms used in the book:

ABA – Applied Behaviour Analysis

ASD – autism spectrum disorder

AS – Asperger's syndrome

FBA – Functional Behaviour Assessment

HFA – high functioning autism

ID – intellectual disability

IEP – individual education plan

NT – neurotypical

PBS – Positive Behaviour Support

PMT – premenstrual tension

SNA – Special Needs Assistant

SRE – sexuality and relationship education

STI – sexually transmitted infection

UPSR – Understanding, Preventing, Supporting and Responding

Some of the concepts in this book may be sensitive for families from various cultural or religious backgrounds. As discussed throughout the book, sexuality and relationship education (SRE) programmes should at all times be cognisant and respectful of a family's belief system.

Part I
Understanding

1

Introduction

There is currently a gap between the need for SRE for children with ASD and its provision, with one of the main reasons cited for this being lack of suitable resources and materials. This book aims to help fill that gap. It is written for professionals working with children up to the age of 18 who have been diagnosed with ASD (encompassing the broad spectrum of autism, AS, HFA, and children with additional significant intellectual needs). It is also relevant for parents as well as those working with young adults with ASD, in particular if they experience additional learning needs.

It is widely accepted that parents should be the primary source of SRE for their children, and that it should encompass the values and beliefs of a child's family. However, as in many other areas related to ASD, parents can feel disempowered in relation to what information regarding sexuality to impart to their children, or how to go about teaching them in this area. The aim of this book, therefore, is not only to help professionals improve their own practice in relation to SRE but, more importantly, to help those professionals support parents to have the confidence and skills to become the primary sexuality educators of their children.

Sexuality and Relationship Education

The term SRE is used in this book to replace the more traditional 'sex education' due to a perception that such a programme is all about sexual intercourse (and possibly STI prevention) – which may in turn impede its implementation in organizations and homes. SRE is *not* all about sex, and any teachings about sexual intercourse are minor and included in a broader teaching curriculum that includes concepts such as identity, safety, love, intimacy and relationships (which may or may not have a sexual element).

The goals of any good SRE programme should include promoting positive and prosocial adaptive behaviours, maximizing integration, increasing self-understanding, self-esteem and self-determination, encouraging independence in making healthy sexual choices, and replacing inappropriate behaviours with more prosocial behaviours that serve the same function. The *primary* goal of SRE should be to support children in developing a healthy sexuality, i.e. the understanding that sexuality is a normal, healthy and valuable part of being human, which includes having:

- an appreciation for and understanding of one's own body
- the ability to make informed and independent decisions about one's own sexuality and sexual activity
- the ability to develop and maintain meaningful relationships
- the ability to express sexual feelings, intimacy and love in socially appropriate ways.

A good SRE programme will provide children with opportunities to learn, question and explore all of these concepts. It will also help them to understand cultural values, their families and the communities in which they live, and the law in relation to sexual behaviour, as well as to understand and accept individual difference. Unfortunately, the reality is that the majority of *typically* developing children may not receive appropriate Sexuality and Relationship Education for their needs, and there are even greater societal barriers to its provision to children with special needs. These issues will be addressed in later chapters. As a guideline, SRE has not been shown to be harmful unless it is developmentally inappropriate for the child or makes them feel bad about themselves. Research (albeit research on typically developing children) indicates that it is those with *little* information in relation to SRE who have early sexualized experiences and may not have the confidence to make safe sexual decisions, including negotiating contraception (Alford 2008). Children who have been taught an understanding of sexuality and safety issues relevant to their age and developmental level are instead provided with a platform to develop healthy, safe sexual identities and relationships.

SRE and Disability

> *The issue of sexuality cannot be separated from the issue of segregation. There is no denying that the 'differentness' of people with disability leads people to fear, and in this case the fear is based, at least partially, on attitudes towards sexuality of people with disabilities. (Hingsburger 1995, p.26)*

Historically, individuals with disabilities have been denied rights to sexuality. In contrast, modern international human rights documents acknowledge that *all* people have the right to receive knowledge about sexuality in a way that they can understand. They have the right to choose a partner, marry and have children, love and be loved, receive information in relation to sexuality and SRE, obtain the highest standard of health care available to them, express their sexuality in ways that are socially appropriate, and to pursue a satisfying, safe and pleasurable sexual life. They also have the right to be provided with *opportunities* for socializing and sexual expression. The United Nations Convention on the Rights of Persons with Disabilities (which has been ratified thus far by 119 countries) addresses many of these issues (United Nations Enable 2012).

While there has recently been a shift in the agenda in relation to sexuality and disability from one concerned with pathology and suppression to one concerned with empowerment and rights with regard to a healthy sexual identity, thinking appears to be ahead of practice and research even still. Societal beliefs regarding sexuality and disability often lead to the sexuality of individuals with disabilities being avoided, ignored or punished, and their relationships and friendships controlled. Many describe having learned about sexuality only through experiences that led to punishment or shame, a problem or a crisis that led to them viewing their own natural feelings as bad and wrong.

In 2000, Chivers and Mathieson looked at the dominant discourses impacting on sexuality and relationship curriculum development for individuals with IDs and found that typical course content focused on STIs, pregnancy and contraception, with an implied emphasis on danger and risk. Main themes that arose included: 'Sexuality has solely a biological function', 'Sex is dangerous' and 'Sex is only penetration', leaving no room for the possibility of pleasure, love, intimacy, touch or consent. In fact, research indicates that the more knowledge individuals with disabilities display in the area of sexuality, the more negative their attitude towards it (Konstantareas and Lunsky 1997), suggesting that this emphasis on danger and risk has the effect of separating sex from intimacy, and most likely further reinforcing isolation.

SRE and ASD

Since the late 1980s, things have improved dramatically for children with ASD. Early recognition and intervention are now common in developed countries. Families have more access to support and advice. Early intervention programmes focusing on behavioural approaches, joint attention and positive interactions have resulted in gains in the areas of development and communication (Howlin and Moss 2012). In addition, factors such as increased life expectancy, de-institutionalization, inclusion and the advocacy movement have all contributed to a shift in focus from exclusively early years to lifespan and adult issues such as transition planning, preparing for independent community living, employment and college. However, follow-up outcome studies show no major improvements in outcomes for adults with ASD, and still little is known about the factors within educational programmes that are likely to have the greatest impact on later progress (Howlin and Moss 2012).

What *is* known is that adults with ASD are still more likely than the general population to be isolated, unmarried and economically deprived, and to have received a poor education; and even those adults with IQ scores in the average range and above appear to be significantly disadvantaged with regard to social relationships, employment, physical and mental health and quality of life (Howlin and Moss 2012). Outcome studies indicate that fewer than half are living independently and most are highly dependent on their families (Howlin and Moss 2012). Just 15 per cent report to be now, or in the past to have been in a long-term sexual relationship or to have married, and only one quarter report having at least one friend (Howlin and Moss 2012). Adults with ASD are also more likely to experience significant mental health issues, with the presence of psychiatric disorders appearing to be independent of IQ and onset related to environmental factors such as life transitions, social isolation, loss and inadequate support (Hutton *et al.* 2008).

So how is it that, despite increased early recognition and intervention, and reported gains in communication and development during childhood, older children with ASD appear not to be successfully navigating the transitions through adolescence to adulthood?

Adolescence is the time following the beginning of puberty (i.e. when physical changes begin in the body) and is characterized by hormone variability and spurts of rapid growth. The hallmarks of adolescence include increased autonomy, independence and peer influence, the beginning of sexual relationships and the transition to work or college. For children in mainstream education it marks a time of significant change, with increased academic demands and responsibility, more teachers and less supervision. It is also a time when the pressure to 'fit in' dramatically increases, a time when many children with special needs are often left behind as the difference between them and their typically developing peers widens. Children with ASD have not only to grapple with these tasks of adolescence, but also to deal with them through the prism of ASD, including core difficulties with change itself.

Research indicates that, physically, children with ASD begin puberty at roughly the same time as their typically developing peers (Murphy and Elias 2006), although some unusual patterns of pubertal development have been reported in females with ASD (Knickmeyer *et al.* 2006). Individuals with ASD are also more likely than the general population to have epilepsy, with seizure activity reported to increase during adolescence (Robinson 2012). There are also some indications that comorbid mental health issues, including depression and anxiety disorders, are more common in adolescents with HFA than in their typically developing peers (Bellini 2006; Farrugia and Hudson 2006; Stewart *et al.* 2006).

There is currently a lack of understanding of the *developmental* and *behavioural* trajectory from early childhood into adolescence and young adulthood for individuals with ASD. Although some studies have noted a deterioration in behaviour during puberty, with females and adolescents with significant ID being primarily affected (Gilberg 1984; Knickmeyer *et al.* 2006; Lee 2004), other studies with larger sample sizes have noted that the core symptoms of ASD can either abate in adolescence and young adulthood (in particular for those individuals with no additional ID) (McGovern and Sigman 2005; Seltzer *et al.* 2004) or remain stable (Shattuck *et al.* 2007).

The results are also inconclusive from studies related to the *relationships* experienced by individuals with ASD in adolescence. Some studies have reported improved social skills and interest in social relationships, although improvements are generally only reported for those higher functioning adolescents (McGovern and Sigman 2005; Volkmar and Klin 1995), while others report continued social difficulties throughout adolescence and adulthood (e.g. Seltzer *et al.* 2003). In 2004, Orsmond, Krauss and Seltzer examined the families of over 200 adolescents and adults with ASD and reported poor participation in social and recreational activities and few positive peer relationships. Conversely, the presence of friends was predicted by younger age and better social skills, while greater participation in activities was predicted by better social skills, independence skills, maternal participation in social and recreational activities and inclusion in integrated settings while in school (Orsmond *et al.* 2004). Pre-adolescents and adolescents with ASD also report greater levels of emotional and social loneliness than their typically developing peers (Bauminger, Shulman and Agam 2003); interestingly, in this 2003 study, increases in social interaction were not found to decrease loneliness, leading one to speculate that it is the *quality* of social interactions that is important, rather than token inclusion in activities.

In relation to sexuality and intimate relationships, research indicates that the majority of adolescents with ASD are going to have normal sexual feelings and will be as interested in romance, sexuality and relationships as the typically developing population (see Chapter 2 for a summary and review of the research). However, difficulties with social understanding and limited socialization opportunities may lead them to try to fulfil these interests in socially inappropriate ways, thereby further isolating themselves from the relationships that they long for. This may be further compounded by difficulties accessing SRE through typical channels. Following are some of the ways in which children with ASD may experience a socio-sexual developmental learning trajectory that differs from that of their typically developing peers:

- They may not have been socially rewarded for the subtle, natural interactions that support a healthy sexual identity.

- They are likely to experience fewer friendships and intimate relationships.

- They may attend special schools and therefore experience fewer opportunities to engage with and learn from typically developing peers.

- Girls with ASD who attend special schools or classes may spend a good deal of time with male peers due to the gender ratio difference in ASD.

- Difficulties with communication may mean that they do not check in if unsure about something.

- They may have less access to books and magazines due to literacy difficulties.

- They experience greater dependence on their parents, and for longer.

- They are less likely to have received SRE.

- They are less likely to have learned anything related to sexuality from their peers.

- They experience less privacy and spend less time unsupervised.

- They are less likely to have played typical childhood games such as 'doctors and nurses' or to have experienced typical childhood parties or sleepovers.

- They are less likely to have experienced flirting or dating.

- Sensory sensitivities may have led them to avoid certain sensations, e.g. touch.

- They find interpreting media representations of sexuality difficult.

- They have difficulties distinguishing fact from fiction, interpreting sarcasm and humour.

- They experience very few positive role models with disabilities who are leading fulfilled, adult, sexual lives.

Yet, despite these differing learning experiences, the difficult developmental tasks of adolescence that they face, their increased chances of social isolation and mental health issues and physically maturing at a faster rate than their social and emotional knowledge, we expect children with ASD to make complex decisions related to sexuality and relationships without any targeted input. Instead, just as we supported these children through their early developmental milestones (e.g. joint attention and communication), we now need to move towards helping them navigate the equally important developmental milestones of adolescence (of which an emerging healthy sexuality is one) in order to prepare them for healthy and fulfilled adult lives. One of the most important ways of doing this will be to provide an individualized and comprehensive personal curriculum in the area of SRE.

Vulnerability to Abuse

When people with disabilities are denied access to sex education they become perfect victims because they can't report what they can't say. (Hingsburger 1995, p.20)

The stories of abuse other females with ASD share with me are insanely numerous. I am wise enough to know abuse stories are not unique to women on the spectrum, but I worry most about my Aspie friends because we are made up of all the things that make it so hard to know when we are being taken advantage of, until it is too late. On some level, we are just the sort of human that sits like a wide-eyed doe too innocent to run away from the hunter... We are mind-blind, too often desperate to have friends, unaware of mixed messages, and on some real level, forever handicapped when paired with the wicked neurotypicals of our world. (Holliday Willey 2012, p.36)

Many research studies have reported that individuals with disabilities are at a significantly higher risk of being sexually or physically abused than the general population. In 2000, Sullivan and Knuton carried out a population-based epidemiological study which assessed the prevalence of abuse and neglect amongst a population of over 50,000 Nebraskan children identified as having a disability. The results of this study indicated that children with disabilities were 3.4 times more likely to be maltreated than their non-disabled peers. Other studies have reported the rates of sexual abuse of children with developmental disabilities to be close to two times greater than for typically developing children (Mansell, Sobsey and Moskal 1998).

While no research exists looking specifically at the risk of abuse for children with ASD, the research on developmental disabilities in general suggests that they are vulnerable. It is also possible that they are at even greater risk of exploitation due to core difficulties in social understanding and interpreting the emotions and behaviours of others, in addition to difficulties reporting abuse due to communication needs. They may also be at increased risk due to their desire to be accepted socially and their uncertainty about what a real 'friendship' constitutes (Edelson 2010). Overprotection from decision making and relationships, as well as a lack of SRE, in turn leave these children even more vulnerable (Hingsburger 1995).

In addition to being vulnerable to abuse, some adolescents and adults with ASD who have not received SRE in areas such as boundaries, relationships, appropriate touch, social skills and flirting may themselves be vulnerable to accusation of harassment, stalking or abuse if they are romantically or sexually interested in someone but do not have the social and emotional maturity either to display appropriate 'courting' behaviour or to interpret their crush's reactions to their overtures (Stokes, Newton and Kaur 2007).

However, while there are real and genuine risks of abuse in this population, discussions around SRE should not focus on the prevention of sexual abuse alone, but also on supporting a healthy sexuality, which will in turn have a preventative function. If a person does not know what is healthy and good, how will they be able to discriminate what is bad and wrong and therefore protect themselves? For example, Hingsburger (1994) queries how it is possible to discriminate between sex and rape unless the person knows that rape is not about sex, but power. The difference can only be seen by comparing the two. A focus on abuse prevention alone can also lead to the sexual rights of individuals with ASD being curtailed under the guise of protection (Gougeon 2010), and fails to contextualize the normal developmental sexual needs of children with ASD.

Information on the prevention of abuse can be found in Chapter 13, 'Teach Safety Skills'.

Why SRE needs to be Embedded within a Wider Social Skills Programme

> *Listening to another person talk about who they are, what they like and want from us is a vital aspect of any relationship. The difficulty for us though is that we might not find this interesting. Even though we are interested in the person themselves, listening to them talk might be uninteresting. We still need to listen though. When I first encountered this I got really uncomfortable in these situations, I wasn't interested and couldn't see the point of the conversation. Now I know that the point is 'this person needs to talk and express these things to me.' They feel comfortable and confident with me: enough to share who they are, what they like, and so on. They need to do this, and I am honoured that they feel safe enough to do this with me. I don't have to 'feel' interested, but I do have to 'show' interest. I do this by listening to them and by giving them my support. (Lawson 2005, p.65)*

> *If you hope to have a job and at least play nicely with those NTs around you who may never truly understand or even accept ASD, you will need to know how to speak the NT social language. (Holliday Willey 2012, p.28)*

Research indicates that social learning from peers and friends is a significant predictor of overall social functioning, and some research indicates that social functioning is the *only* significant influence on the level of romantic functioning in adolescents and adults with ASD, in itself dependent on learning from peers (Stokes *et al.* 2007). This indicates that without an appropriate level of social functioning, children with ASD may be left without even the foundation required for more complex romantic relationships.

SRE should never be taught as an isolated phenomenon. The intimacy of sexual relationships is not separate from the intimacy of social relationships. Children with ASD need to be helped to make connections with others and to develop a range of relationships, the most important of which will most likely be friendships. There is therefore no meaning to an SRE programme that does not have its basis in a good social skills programme that supports children in developing and maintaining social relationships.

Outlining a social skills programme is beyond the scope of this book and also unnecessary, as there are many good resources for supporting children with ASD in this area. However, one important note on social skills programmes: social skills will not develop or generalize unless the child is supported in developing these skills in the real world, through real world social situations. Worksheets in the isolation of the classroom do not a social skills programme make.

How to Use This Book

This book is not divided up according to age, developmental level or severity of ASD symptoms, and is not a curriculum or a series of lesson plans. It is instead divided into topics that will support professionals in developing their own individualized and developmentally appropriate programmes and curricula to meet the needs of a diverse client group.

This book follows a UPSR (**U**nderstanding, **P**reventing, **S**upporting and **R**esponding) approach, which aims to promote a holistic, individualized and systematic method of supporting children in the area of SRE. Thus, it is divided into the following four sections:

1. Understanding

This section aims to support professionals to understand the issues involved in SRE and ASD. It looks at what to include in a best practice SRE programme, the research base in this area, typical sexual behaviours of children, how to understand behaviour in general (in order to respond in child-centred and appropriate ways to sexualized behaviours), and outlines best practice teaching tools and recommendations. This section also includes important information on working collaboratively with parents and carers and developing an organization's SRE policies and procedures.

2. Preventing

This section aims to provide information on the concepts which should be included in all SRE programmes, with the aim of preventing issues occurring in the future. Teaching activities and recommendations are provided for each concept, with lists of learning concepts to support curriculum development, as well as sample resources including instructional stories.

3. Supporting

This third section emphasizes those aspects of an SRE programme that are not only about preventing issues, but also about supporting individuals with ASD to develop a healthy sexuality and intimate relationships. Again, teaching activities and recommendations, learning concepts lists and resources are provided.

4. Responding

The 'Responding' section aims to support professionals who are looking for information and interventions tactics on how best to respond to 'inappropriate' sexualized behaviours that are already occurring. It then details the steps to putting together curriculum and behaviour management plans in relation to SRE, including how to use the resources provided in the book.

Resources

There are a number of resources included in this book which aim to help professionals with curriculum planning, behaviour management and developing individualized resources for their client group, all of which can also be used to support IEP planning:

- **Instructional stories** (some illustrated) can be found at the end of most SRE curriculum concept. It would not be possible to provide instructional stories for all areas of such a curriculum covering all children's differing developmental and language levels. Therefore, the instructional stories provided are designed to illustrate a range of *examples* only. Be aware that some may be inappropriate for younger children.

- The **SRE: Child Checklist** provided in Appendix B can be used prior to any programme being implemented, in order to gain a baseline of skills. It can also subsequently be used to measure the progress of a programme or intervention.

- The **SRE: Organization Checklist** (Appendix C) aims to help professionals analyse how closely their organization compares to best practice with regard to SRE, to help with programme planning and, again, to help measure progress.

- The **SRE: Individual Curriculum Plan** (Appendix D) allows professionals to plan specific goals for individual children in each of the SRE curriculum areas.

- A **Functional Behaviour Assessment (FBA)** (Appendix E) will support those professionals investigating challenging behaviours.

- The **UPSR SRE: Individual Behaviour Plan** (Appendix F) is included to support professionals in putting together a child-centred, easy-to-use behaviour management plan in relation to 'inappropriate' sexualized behaviours.

- **Illustrations** are provided in Appendix G to support the development of individualized SRE resources. These can be photocopied or scanned into a computer, enlarged or reduced, and used in a variety of creative ways, including:
  - instructional stories
  - flashcards
  - booklets
  - posters.

START EARLY!

Children with ASD often have significant difficulty coping with even minor changes in their lives. Remember, too, that learning can be slow and confusing, in particular in the social realm. For example, trying to 'retrain' skills such as 'where to undress' during puberty, an already turbulent time, could cause unnecessary confusion. A child is never too young to begin learning developmentally appropriate SRE concepts.

2

Sexuality, SRE and ASD

A Review of the Research

This research review focuses on the period 1990–2012, as it was not until relatively recently that distinctions were made between the categories of *intellectual* and *developmental* disabilities. Furthermore, it was not until 1987 that the definition of 'autistic disorder' (similar to the one used today) was added to the Diagnostic and Statistical Manual of Mental Disorders (DSM III-Revised).

> *It was quite a shock when she told me, about ten minutes into our first session, that she thought I might have Asperger's. I'd always heard that people on the spectrum weren't interested in deep connection with people, didn't like affection, didn't like sex, didn't even seem to care about anyone around them, and that just wasn't me. (Andee Joyce in Ashkenazy and Yergeau 2013, p.5)*

There is currently a paucity of research relating to sexuality, SRE and ASD. Out of 38 published (and two unpublished) articles during this time period, just 20 constitute research studies, five of which are case studies. Ten studies make reference to sex education: four are case studies, and just one (Nichols and Blakeley-Smith 2010) moves beyond a descriptive research approach to use outcome measures to measure efficacy. A list of these articles can be found in Appendix A.

In this area, the majority of the research studies to date aim to investigate whether individuals with ASD display sexual behaviours or have sexual knowledge. However, it is important to note that most of the data are gained from parents and professionals (with some exceptions, e.g. Konstantareas and Lunsky 1997; Mehzabin and Stokes 2011; Ousley and Mesibov 1991), so that the bulk of research findings are related to the perceptions of others as opposed to the individuals themselves. Methodological and validation challenges are also common, with issues including small sample sizes, lack of control groups and randomization and questionable data analysis. In many the aims are unclear, bias is not critically examined and there is a general lack of discussion about the appropriateness of the research design. The studies also vary in their topics, participants and methodology, so that generalizability is limited, and there is a significant male sexuality bias (perhaps understandable given the male–female ratio within ASD). Some studies make the distinction between subjects who are low or high functioning but little argument is given to the nature of ASD, that is how different individual presentations can be notwithstanding these labels, and how inconsistently the labels are attributed. There are also issues with the case studies, which focus on low-incidence, complex issues (often contextualized as 'problematic sexual behaviours') which are not put into context of the general population or even the population of individuals with ASD.

However, there *are* a few studies which are methodologically robust (Mehzabin and Stokes 2011; Nichols and Blakeley-Smith 2010; Stokes and Kaur 2005; Stokes *et al* 2007; van Bourgondien, Reichle and Palmer 1997), and others that are valuable in terms of increasing knowledge in an under-researched field (Ballan 2012; Hatton and Tector 2010; Ray, Marks and Bray-Garretson 2004). Although not a research study, Gougeon's (2010) 'Sexuality and autism: A critical review of selected literature using a social-relational model of disability' deserves credit as a well written and thoughtful summary of the relevant research, reviewing it according to recurrent themes using a pragmatic social-relational model of disability and highlighting the problem-based perspectives and curtailment of individual rights so common in the literature.

What Can be Learned from the Research Base?

- What is reported consistently throughout the research base (Ballan 2012; Haracopos and Pedersen 1992; Hatton and Tector 2010; Hellemans *et al.* 2007; Hellemans *et al.* 2010; Konstantareas and Lunsky 1997; Mehzabin and Stokes 2011; Ousley and Mesibov 1991; van Bourgondien *et al.* 1997) is that individuals with ASD display typical sexual needs, a wide variety of sexual behaviours, wish to engage in intimate relationships, and are neither hypersexual nor asexual (Gougeon 2010).

- Individuals with ASD can display what are often considered 'problematic' sexual behaviours (Haracopos and Pedersen 1992; Hatton and Tector 2010; Hellemans *et al.* 2007; Hellemans *et al.* 2010; Konstantareas and Lunsky 1997; Mehzabin and Stokes 2011; Ousley and Mesibov 1991; van Bourgondien *et al.* 1997). This appears to be largely due to deficits in social and communication skills.

- There is insufficient availability of suitable *materials* designed for parents, professionals or individuals themselves looking to support the development of a healthy sexuality and intimate relationships in children or adults with ASD (Ballan 2012; Hatton and Tector 2010; Tissot 2009).

- There are societal barriers in place that prevent SRE from happening (Griffin-Shelley 2010; Hatton and Tector 2010; Nichols and Blakeley-Smith 2010 – cited in Gougeon 2010).

- Caregivers are aware of, and concerned for, the sexual needs of their children (Ballan 2012; Kalyva 2010; Nichols and Blakeley-Smith 2010; Ruble and Dalrymple 1993; Stokes and Kaur 2005; Stokes *et al.* 2007). Primary concerns noted by parents thus far surround their children's safety and others' understanding of their behaviours (Ruble and Dalrymple 1993; Nichols and Blakeley-Smith 2010; Stokes and Kuar 2005). Ballan (2012) reported that parents expressed a strong desire to communicate with both their children and professionals about sexuality, with the majority indicating that they would like to learn from professionals how to better communicate with their children about sexuality issues.

- Individuals with ASD have difficulty translating theory into practice, that is using the information that they have received about sexuality, relationships and appropriate behaviours in their everyday lives (Griffin-Shelley 2010; Hellemans *et al.* 2007; Konstantareas and Lunsky 1997; Realmuto and Ruble 1999; Ruble and Dalrymple 1993; Stokes and Kaur 2005, cited in Gougeon 2010). Therefore, they may be aware of sexual terminology, but do not display a complex understanding of these terms. This gap between knowledge and practice can be a common difficulty for many individuals on the ASD spectrum.

- There is a demonstrated need for evidence-based SRE programmes (Haracopos and Pedersen 1992; Hatton and Tector 2010; Hellemans *et al.* 2007; Kalyva 2010; Konstantareas and Lunsky 1997; Mehzabin and Stokes 2011; Stokes and Kaur 2005; Stokes *et al.* 2007), and in particular parent sexuality training programmes (Ballan 2012; Nichols and Blakeley-Smith 2010). Therefore, for systematic and proactive SRE to be provided, the needs of parents and teachers should be addressed, alongside the needs of children with ASD. Gougeon (2010) notes the fact that while much of the research conducted thus far indicates the need for SRE, by the nature of the research and the language used the studies also concurrently perpetuate the stigma of sexuality as a problem in need of management.

- As is the case for individuals with ID, the sexual rights of individuals with ASD are routinely denied (Galluci, Hackerman and Schmidt 2005; Tissot 2009; van Bourgondien *et al.* 1997).

- Last, a consistent finding is that the sexuality of individuals with ASD is addressed from a problem-based/deficit perspective (Galluci *et al.* 2005; Griffin-Shelley 2010; Hellemans *et al.* 2007; Hellemans *et al.* 2010; Realmuto and Ruble 1999; Tissot 2009 – cited in Gougeon 2010). Sexual 'problems' are questioned within a framework of deviancy and a discourse of fear pervades (Gougeon 2010). Terms such as 'obsession', 'stalking' and 'fierce attachment' are routinely used (as opposed to 'falling in love' or 'having a crush'), implying a pathological quality in the way a person with ASD behaves and feels, rather than the possibility of behaviour arising from lack of experience and immaturity compared to their peers. Unfortunately, but perhaps understandably, even when researchers themselves do not address the issue from a problem-based perspective, parents can (Ballan 2012).

3

Understanding Sexual Behaviours in Children

IMPORTANT NOTES

- Professionals must be aware and knowledgeable about child protection issues, including recognizing and reporting child abuse, and dealing with disclosure. Child protection procedures and policies may vary from state to state or country to country. If for any reason child abuse is suspected, it is necessary to follow the correct child protection policies and procedures of your organization or country before embarking on any behaviour investigation or intervention. If you are aware that a child has been abused in the past, a behaviour investigation, as outlined in this book, may not be appropriate unless you have first liaised with the correct professionals and authorities involved with the child.

- Any behaviour change that happens out of the blue needs to be investigated, as it may be caused by pain, illness or acute distress.

Due to the nature of the difficulties experienced by individuals with ASD, some may present with maladaptive socio-sexual behaviours such as masturbating or undressing in public places, acting in socially inappropriate ways or misinterpreting relationship boundaries. However, before implementing a plan in relation to a child's 'inappropriate' or sexualized behaviour, it is important to have a good understanding of behaviour in general, common and less common sexual behaviours in children, behavioural signs of sexual abuse, and strategies to help investigate and understand behaviours as they are occurring. With this understanding, child-centred and developmentally appropriate intervention methods can be implemented effectively. Information on how best to *respond* to these behaviours is provided in later chapters. However, it is hoped following the guidelines in this book will result in less time and energy spent in dealing with 'crisis' behaviours. It is also hoped that, as a result of increased understanding, these behaviours will not so readily escalate to crisis stage within organizations and families.

This book advocates a PBS model, which looks not only at eliminating problem behaviours but also teaching new skills, increasing success, and enhancing personal satisfaction, dignity and positive social interactions. It is a holistic approach that encompasses all settings. PBS is a technique that also helps us best understand a child's challenging behaviours, so that we can work to prevent them happening in the future. It involves a focus on increasing quality of life and making positive lifestyle changes as per the individual strengths and wishes of the child.

CASE EXAMPLE

Tommy is an 18-year-old young man with ASD and mild ID who attends a special school for children with ASD. Although it is a mixed-sex school, no girls who attend are in his age group. Recently, Tommy began rubbing his pubic area against female staff as he walked by them in the hall. A behavioural intervention was implemented which included punishment and lack of privileges (i.e. 'time out' and his computer being taken away) when he displayed the behaviour. Although this behavioural intervention appeared to be working (i.e. the number of incidences had reduced), during class one day Tommy purposefully knocked his female teacher to the floor, straddled her and began thrusting his pubic area into her leg. This was clearly very distressing for the teacher involved and Tommy was suspended from school, with the possibility of expulsion. When his parents asked him why he had done it that night, Tommy said 'No girlfriend, never girlfriend.'

When Tommy first began displaying inappropriate behaviours with female staff, rather than focus on punishment alone, a PBS intervention would have begun by looking at the reasons *why* Tommy was displaying this behaviour.

Tommy is an 18-year-old young man with normal 18-year-old feelings and the right to intimacy. It is developmentally appropriate for him to want a girlfriend and seek sexual experiences, but he was, of course, doing so in highly inappropriate ways and with inappropriate people. Following are some questions that could have been asked at that time.

- Has Tommy received any SRE in the past?

- How much insight does he have into his own behaviour?

- Has anyone asked *him* why he is displaying the behaviour?

- Does he understand his feelings?

- Does he want a girlfriend?

- What does having a girlfriend mean to him?

- What explicit or implicit messages has he been given with regard to his having a girlfriend?

- Does he know that teachers cannot be girlfriends?

- Does he have any opportunities to meet girls of his own age who would be more appropriate objects of his desires?

- Is displaying this behaviour the only opportunity that Tommy has to touch another human being (or be touched)?

- Does he know how to talk to a girl, or ask someone to be his girlfriend?

- Does he know the 'rules' of appropriate touch with different people?

- Does he display these behaviours in the home (for example, with his sister or his sister's friends) or out in the community?

- Is he able to communicate his feelings, wishes and frustrations? Could he be taught ways to do this?

- Does he have the time and privacy at home in his own bedroom to masturbate?

- What replacement behaviour could he be taught that might meet the need that the challenging behaviour did?

Following an in-depth analysis of the situation, an informed intervention could then have focused on developing Tommy's knowledge and skills, supporting him in dealing appropriately with his sexual feelings when in public, increasing his participation in community activities where he would have the opportunity to meet appropriate girls and ensuring that he had adequate private time at home in his bedroom, as well as a behavioural intervention to support him in reducing his inappropriate behaviours.

What is Behaviour?

Behaviour is anything a person does that can be seen, counted or described. It is anything we do, and can be positive, negative or neutral. *Internalized* behaviours are behaviours that direct the problem behaviour towards the self. *Externalized* behaviours directly affect other people.

Behaviours have a function. They are a child's way of telling us something, and are there because they have worked for the child in the past. This, of course, implies that the people around the child have a significant part to play in the shaping and development of behaviours. Behaviours are learned, which means that they can also be unlearned, and new behaviours can always be taught.

What Makes Behaviours Challenging?

Behaviours can be described as problematic if they are happening too frequently, are developmentally inappropriate, interfere with learning or functioning, stop the child using already learned skills, are disrupting others or cause harm to the child or others. However, how we interpret behaviours is entirely subjective and dependent on a person's living situation, family, community, history, school and societal context. What may be considered a problem behaviour in one family may be accepted in another (e.g. masturbation or pornography). When working with children with ASD in the area of 'inappropriate' behaviour, we need to analyse not only why a behaviour is occurring but also why we consider it challenging and wish for it to change. We also need to consider whether the child's family have any issues with the behaviour continuing.

If a behaviour is dangerous to the person or others, or illegal (or will become illegal once the child turns a certain age), it clearly needs immediate intervention. If the behaviour is one that is considered morally or ethically 'wrong', or indeed socially unacceptable, then one needs to think critically before implementing any plan. However, it does not follow that we should be tolerant and accepting of behaviours that are not acceptable in the child's social environment. Allowing these behaviours to continue due to, for example, beliefs that the child can't learn, or that they will grow out of it, or due to a professional or parent having different standards for that child because of their disability, is in itself a grave mistake. Sentiments such as 'Leave the poor girl alone, she doesn't know what she's doing' only serve to further isolate the child, in addition to damaging the reputation of people with disabilities in general. From a behavioural perspective, allowing behaviours to continue without interruption or intervention teaches children that the behaviour is OK and gives them 'permission' to continue. Not teaching therefore becomes a form of teaching, and often leads to more challenging and engrained behaviours which become even harder to tackle in the future.

Behaviours can also be challenging because they occur too often, there are too many of them, or they occur at the wrong time or place (i.e. 'too often, too many or bad timing'). For example, if an adult masturbates in their own bedroom, this is not a problem. If they do it in a public park, it is illegal. It is also a problem if they are spending *all* of their time masturbating in their bedroom to the exclusion of all other activities.

Why Do Behaviours Occur?

> *For most of us we react, rather than choose to act. In fact, if you don't give us the tools to choose to act, we can only react! Just like NT individuals I am driven by my emotions, feelings and (definitely) hormones, but this is only part of the picture. I need information that helps me access the rest of the story. The outcomes of too little information and incomplete concepts can mean that I say and do things that might embarrass others. This is not my intention, I just may not realize how other people will be affected by my literal and incomplete understanding. If I don't access the appropriate understanding I may just be the product of my feelings. (Lawson 2005, p.35)*

> *The psychologist never discussed my child's changing behavior could be due to raging hormones or not understanding the changes in his body, even when I asked if that was possible. She only wanted to talk about it when he got into trouble for kissing his piano teacher and trying to touch her breast. (Parent of a child with ASD, in Ballan 2012, p.680)*

There are three main functions of behaviour:

1. to get something (including tangibles or interaction/attention)

2. to avoid something (including specific people, activities or settings)

3. to feel something (including control and sensory experiences).

A question frequently asked by both parents and professionals during the teenage years is: 'Is it the autism or is it hormones?' It can be hard to distinguish whether a behaviour is occurring due to a core difficulty relating to ASD, or as a normal part of teenage development (e.g. if a 16-year-old girl becomes moody and increasingly isolates herself in her bedroom or talks obsessively about a boy in her class). It is certainly very important to be cognisant of 'overshadowing' (Hingsburger 1995), as when a doctor, for example, can see only the person's disability, and therefore attributes all issues to it. It is also true that the concept of 'raging teenage hormones' is culturally laden and not identified or accepted in many parts of the world. However, whether or not a behaviour is occurring due to hormones, a developmental stage or as a consequence of ASD, the function of the behaviour (i.e. to obtain, avoid or feel something) remains the same. All children display issues with behaviour at some stage in their lives, and one shouldn't attribute everything to ASD if this leads to the adult becoming confused and disempowered in attempting to support the child with their behaviour.

There are innumerable reasons why a behaviour may be occurring in a specific context. Before we look at why children with ASD may exhibit what we interpret as sexual behaviours, we need first to recognize and understand sexualized behaviours that occur as a normal part of a child's development.

Sexual Behaviours in Children

Sexual behaviours in children are a normal part of child development, and occur within a developmental trajectory that includes testing of personal boundaries, curiosity-seeking behaviours, and situational factors that elicit such behaviours (Kellogg 2009). For both professionals and parents, differentiating between normal and unusual (or developmentally inappropriate) sexual behaviours is critical, not only so that typical behaviours can be responded to in a child-centred, calm and appropriate manner, and atypical behaviours can be highlighted as needing further investigation, but also in order to understand that there are concepts that need to be taught (e.g. gender and modesty) during these developmental periods to help keep children on a typical developmental track (Hingsburger 1995).

> *I was in this little ignorant cocoon and it kinda crept up. Parents need to know that just because their child does have a significant developmental delay doesn't mean that their sexuality is going to be delayed. Because no one ever, I mean I go to all of the paediatrician, I go to the developmentalist, and no one said to me this will happen. (Parent of a child with ASD, in Ballan 2012, p.680)*

All children are different. They may or may not display certain sexual behaviours and will not necessarily meet their developmental milestones in a linear fashion (this is in particular true for children with ASD). However, the following table summarizes some typical sexual behaviours displayed throughout childhood. Age guidelines are rough estimates.

TABLE 3.1 TYPICAL CHILDHOOD SEXUAL BEHAVIOURS

AGE	TYPICAL BEHAVIOURS
Birth to two years	Touching genitals for pleasure. Discovering body. Initiating and responding to physical touch, including hugging and kissing.
2–5 years	Continued exploration of body. Touching genitals in public. May rub genitals for relaxation. Some reflexive sexual response (erection or lubrication). Curiosity about private parts. Trying to view adult or peer nudity. Enjoys touch and nudity. Playing games such as 'doctors and nurses' and 'I'll show you mine...' i.e. showing genitals to peers and exploring peers' genitals. Consensual exploration of same age peers' bodies. Dressing up (including boys dressing up as girls). Questioning how babies are made and delivered. Joking about genitalia and body functions.
5–10 years	Interest in how babies are made. Masturbation for pleasure. Continued curiosity about bodies. (Can be same gender and is not indicative of future sexual preference.) Play involving touch may still occur. Beginning to adhere to peer group style and gender roles in clothing and play.
10–14 years	Continued sexual play and exploration between same and opposite sex peers (secretive and hidden from adults). Thinking, talking and dreaming about sex. Watching sexually explicit material and masturbating to orgasm. Interest in the opposite sex. Feelings of attraction may become sexual. Sexual fantasies. Dating, kissing and 'petting'. Interest in sex in the media. Peer discussions about sexual behaviours. 'Boyfriends' and 'girlfriends' often established.
14–18 years	Continued masturbation for pleasure. Becoming self-conscious. Body-image and self-esteem issues may arise. Continuing to be influenced by peer group. Fitting in is important. May begin having sex. Sexual wishes and fantasies.

(Friedrich et al. 1998; Kellogg 2009; Realmuto and Ruble 1999)

For those working with children with developmental disabilities, it is important to look at developmental level as well as age when assessing behaviours, as children with ASD (in particular those with added ID) may engage in 'typical' sexual behaviours at an older age. For example, an adolescent with ASD whose intellectual functioning is comparable to a child of five years of age may exhibit self-stimulatory behaviour that is consistent with their developmental level, including a lack of awareness of appropriate public behaviours. Even those children with ASD and normal to high IQs may experience a developmental delay in this area due to their particular learning needs and differences in socio-sexual learning experiences explicated in the introductory chapter. These age inappropriate yet developmentally appropriate sexual behaviours have the potential either to have their intention misinterpreted (particularly if they are challenging to others) or to be misinterpreted as signs of sexual abuse (in particular if parents, or indeed professionals, hold beliefs about children with disabilities being asexual) (Ruble and Dalrymple 1993).

It would be a mistake to assume that all unusual sexual behaviours are a sign that abuse is taking place (Kellogg 2009). However, it would also be a mistake to assume that all behaviours exhibited by children with ASD are part of a delayed sexual development, in particular given the statistics with regard to the sexual abuse of children with disabilities. Cavanagh Johnson (2002) has described a continuum of sexual behaviours displayed by children, including 'typical' sexual behaviours, 'sexually reactive' behaviours, 'excessive but mutual peer' sexual behaviours and 'sexually abusive' behaviours. 'Problem' sexual behaviours are described as arising not only due to abuse, but also in reaction to traumatic events and/or overstimulating environmental experiences.

The Australian South Eastern Centre Against Sexual Assault (CASA) 'Age appropriate sexual behaviour guide' uses a traffic light colour coded system to classify childhood sexual behaviours as 'Age Appropriate', 'Concerning' (signalling the need for further investigation) and 'Very Concerning' (requiring immediate professional advice). Sexual behaviours are classified as such within age ranges from 0 to 18. This useful guide can be accessed for free at the South Eastern CASA website (South Eastern CASA 2013).

The American Psychological Association (2012) reports that while not all sexually abused children exhibit symptoms, there are some documented signs including sexual knowledge and language that is unusual and inappropriate for their age, sleep difficulties, anger, anxiety, depression, difficulties walking or sitting, pregnancy, contracting an STI, running away, regressive behaviours, and a reluctance to be left alone with a particular individual or group. Be aware that this list relates to typically developing children, and children with ASD may be more likely than the general population to experience some of these concerns.

There is a scarcity of research into the sexual behaviours of children with ASD, and there is currently no research into the behavioural manifestations of sexual abuse in this population. Although they develop *physically* at the same rate as their peers, *cognitively*, individuals with ASD display not only delayed development, but also *atypical* or *disordered* development. Therefore, parents and professionals need to be cautioned about coming to easy conclusions about 'typical' or 'unusual' sexual behaviours for this population at this time.

Other Reasons Why a Child with ASD May Display Sexual Behaviours

Difficulties Understanding Social Rules

Social skills issues are part of the triad of impairments inherent in ASD and children with ASD have typically not accessed the same learning experiences as their typically developing peers. Therefore, a child may display a sexual behaviour in public because they have not yet learned the rules (i.e. 'the hidden curriculum') with regard to appropriate touch in a public place.

Difficulties with Communication

Children with ASD can often have difficulties understanding the messages we give to them (whether they be verbal, nonverbal or written). They also have difficulties expressing their own thoughts and wishes or seeking clarification for misunderstandings. Issues in both of these areas may lead to frustration, misunderstandings and behavioural issues.

The Behaviour Has Become Learned

A child may initially have displayed a behaviour for another reason. Perhaps he was too hot and so decided to take off his trousers during maths class. However, the reaction to this behaviour then met some need. For example, it may have caused a big, enjoyable 'fuss'. The child may also then have been removed from a boring lesson to go outside and put his trousers back on. Over time, this may become a learned behaviour, as the child *learns* that if he takes off his trousers, he gets to leave the classroom, and this has now become the only reason he takes them off (i.e. it has nothing to do with his being too hot any more). He may have learned that if he takes off his underwear also, he will *definitely* be sent out. However, as he is 14 years old and now taking off his clothes regularly, which he never did before, it may be understandable for his teacher to hypothesize that he is stripping for reasons related to puberty and sexual feelings.

Emotional Upset

The issue of 'diagnostic overshadowing' is particularly pertinent here. Children with ASD are subject to the same emotional upsets as all children. They are affected by changes in family or school circumstances, illness and loss. For example, a child with ASD is just as likely as their typical peers to regress somewhat upon the arrival of a new sibling. Renewed wetting themselves in school should then be seen not as a new 'behaviour' to be tackled, but as an understandable reaction to what is going on within the family.

Changes in Routine

In general, children with ASD thrive on routine and sameness and can become genuinely distressed by even minor changes to their routine or environment. It is important not to overlook these changes when analysing what could be upsetting the child and causing any challenging behaviours which may have a sexual component.

Sensory Issues

Although it is not part of the diagnostic criteria of ASD, the majority of authors with ASD document how sensory issues have significantly affected them throughout their lives. An example of this might be a child taking off their clothes and rubbing themselves against a window. While this may be embarrassing for families and causes serious issues for schools, the child may be doing it purely for the feel of the glass against their skin and not out of any desire to display themselves to others, shock, or for any other reason why a typically developing child might display this behaviour. However, it is possible that the reaction of the people around the child will lead to the behaviour being reinforced, and therefore even more likely to occur in the future.

Medication

Some medications frequently prescribed to children with ASD to help with anxiety or repetitive behaviours can cause a decrease in sexual desire or make orgasm significantly more difficult (Urbano *et al.* 2013) which may lead to behavioural concerns.

Medical Issues/Genital Discomfort/Pain

Many children with ASD have difficulties communicating when they are hurt or feel sick. They are also subject to the same illnesses, infections and allergies as everyone else. A child may be acting out because they are in pain. They may be touching their genitals because they have a urinary tract infection, thrush or eczema. Their trousers may be too tight. They could be allergic to the washing detergent being used on their clothes, leading them to itch and therefore remove them. Medical concerns *always* need to be ruled out before embarking on a behaviour management programme, even if it seems unlikely that these are the cause.

Menstrual Pain

Children with ASD also suffer from the same menstrual pain as other girls, but again have difficulties both recognizing the pain and communicating to others about it. For girls, it is helpful to track behavioural concerns on a monthly calendar in order to rule out whether behaviour issues are arising due to premenstrual pain or discomfort.

Boredom

Children can often display challenging behaviours due to boredom or lack of environmental stimulation. Look at the child's daily schedule, observe them in class or during leisure activities. How much fun are they having? Are they stimulated by what they are doing? Are they smiling? A bored and understimulated child will find other ways of occupying themselves or gaining stimulation from their environment.

Overstimulation, Noise and General Disruption

In contrast, overstimulation, noise and general disruption can also cause challenging behaviours, in particular for children with ASD.

Seeking Attention

A child may have learned that displaying a certain sexual behaviour means that they receive a lot more attention than for other behaviours. If the child is using a behaviour to gain attention, giving that behaviour attention is the best way to ensure it continues. They may also display a certain behaviour to annoy, impress or win approval (all variations of attention). For example, a teenager may learn that telling dirty jokes in class gets a big laugh from their peers, without any real understanding of the jokes he is telling. As someone who has most likely been ignored, bullied or rejected in the past, this perceived social acceptance is hard to deter by adult disapproval.

Inability to Masturbate Effectively

Anecdotally, it would appear that this may be a common occurrence, with children unable to masturbate effectively due to lack of privacy, poor technique or medication. They may masturbate with inappropriate objects, or indeed other people, and may become frustrated by not being able to masturbate to climax. This can cause considerable distress for those around the child, and may lead to the child masturbating more frequently as a result.

Lack of Choice and Control

It is a basic human and developmental need to have choice and control in one's life. Without either of these, challenging behaviours can become common, as the individual attempts to assert some control over their lives. Unfortunately the life of a child with a disability may be controlled for most of the time, with significant repercussions in terms of their behaviour.

Mistakes in Behaviour Management

As mentioned previously, undesirable behaviours can be inadvertently reinforced by the way we respond to them. Conversely, there may be no clear reinforcement for positive behaviours. Observe the child in different settings. How often do the adults around them praise or reward them when they are behaving appropriately? Or are they ignored until the 'crisis' behaviour rears its head, and then punished? Remember that rewarding positive behaviours is always going to be more effective than punishing unwanted behaviours.

No Opportunities to Express their Sexuality in Appropriate Ways

If a teenager has no access to a healthy sexuality or sexual relationships, inappropriate sexual behaviours may occur, as, wishing to make a connection with someone else, the teenager may perceive these as the only alternative for accessing these things.

Investigating Behaviour

A good assessment is the foundation of a child-centred, supportive and effective intervention plan. A systematic problem-solving approach will also help to organize an approach and formulate a theory, as well as identify solutions.

First of all, remember that it is better for people who know the child well to do any investigating, rather than any outside 'expert'. Also, nobody is more of an expert on a child than their parents.

Selecting the Behaviour

It is best to decide on one behaviour to work on at a time. Everyone involved with the child needs to agree on which behaviour to choose. It is probably most helpful to choose the behaviour that is causing the most distress to the child or others. However, it can also be useful to choose a relatively 'easy' behaviour to work on first, so that the team (and the child) can experience some success.

Deciding Whether the Behaviour Needs to be Changed

Thinking about the information in Chapter 3 on the typical sexual behaviours of children, do you feel that the behaviour still needs to be changed? For example, a child masturbating in their room who is not distressed and is still engaging in a range of other activities is displaying a developmentally appropriate behaviour which does not need to be changed. However, they may be going about it inappropriately – for example, leaving the bedroom door open or not cleaning up after themselves. This could then be targeted to work on instead.

Defining the Behaviour

Now that you have chosen a behaviour to work on, it needs to be clearly defined. Be explicit. Write it down as if you are telling an actor how to act it out. Explain it to someone else and ask them to tell you what they think you mean.

'Ben is showing sexual behaviours in school' tells us nothing. However, 'Ben is staring at specific girls' breasts during class until told to stop. He continues staring for up to ten minutes without looking away' is clearer and therefore something to start working on. We will also know if progress has been made. For example, after intervention Ben may only briefly look at girls' breasts before looking away independently. This is progress that would not have been recorded if the duration of the behaviour wasn't explicitly stated in the definition.

Observing, Investigating and Documenting

Taking the time to do a proper investigation of any behaviour is vital. FBA is a problem-solving process which helps to develop a hypothesis about the function maintaining the child's 'problem' behaviour. It involves figuring out why a behaviour is occurring, so that a replacement behaviour can be taught that services the same function. A sample FBA is included in Appendix E.

A good FBA will include investigation of behaviours that the child is already displaying which involve positive and appropriate ways of communicating with and requesting from other people. Documenting these is important, as you may find that although a child is displaying a certain sexualized behaviour in order to gain attention, they may already have appropriate methods of gaining attention in other settings or with other people. Generalizing these already learned behaviours will most likely be easier than teaching completely new skills. A good FBA will also include investigation of medical issues which could be causing or affecting the behaviour, as well as sensory, social and environmental issues.

A number of tools can be used to do an FBA, including interviews, observations and checklists of preferences or motivations. It should include all settings the child engages in. Previous reports and assessments may be viewed for information, although some professionals prefer not to, so that they are not influenced by other people's opinions (in particular if they are negative or include low expectations for the child). Both methods have their merits.

Although self-report is difficult for children on the spectrum due to the nature of their communication difficulties, attempts should also be made to elicit information from the child regarding their understanding of the behaviour. If they cannot verbally report, attempt to gain information in different ways – for example, worksheets with closed sentences ('I hit Dad because…', 'I felt…before I took my clothes off'). Or draw pictures and ask the child to circle the one that fits the best (e.g. emotions faces). If you are finding it difficult to elicit any information from the child, ask other people who know them well for ideas.

Part of your FBA should focus on establishing a baseline for the challenging behaviour, which means clearly stating how often, how intense and for how long the behaviour is occurring (i.e. duration, intensity and frequency). This can then be compared to any behaviours occurring after having implemented a behaviour plan. Without a baseline, how are you to know which approach is working?

Observations of the child should include filling in ABCs, which is a simple method of collecting information on the behaviour: once a behaviour has been clearly defined, whenever it is observed, note what happened 30 seconds before it (**A**ntecedent), the exact **B**ehaviour, and then what happens 30 seconds after it (**C**onsequence).

TABLE 3.2 ABC

ANTECEDENT	BEHAVIOUR	CONSEQUENCE
• What happened before the behaviour? • Where was it? • Who was there? • What was happening? • Who said/did something?	Clearly defined behaviour.	• What happened directly after the behaviour? • What was used as a consequence? • Who said what?

SOME SAMPLE ANTECEDENTS

- Something is taken away from the child.
- The child requests a preferred item.

- There is a change in the routine.

- A request is made.

- The child's attempts at communication are ignored.

SOME SAMPLE CONSEQUENCES

- The adult walks away from the child.

- The child is sent to 'time out'.

- The child is given a food item.

- The child is given a different task to do.

- The child is given a hug.

TABLE 3.3 ABC: EXAMPLE

ANTECEDENT	BEHAVIOUR	CONSEQUENCE
Teacher tells Mary to sit at her desk.	Mary hits her pubic area, over her clothes, with both hands.	Mary is taken out of the classroom by Judith to go for a walk.

ANALYSING THE INFORMATION GATHERED

At this stage, gather all of your information and look for patterns. It is a good idea to look for exceptions first, that is where the behaviour is least likely to occur, and with whom. A lot of meaningful information can be gained by focusing in this area. Next, look at where it is most likely to occur. Analyse your ABCs. What are the main triggers for the behaviour? Looking at the consequences you have noted, what do you think is maintaining the behaviour? What is the child getting out of the behaviour? Under what conditions does the child never display the behaviour? Why under these specific conditions? Are the conditions replicable?

Coming Up with a Hypothesis

The last step in your investigation involves coming up with a hypothesis as to *why* the behaviour is occurring, including what you feel the triggers are and why the child continues to display the behaviour. Remember that this will be just your best guess. Having a hypothesis as to why somebody is doing something will *always* be a hypothesis, so don't be afraid of getting it wrong. You can come up with a new hypothesis if new information comes to light or if the intervention you put in place is not successful. Remember that if the intervention strategies chosen are child-centred and preventative, they should cause no harm to the child, who will learn new skills in the process, even if your hypothesis turns out to be incorrect.

4

Teaching Tools and Recommendations

Following is a list of practice- and evidence-based teaching tools and recommendations for those working with children with ASD, many of which are specific to implementing an SRE programme.

Be Aware of Child Protection Issues

This should be your number one priority before implementing any SRE programme with a child. Know the child protection policies and procedures of your organization and home country. Be aware of the limits of confidentiality within your sessions. Have a clear plan for exactly what you will do if certain information comes to light, what you will say to the child and their parents, who you will report to, how, why, in what time frame and what the implications of any reporting will be for you, the child, their family and your organization. Being aware of and following policies and guidelines will help to keep both you and the child safe.

Network with Other Professionals

Working with children with ASD can be extremely challenging for even the most skilled and experienced of professionals. Even (in fact, especially) if you are working in a solo capacity, make the effort to network and liaise with other professionals. This could involve joint working, shadowing, receiving supervision, mentoring or liaising with other schools or agencies. There are plenty of professional groups (including many online groups) who regularly share information and resources. Linking in with other professionals will not only improve your practice and be professionally stimulating, but will also help build your confidence in your own abilities to address sensitive topics. It will also help you locate appropriate resources, which may mean your workload is reduced as you do not need to reinvent the wheel at every stage of your programme.

Take a Multidisciplinary Approach

Multidisciplinary working is one of the basic best practice requirements when working with children with ASD.

Value Evidence-based Practice

It is important to keep up to date with research into ASD. Regularly reference best practice guidelines in terms of teaching and therapeutic approaches. Learn skills in evaluating research. The book *Bad Science* by Ben Goldacre (2008) is recommended as an easy-to-read and entertaining way to go about this, if needed. It includes a chapter debunking the false measles, mumps, rubella (MMR) vaccine–ASD link, which should be required reading for anyone working with or parenting a child with ASD.

Don't Rely on Outside Agencies

All too often, schools rely on outside agencies to provide SRE to their pupils. This is inappropriate in particular for children with ASD, who will most likely need repeated learning over a variety of contexts for information to be retained. Having an outside agency come in and provide SRE isolates it from the rest of the child's curriculum and is not good practice.

   If training is needed, it is more appropriate for staff who know the child well to be trained (and given the confidence) to provide SRE themselves.

Use the IEP

SRE goals can be added to children's IEPs in the same way as other learning goals. This will also ensure that parents are involved and carrying out their own responsibilities in the home.

Work Collaboratively with Parents/Carers

Parents/carers will need to be fully involved in planning and implementing any SRE programme. This is fully discussed in Chapter 5, 'Working with Parents'.

Take the Time to Build Rapport

Don't forget to put time into building rapport and a good relationship with the child. Establishing rapport implies that two people *want* to interact with each other. Although the child you are working with may experience the world differently from you, it would be a mistake to assume that whether they like you or not will not affect the outcomes of any intervention, or that they would not appreciate the positive regard and genuineness of a real relationship. Putting time and effort into establishing rapport will increase the likelihood of engagement with a relaxed child who will want to spend time with you, to learn more and to do well. It will most likely have the added benefit of reducing your need for behaviour management strategies during sessions.

Enter the Child's World

More important than learning any teaching method will be learning about ASD, understanding the individual and unique world of a child with ASD and seeing the outside world from their perspective. This can only lead to creative, empathic and successful teaching methods. As well as learning as much as you can about the child, reading books by authors who have ASD is one of the best ways to go about this.

Use What Already Works

Presumably, teaching tactics and methods have already been found that are successful with particular children. Use these same tactics when teaching SRE, that is, treat the subject as you would any other part of the child's curriculum.

Provide Role Models

Children with ASD experience very few positive role models who are also on the ASD spectrum. Make links with advocate groups. Consider involving an appropriate person with ASD in presenting your SRE programme – for example, they could give short talks on specific topics or answer questions from the children. Meeting these individuals and hearing their perspectives will be a very powerful experience for the children. Of course, it would be important to choose a suitable candidate and to 'train' them for the role.

In addition, provide children with books by authors with ASD, ensuring appropriate content. Teenagers may be especially interested in reading books written by teenagers with ASD.

Be Flexible

Working with children with ASD requires professionals to be flexible. This means learning to teach in different ways, through different modes, with different class sizes, and being able to change your teaching style and methods depending on the child you are with, their mood or even the time of day.

Be Fun

Make yourself someone who is worth attending to and interacting with. Much more will be accomplished if the child is in a positive environment filled with reinforcing people and activities.

Provide One-to-One Instruction

Children with ASD (including those with AS) usually learn best on a one-to-one basis. However, if you have a small group of children with similar needs and communication skills, based on what you know about the children, you will need to decide which key concepts of the SRE curriculum could be taught on a one-to-one basis, and which could be taught in small groups.

Be a Good Communicator

- When communicating with the child, use the communication system already known to be most effective with that particular child.

- Back up language with visual information.

- Reduce your language, even with children with AS.

- Use concrete language and terminology as opposed to abstract, i.e. talk about the penis and the vagina, sex and masturbation, not 'the birds and the bees'.

- Beware of the jokey, 'nudge nudge, wink wink' language that accompanies many SRE books for children. Information presented in this way is less likely to be understood by the child with ASD.

- Don't expect or force eye contact, which may be uncomfortable for the child.

- Respond to all questions calmly and with a positive tone, even if they surprise you. If you cannot answer in the moment, assure the child that it is a good question that you will answer later if you can.

- Talk about 'what people do' not what 'you' or 'I' do.

- With the child's parents, decide on terminology for the body and stick to it. Inform all those working with the child of the terminology to use. If appropriate, differentiate between more medical terms for different parts of the body and those words which the child might hear in the school yard. This will help ease confusion when they hear the words being used, and prevent them from making innocent mistakes which could lead to teasing.

- It is recommended that the term 'rude' is used to define sexual slang, rather than the more abstract 'inappropriate' or 'offensive'.

- You may need to be careful about *your* use of language, particularly if the child is literal with language. For example, describing a child's voice as 'breaking' could upset them. 'Your voice is changing. It will become deeper, like your brother's' is more appropriate.

Emphasize the Private Nature of the Topic

When discussing private, sexual topics, it is most appropriate to do so when there is noone else around, in order to emphasize their private nature. If you are undertaking an SRE programme with a child, have clear definitions for where sessions will take place (i.e. somewhere private) and why. Also define clearly who else may be there or come in, and who else the child may wish to discuss what they have learned with.

Be Explicit about the Ground Rules

Due to the sensitive nature of SRE, it is important to be very clear on certain ground rules with regard to information shared, either by yourself or by the child. Children with ASD often need guidance in areas such as defining types of relationships (e.g. understanding that a psychologist is not a personal friend) or what information is relevant to be shared within different relationships. Remember that a child with ASD is not only learning new skills during an intervention, but is also having to be an active participant in a social interaction in order to do so (typically the area where they experience the greatest difficulty). They will need support in both of these areas if real progress is to be made. Be clear about the following ground rules.

- Some SRE situations will be different from others in terms of appropriate information to be shared or asked. For example, if a child is being supported in this area by a psychologist, it may be appropriate for the child to share more personal information with that person than with a teacher. In advance of implementing any programme, know the boundaries of appropriate sharing of information in your particular setting.

- Be clear with the child before starting any programme about the limits of confidentiality, what information you will need to pass on, to whom and why.

- Be clear about the type of professional you are, what you do, what will happen in a session, where it will happen and what will be expected of the child.

- If working in a group situation, be clear that there might be some questions that you will not be able to answer if there are others around. Tell the children in advance that this is not because they are bad questions, just that they may not be suitable for class discussions. Tell them that you will discuss those questions with them later in private (if appropriate).

- Some organizations insist that certain questions are answered only by parents. Know these and inform the child in advance, being clear about why.

- If appropriate, be clear with the child that you will not be discussing their private life but talking about what people 'in general' do or feel. If the child raises personal issues, it is still important to affirm and normalize the statement or question. You can then follow this up with talking in more general terms – for example, talking about how 'Many people feel excited when they see naked pictures; this is normal.' They could be directed later to discuss the issue with their parents if they wish to do so.

Provide and Teach Rules

Children with ASD can often learn well through the use of rules, although this needs to be approached with caution as they can also subsequently become rigid in sticking to them.

- Don't assume that the child will naturally pick up rules of behaviour without being explicitly taught them.

- Make rules realistic.

- Phrase them positively.

- Keep rules consistent across people and settings.

- Provide positive choices.

- Encourage good behaviour.

- Explain why you have specific rules.

- Focus on the dos, not the don'ts.

- Put visual reminders of rules in prominent places.

- In terms of teaching children skills, it is often helpful to teach them in rule format, for example, 'Always check your zipper before leaving the toilet' or 'Always thank someone if they give you a compliment.'

Be Sensitive to Sexual Orientation

Be careful in your communications with the child not to assume that they are (or indeed that everyone is) heterosexual. As much as possible, use gender neutral phrases, for example 'partners'.

Be Creative with Multimedia Sources

Be as creative as possible with multimedia sources, for example music videos, video clips, movies, the internet and PowerPoint presentations. Use as many resources as possible and try a variety of media formats to see which ones the child likes best. Examples could include:

- watching a short video clip of teenagers flirting with each other; the child could then point out the overt signs that someone is flirting (or indeed not flirting)

- searching through a specific SRE website for information on STIs

- presenting homework in a PowerPoint presentation (i.e. heavy on visuals with short sentences) on what a healthy body looks and feels like

- reading an online newspaper article about internet dating, followed by a clozed sentence exercise

- designing an app relating to finding local women's health centres.

Individualize

Differentiation and individualization of work is *key* with children on the spectrum, who present with an extremely varied profile of cognitive and language skills. Although there are many SRE resources available for typically developing children, as well as some for children with developmental disabilities, you are likely to find quickly that these are not suitable for the particular child you are working with. Rather than spending time searching for resources, creating individualized resources yourself is usually a much more productive use of time. These do not need to be elaborate or 'pretty', and become quicker and easier to make as you gain practice and confidence.

Of course, the curriculum itself, as well as the format it is delivered in, will also need to be individualized for the child.

Utilize Areas of Strength

Instead of focusing on the child's areas of need (for example, their memory or verbal skills), focus instead on their strengths and teach through these.

For example, the steps to changing dirty sheets include the following:

'Check if the sheet is dirty', 'Take old sheet off', 'Take mattress cover off', 'Put both in wash basket', 'Put new mattress cover on', 'Put new sheet on', 'Check all corners' and 'Put back on duvet and pillow'.

- If the child is good at rote learning and likes music, the sequence of steps could be made into a short rhyme and taught to the child in a repetitive manner until learned by rote.

- If they have good computer skills, encourage the child to search for pictures on the internet for each step before putting them together into a poster to print out for their bedroom wall or a PowerPoint presentation format.

- If the child enjoys drawing, they could draw the steps and again make a poster for their bedroom wall.

- If they are good at science and enjoy logic, they could be asked to investigate the reasons why it is important to have clean sheets regularly.

- If they are sociable, they could take a survey of a number of (briefed) adults, investigating topics such as how often they change their sheets, what detergent they use, what temperature they wash their sheets at and how they dry them.

Use Visuals

The majority of people with ASD have more developed visual than verbal skills, and therefore learn best visually. Temple Grandin (an author with AS) has described herself as a 'visual thinker' who accesses information more readily if it is presented in visual rather than verbal format. Visual strategies can include objects, black-and-white photographs, colour photographs, symbolic representations (such as icons), line drawings and written words, as well as visual organizers, such as relationship circles, timelines and hierarchies. In general, visual information should be clear, with no background information to distract. The type of visual used should be determined by what the child understands.

Creating a Visual Schedule for a Specific Task (e.g. Brushing Teeth)

Step 1: Decide on the type of visual the child learns best with.

Step 2: Do a task analysis for 'brushing teeth', i.e. determine all the steps needed.

Step 3: Make a visual for every step.

Step 4: Pick a location for the visual schedule.

Step 5: Model the schedule for the child.

Step 6: Teach the child the sequence.

The child may take each visual off and put them all in a 'Finished' envelope, once completed. Alternative, when moving to the next step of the sequence, the child could physically bring the picture symbol over to the activity (e.g. bringing the 'wash hands' symbol over with them to place beside the sink).

Within an SRE programme, it would be most useful to use the type of visual supports that the child is already using. Where professionals may run into difficulties is when a child uses photographs to support learning. Some professionals (and parents) may feel that some of the visual teaching strategies which have been successful in the past are not appropriate for this area of the curriculum, due to the graphic quality that would be necessary. Many may feel uncomfortable giving such materials to children and worry about the child protection implication for themselves. However, if it is legal and allowed within your organization, and if you follow the policies and procedures of your organization, the benefits for the child in terms of learning a lifelong, adaptive and appropriate, prosocial behaviour should outweigh these concerns.

Support Multisensory Learning

As much as possible, learning should be multisensory, incorporating visual, auditory and tactile methods. For example: when teaching body parts, use anatomically correct dolls, pictures, cartoons and the song 'Head, Shoulders, Knees and Toes'.

Be Aware of Sensory Sensitivities

In general, background noise should be kept to a minimum. Ensure that the lighting is not too bright or distracting for the child. Fluorescent strip lighting, for example, can be experienced as painful and distracting by some children with ASD.

Organize Learning

Make learning structured and predictable for the child. Most children with ASD like their time to be structured. They like to know the exact time something is to happen, and how long it is going to take, who will be there and how many times something is going to happen. Tell them by using visual timers and schedules that they understand and which work for them. And then stick to them.

Organize the Environment

Some children with ASD need their environment to be highly structured also. They may need to be blocked off visually from other children, using partitions, when they need to concentrate. Keeping books, visual schedules and other work in specific places on their desk or in their class will also help. The use of 'To Do' and 'Finished' trays for work can also be useful.

Organize Information

Children with ASD learn well when information is organized for them and the world is made a more ordered place. Look at the information that you need to impart and:

- make lists
- organize information into charts, graphs and webs
- classify and label
- colour code
- keep information in specific places (i.e. colour coded ring binders).

Use Reinforcement

Giving rewards, using whatever the child finds reinforcing, can be a highly successful tactic with children with ASD (but continue to use natural reinforcement in the form of smiles and praise). However, there is no point trying to second-guess what a child on the spectrum will find rewarding. Instead, ask them, ask people who know them well, or observe what they naturally gravitate to or speak about. Rewards can be given immediately, interspersed throughout activities, or by means of 'start charts' or other reward systems.

Use Special Interests

Special interests can be an excellent teaching tool to make learning interesting, fun and meaningful for the child. Make analogies with special interests during teaching. If a child is interested in a particular superhero, you could create problem-solving scenarios where the child needs to work out what the superhero would do in specific contexts. Or make a poster where the superhero teaches the 'rules' of touching in school. Or, if looking at sexuality in the media, a superhero movie could be thematically analysed. Alternatively, use a special interest just to add interest to worksheets – for example, adding logos to the top of every page.

Good work or behaviour can also be reinforced using the child's special interest (e.g. superhero stickers, time talking to you about the superhero, tokens with the superhero logo on them or time watching a specific cartoon).

Ensure Generalization of Skills

We learn our lessons so slowly. As a group, people with ASD are not wired to generalize. Experiences do not transfer from one situation to another. For example, after my episode with the deputy sheriff, all I learned was that deputy sheriffs were not to be trusted. First of all, this lesson is far too specific. Who is not as important as how and why, but I missed that concept for years... Frustration barely scratches the surface of how annoying it is to know I can go from one bad experience to another like the little silver ball slapping around a pinball machine. (Holliday Willey 2012, p.36)

Children with ASD find it difficult to understand the big picture. They struggle to connect concepts together and learning is not often generalized. For example, if correct condom use is taught in one class and sexual intercourse in another, it cannot be assumed that the adolescent will make the link that condoms should be used during sexual intercourse. Therefore, concepts across an SRE curriculum will need to be explicitly linked together.

It is also important that skills are generalized to contexts outside of the isolated situations for which most SRE programmes are delivered. A child may learn the rules of appropriate touch during greetings through role plays within their special education classroom. They may also be able to discuss at length how and why people should be greeted in specific ways. However, without being specifically taught, they are unlikely to follow these skills through to the 'real world' and may continue to touch strangers inappropriately. Continuation of education outside of classroom will therefore be vital if skills are to be generalized across people and settings.

Teach Problem-solving Strategies

Think of the saying, 'Give a man a fish and you feed him for a day. Teach him how to fish and you feed him for a lifetime.' Teaching a child to solve one specific problem will teach them just that, especially children with ASD, who have difficulties generalizing information. More useful for that child would be to teach them problem-solving strategies that they can apply to a number of situations.

Good problem-solving strategies are visual and simple and include methods such as 'decisions worksheets' which help the child work through problem-solving steps, for example coming up with solutions, picking one and evaluating the results. Remember that all children need to be allowed to make mistakes.

Teach Self-management Skills

In a similar vein, self-management skills include the child taking control of their own behaviour management by learning to use self-assessment tools, checklists and rating scales.

Steps for Putting a Self-management System in Place with a Child

Step 1: Choose the behaviour to work on.

Step 2: Decide how the child will measure the behaviour (e.g. after a specific time interval or after each incident). It is usually easier to measure time intervals, but if measuring incidents the child can use a wrist counter or clicker every time they perform a desired behaviour.

Step 3: Find the baseline for the behaviour (i.e. how often it is occurring) so that an appropriate time interval can be decided on in order to promote success (too long and the time interval will be unobtainable, too short and it will lose its reinforcing value).

Step 4: Make or buy a recording device, which could be a sheet of paper, a wrist counter or an app on a smart phone.

Step 5: Decide on a reward (with the child).

Step 6: Teach discrimination. Before the child can self-monitor, they need to understand *what* they are monitoring and the difference between doing and not doing the behaviour. Focus only on when the child displays the behaviour appropriately, i.e. don't track failures, only successes.

Step 7: Record successes. Once the child understands the system, they can begin evaluating themselves. They may need prompting in the beginning but over time should learn to self-evaluate without prompts.

Step 8: Provide rewards paired with praise.

Step 9: Fade back the system. This can be done by increasing the number of points or time recorded, gradually and systematically.

Repeat, Repeat, Repeat

It is vital that concepts are continually reinforced and practised. A single lesson is unlikely to have a significant impact on future behaviour or quality of life.

Provide Choice

Ensure that the child experiences choice throughout the day in terms of what they will do, when, with whom, and the rewards they will receive. This gives them a sense of ownership of their learning and their environment and increases personal responsibility, and therefore motivation.

Check in for Understanding

Although they may seem able, do not assume that the child you are working with has even the most basic knowledge in the area of sexuality and relationships. Most people grow up with half-beliefs about sex and reproduction (e.g. a belief that you will not get pregnant if you have sex standing up) but these can be especially upsetting, and in fact dangerous, for children with special needs, who may never learn the truth. If they take language literally, it is very easy for information to be misinterpreted (e.g. the eggs inside a woman's body have a hard shell like hen's eggs). Always check in that the child understands what you are trying to teach.

Utilize Teachable Moments

Capitalize on 'teachable moments' (e.g. a member of staff being pregnant or a pet dog having puppies), that involve being familiar with the SRE programme. Clarify and label daily interactions with the child. Comment on what is going on around them.

Instructional Stories

The use of short written stories or picture stories is a great way of supporting all areas of an SRE programme. These stories are used to aid understanding, but can also instruct the child as to how to handle different social situations (e.g. 'asking a girl on a date'). They are most successful if the child is involved in writing or making them. Although it is possible to access instructional stories online or in books, it is more appropriate and meaningful for the child if they are tailored to the child, their individual situation and ability and language level. In general, stories are best when accompanied by simple visuals and with no background information to distract. Instructional stories:

- can be produced in a number of different formats
- are best if they reference the child specifically in the story
- should be specific to the child and situation
- should identify the behaviour you want to change or the area you want to teach
- should include areas that the child does well in or is successful at
- can be used to explain sarcasm and interpreting other people's thoughts
- can include stick figures, speech and thought bubbles
- are better if they are attractive and colourful
- can include text written in different colours, which can be chosen by the child.

Examples of instructional stories are provided throughout this book.

Create Social Scripts

Social scripts involve the use of either an audiotaped or a written script which focuses on a specific situation (e.g. 'Dealing with rejection when you have asked someone on a date'). It involves the child learning the script with visual supports (e.g. on cue cards). The script is then faded until the skill is mastered without the visual supports being present. Social scripts can be practised during role plays before moving on to 'real world' interactions.

Teach through Role Play and Drama

I think when it comes to relating to anyone at any level, after reading the books, watching the videos and engaging in conversation, appropriate *role-play can be useful. Role-play is like putting the final bricks in the wall — the top layer that completes the building. For this level of understanding to register, a significant amount of role-playing is needed… Role-playing creates a more concrete setting, and enhances our learning. (Lawson 2005, p.41)*

The use of role play and drama has been highlighted as a method which can be useful in teaching children with ASD social skills. Through repeated role play and drama classes, children can learn in a safe environment how to express certain emotions with their face or voice, and how to act in certain social situations, and so they can develop confidence in their social abilities.

Teach the Use of Journals

Children with ASD generally find it hard to express themselves verbally, especially in writing. However, for those children with good language skills, it may be a valuable exercise to support them in writing in a journal or diary about themselves and their lives. They can then be encouraged to keep note of their own successes as well as the areas that they need to work on. Ground rules around privacy and who can access these journals will need to be established from the start.

Use Video Modelling

Video modelling, a positive and highly visual approach, has led to some success in teaching tasks and social skills to children with ASD (Rayner 2010). In video modelling the child first watches a video of someone else performing a certain behaviour, following which they try to imitate the behaviour. Video *self*-modelling involves the child watching themselves displaying a certain behaviour successfully.

Steps to Using Video Modelling with a Child

Step 1: Choose a skill to teach.

Step 2: Write a script (addressing the target behaviour or skill).

Step 3: Make the video (using adults, peers, siblings or the child themselves).

Step 4: Watch the video with the child.

Step 5: Practise the behaviour shown in the video (providing feedback and positive reinforcement). This can be done through role play and then in more natural environments.

If video self-modelling is used, only positive behaviours should be shown and all unsuccessful clips should be edited out.

Of course, there will be some areas of an SRE programme that are inappropriate for a video modelling teaching technique.

Shape Behaviour Gradually

Shaping is a way of adding to a child's repertoire behaviours that they have not yet mastered. It involves *approximations* of a behaviour being reinforced (i.e. those behaviours that either resemble the target behaviour or are a step closer to it). The general rule is to reinforce any behaviour that is closer to the target behaviour than the last reinforced behaviour.

Do Task Analysis

Task analysis involves analysing the sequence of steps needed for a particular task (e.g. brushing your teeth, putting on a condom, having a shower or shaving your legs), so that it can best be taught to a child. Without a full analysis steps may be left out, as they are often things that we have learned to do automatically.

Undertaking a Task Analysis

Step 1: Choose a task to work on.

Step 2: Do the task several times yourself.

Step 3: Write down every step.

Step 4: Have the child follow the same steps (with guidance) to see if it is the best way for them to complete it.

Step 5: Make a final list of the steps in the visual format that works best for the child.

Step 6: Watch the child do each step. Note which steps they are able to do independently, which need prompting, and the type of prompts the child needs. This is your baseline.

Step 7: Begin teaching any steps the child cannot do independently.

Forward Chaining

Forward chaining involves teaching the sequence of steps for a specific task in chronological order. For example, in the steps for changing a menstrual pad, the first step to teach might be pulling down their underwear, the second would be taking the pad off their underwear, and so on. Teaching is continued until the child can do all of the steps independently.

Backward Chaining

Backward chaining involves teaching the last step of the sequence first, prior to teaching the rest of the sequence in reverse order. This means that the child always finishes the routine, which is in itself rewarding. It also teaches completion of tasks. In the steps to changing a menstrual pad, the last step may be washing hands, taught before the second last step, which may be checking that all of your clothes are tucked in, zippers zipped, and so on.

Behavioural Momentum

Behavioural momentum involves teaching the easy and less frustrating tasks first. Which steps these are will depend on observations and your knowledge of the child's individual strengths and needs. This allows the child to experience success, gain rewards (both internal and external) and can lead to enhanced engagement with future, more difficult tasks.

Intersperse Easy and Hard Tasks

Alternatively, intersperse easy and hard tasks to keep the child interested, motivated and engaged.

Support Motor Memory

Motor memory is involved when skills are taught using guided 'hand over hand' – for example, for self-care tasks such as brushing teeth or putting on deodorant. After repeated guided movements, the child's motor memory will assist them in completing the task independently. There is some controversy over the idea that masturbation may need to be taught in this manner to some teenagers and adults with significant disabilities (discussed later in Chapter 19, 'Masturbation').

Use Music

The use of rhythm, song, repetition, melody and rhyme can aid memory recall for all children, as well as making learning more fun in the process.

Emphasize Peer Modelling and Support

Peer modelling, support and teaching can be an extremely valuable tool for teaching in a number of areas. Peers can include classmates, older children or siblings, who can be trained to model appropriate skills, as well as how to engage with the child and give meaningful feedback.

Particularly in the teenage years, children may pay more attention to what their peers say about a particular topic than their parents or teachers. For example, you might decide to enlist the help of an older (and admired) sister to talk to a girl about the dangers of internet dating. Or a small group of boys could be taught how to sensitively support another boy with ASD in learning about the importance of good body odour and washing.

Applied Behaviour Analysis

ABA is a set of principles that form the basis of many behavioural interventions. It is currently one of the most researched and empirically based strategies for instructing children with ASD. ABA looks at behaviour as a science, including certain 'laws' about how learning takes place and why behaviours occur. Basic principles associated with ABA include the use of prompts, chaining and modelling, all of which focus on antecedents (what happens before the behaviour) and consequences (what happens after the behaviour).

One technique that is particularly emphasized in ABA is the use of reinforcement so that behaviours are more likely to be repeated. ABA also emphasizes the collection of data at every stage. The principles of ABA can be applied to teaching any skill or behaviour, including components of an SRE programme.

TEACCH

TEACCH is a comprehensive programme designed for children with ASD which emphasizes structure and has a strong behavioural modification emphasis. It covers all areas of functioning and includes a Sexuality and Relationship Education curriculum with an emphasis on seeing sexual behaviours in the context of social skills, communication, cognitive ability and an individual's strengths and weaknesses.

The TEACCH Sexuality and Relationship Education curriculum includes four developmentally sequenced levels chosen according to level of cognitive functioning (Schopler 1997). Those individuals with a significant ID may receive only the first level of the curriculum, whilst 'high functioning' individuals may be exposed to all four levels. The first level of the TEACCH programme focuses on developing appropriate social behaviours and habits through the approach of behaviour modification. The second and third levels focus on issues of personal hygiene and understanding sexual anatomy and functioning. Level four focuses on interpersonal relationships.

CASE EXAMPLE

Mia is a 15-year-old girl with ASD who attends mainstream education. Although she has good verbal ability, Mia has never spoken to anyone in her class. On Valentine's Day, Mia sent a sexually explicit Valentine's Day card which she had bought in a local shop to Peter, a boy in her class. Following an investigation by her teacher (who heard her classmates laughing about it), it turned out that Mia had not been aware of the inappropriate content of the card. Not only that, but she had misunderstood Valentine's Day, thinking that it was a day to ask a boy to be your friend. Mia stated that she had no romantic interest in Peter, that boys were generally 'loud' and 'boring', but because Peter had Doctor Who badges on his bag (her current top special interest), she had deduced that he would make a good friend for her.

It would appear that Mia currently has no interest in boys romantically. Therefore, teaching her SRE concepts related to dating and boyfriends would most likely be inappropriate at this time. However, it is clear that she needs support in a number of areas relating to understanding sexual language, socializing with her peers and making friends. Following are some examples of teaching activities to help support Mia in these areas.

- Goals such as 'Appropriately greeting peers' could be added to Mia's IEP.

- Teach her the factual meanings of the sexual terminology and images that she had misunderstood.

- Simple instructional stories could be created to teach Mia about friendship, how to make 'small talk' with her peers and ask someone to be her friend.

- A social script could be created to help Mia enquire in a friendly and appropriate way about Peter's Doctor Who badges.

- Video modelling (including self-modelling) could be used to teach appropriate greetings and how to react when someone does not want to talk to you.

- Peter could be supported in dealing appropriately and kindly with Mia's mistake. His teacher could talk to him about ASD, why Mia made the mistake and how it must feel for Mia to have no friends in her class. If willing, he could be enlisted to help teach her appropriate social skills and include her in some activities with his friends.

- Peter and Mia could do repeated role plays of her approaching other children and talking about different topics, with Peter providing age-appropriate but sensitive feedback.

- Mia could be taught a self-management system whereby she records and is rewarded every time she greets a peer appropriately.

- She could be encouraged to keep a journal all about what she would like out of a friendship and what it means to be a good friend.

- Mia could be rewarded for all her efforts to learn new skills with some extra time on the computer researching the history of Doctor Who.

- She could be encouraged to investigate whether there are any online Doctor Who fan discussion sites which would be appropriate for her to join and contribute to (which would be monitored by her parents).

Above all be patient, kind and understanding, both with the child you are working with and with yourself!

5

Working with Parents

Why Parental Involvement in SRE is Key

If you are planning an SRE programme, or working on a child's inappropriate sexualized behaviour, there is nothing more important you can do than support and empower the child's parents (or other primary carers) to feel more knowledgeable about and comfortable in providing SRE to their child themselves. Better outcomes will be achieved if SRE is started from a young age, throughout the school or organization, and parents are supported through every step by combining efforts, maintaining communication and building relationships.

Parental involvement may be one of the only ways of supporting a child with ASD to develop and maintain *lifelong* skills and experiences in this area, due to the more involved and prolonged nature of the role of parents in the child's life, including playing the role of 'gatekeeper' to accessing SRE, sexual health services and experiencing intimate relationships. They are also best placed to act as advocates for their child, ensuring that SRE concepts continue to be part of their curriculum, IEP or person-centred plan.

In addition, parents will need to be involved and committed if skills are to be taught and generalized across settings. Possibly even more than other curriculum areas, SRE needs to span home and school, and is incomplete and potentially harmful if it is not also being carried out in the home. For example, children need to learn that they can explore their bodies or be naked in the privacy of their own bedrooms, as they will not be allowed to do so in other settings.

SRE has strong moral and value-laden components. Children need to learn the values and morals of their core family and community if they are to live and thrive within them. Even if parents are unwilling to take part, it is important that their values are incorporated into any programme. Parents should also be viewed as the experts on their own children. Therefore they are valuable mines of information as well as being best placed to teach their child new skills.

Barriers to Parental Involvement

He gets crushes, so far he is ultimately rejected and devastated. The thing is preparing him for rejection so that it doesn't destroy his self-esteem. Why talk about sex with him when it will most likely never happen? It is cruel to get his hopes up. (Parent of a child with ASD, in Ballan 2012, p.681)

Is my child ever going to get married and have kids – no. That opportunity was taken away from her the day she was diagnosed with autism, without her having a choice. She has discovered (her area) but a partner, nope, it is just not in her future. (Parent of a child with ASD, in Ballan 2012, p.681)

Following is a list of some of the areas where parents report difficulties in becoming involved in SRE.

Skills

Parents may feel that they do not have the competency to provide SRE to their children, who may have needed specialized education and care up to this point, leading the parents to feel disempowered in relation to work on other areas such as sexuality. Educational jargon can contribute to this lack of confidence.

Information

Parents may not have been provided with information about sexuality, typical sexual development in children and SRE in general, or prepared for their child to need to be taught in these areas. They are most likely unaware of the breadth and value of a good SRE programme. They may also be unaware of how to apply concepts to the child's everyday environments. Without this information, they may be uncertain about when to start, and how to handle sexual behaviours or the appropriateness of different topics for their child.

Resources

There is currently insufficient availability of resources and materials developed for either parents or professionals to provide SRE to children with ASD without a considerable investment of time and energy.

Desire to Protect

The gap between physical and cognitive development in a child with ASD can be wide. It is understandable that in these circumstances it is the parent's natural instinct to want to protect their child from inappropriate information. In addition, they may feel that discussing sexuality and relationships with their child will open up to them a world that they will not be able to access because of their disability, leading to hurt and possibly more significant mental health issues. Parents may also perceive sexuality to be an additional burden on their child, who may already struggle in so many other areas.

Beliefs

Parents may be holding culturally laden beliefs that children with disabilities are (or should be) asexual.

Grief

The topic of sexuality may bring up issues relating to parents' hopes and dreams for their child, and the gap between what they had wished for them in terms of relationships, employment and marriage, and the reality. Therefore, adolescence may trigger not only stress for parents, but also a sense of loss and renewed grieving.

Personal History

Teenage sexuality may bring up issues (particularly if they are unresolved) for parents regarding their own sexuality and sexual past. Parents may also have had negative experiences of school or authority, leading to disengagement with professionals involved with their children.

Understanding

Parents may have concerns about their child's ability to understand the information presented to them.

Behaviour

Some parents may worry that SRE could lead to perseveration of a particular behaviour, for example that masturbation could become a substitute for current behaviours such as hand-flapping or rocking. They may also fear that exposure to SRE will overstimulate their child and make inappropriate sexual behaviours worse. (This has not been borne out in the research on cognitive disabilities (Tarnai 2006).)

Time, Stress and Money

Parents may report feeling busy and stressed. They may have other children to look after or be dealing with their own personal issues, including illness, work strain, bills or lack of sleep. All of these factors may contribute to parents feeling that they do not have the emotional or physical energy to become involved with any extra programme. Finding babysitters may also be difficult to organize, and expensive, if parents are asked to come in for parent meetings, training or information sessions.

Negative Experiences with Professionals or Schools

Has all communication to a parent focused on negative behaviours and crises? Have they only been asked to meet with a professional when inappropriate behaviours escalate? If so, parents will be less keen to become involved when asked in to discuss an SRE programme for their child, as they will assume that it is going to be a negative and stressful encounter.

Privacy

Parents living in small communities (i.e. where everyone knows each other) may have higher concerns about the privacy issues involved in their child taking part in an SRE programme than parents in larger urban areas (McCall 2012).

Promoting and Supporting Parental Involvement

Good Communication and Relationships

If you have a good relationship with a child and the child's parents, they are more likely to trust you when you propose introducing new areas to the child's curriculum. To build trust and good relationships, there need to be systems in place whereby parents are consistently supported in all areas and communicated with regularly. Ballan (2012) reported that parents portrayed professionals as lacking initiative and receptivity to addressing sexuality issues unless it presented as a behavioural concern. Instead, involve parents early and on a continuous basis, and not just when there is a crisis. Make the time for regular parent meetings. Be available for and open to phone calls and meetings. Provide parents with regular feedback on their child's strengths and successes.

Consider the religious, ethnic and cultural beliefs of the child's family. Anticipate that the topic of sexuality will be sensitive. Remember that this child is their 'baby', whom they have cared for and loved for years before you came along, and will for a lifetime after you are gone from their child's life. Their views on their child and what they need are more important than yours. Reflect on the reasons they may have for not wanting to engage. Learn to understand their fears and develop empathy for where they are coming from. Let them know before any meeting what will be discussed, that is, don't spring any new information on them. When talking about SRE, be specific about what you are talking about. Ask for their opinions. Acknowledge their concerns and address barriers directly but sensitively.

Collaboration

Collaboration with parents will promote good relationships, build confidence, and support 'buy in' and motivation from parents. Following are some ways in which you or your organization can promote this:

- Undertake parent involvement programmes.

- Divide tasks, with parents responsible for the home environment.

- Recruit someone specific from the child's family to help with the programme.

- Organize parent groups that could be involved in contributing to, approving and evaluating your SRE programme, as well as being given responsibilities – for example, finding out about sexual health services in the region.

- Alternatively, if they do not wish to engage, parents can be involved just by receiving information regularly and being informed about progress.

To ensure a holistic and community-based best practice programme, collaboration with local doctors, health clinics, voluntary agencies and community agencies is also recommended.

Information, Resources and Training

> *The experts have the answer for every situation with my child except the one that could land him in jail if he handles it wrong. I just wish they would be trained to ask us the important questions since we don't know what questions to ask or to who. Why would I think my son would get erections or try to kiss girls at nine when he wasn't even toilet trained until six? (Parent of a child with ASD, in Ballan 2012, p.680)*

Provide parents with relevant, accessible and sensitive information, resources and training. Following are some examples of how to go about this:

- Demystify and normalize SRE for them. Be *specific* about what you will be teaching and why.

- Introduce developmentally appropriate sexuality and relationship topics early (i.e. well before puberty) and label them clearly as SRE topics.

- Ask parents what supports they feel they need to become effective sexuality educators.

- Organize parent information sessions.

- Build confidence through a tailored, parent-based intervention to support them in the areas they have raised. Parents should leave any training thinking, 'I can do this. I know how to teach my child. I have taught my child many things. I have the skills and knowledge to teach them this.'

- Develop materials (e.g. factsheets) which address specific concerns that parents have raised.

- Reassure them that the programme will take a factual, honest approach to presenting information and will not typically promote which decisions are best or condone certain lifestyle choices.

- Inform parents that education is key to preventing abuse and that research indicates that SRE does not increase sexual experimentation.

- Recommend specific books, websites and resources.

- Support parents in finding related talks and information in the community (e.g. in the library or local health centres).

- Bring written information about policies and curricula requirements to all meetings.

- Reassure them that they can 'opt out' of certain sections of the programme.

- Provide them with information on typical child sexual development and what they may expect for their own child.

- Support them in implementing the skill-based techniques that are already in place for the child (e.g. visual schedules) in relation to sexuality and relationships.

- Help them in assessing their child's understanding of sexuality-related topics.

  I don't want someone on the child life study team educating my son about masturbation. I have no idea of that person's morals, values or skills. I often don't even agree with what she wants for my child academically. But I would like for them to help me figure out how to best provide the information to my son, so that he learns it and I know he gets it. (Parent of a child with ASD, in Ballan 2012, p.682)

6
Developing SRE Policies and Procedures

If SRE is being provided within an organization meeting the needs of children with ASD (e.g. a school, respite or intervention service), it is typically in response to a particular child's behaviour and provided to that child alone. Because it is also often provided thanks to the particular interest of an individual professional, it may be done in an ad hoc and haphazard manner, depending on individual values and interests and the needs of individual children. This is far from best practice.

If SRE is to be taught in a planned, staged, organized and preventative manner to *all* children from an *early age*, there need to be clear guidelines and policies in place. What is also needed is strong leadership and a meaningful commitment to improving services, adopting a planned and systematic approach. There needs to be a *vision* for the work to be done, including the changes that may need to be made at a systems level – for example, changes in attitudes towards sexuality at a society and service level, and the recognition that people with ASD need to have opportunities to develop relationship skills. In addition to this, there needs to be within the organization a belief in behaviour change in general, that things will progress for all children with support, and that having ASD does not mean that they will not benefit from strategies aimed at skills development or insight. A strong and confident organizational ethos will not only have a significant effect on staff attitudes and behaviour, it will also form the basis of strong service provision.

An organization's policies should be based on guiding principles, for example:

- Individuals with ASD have the same rights as other members of the community.

- They can live in the community with appropriate supports.

- They have the right to a sexual life.

- They have the right to determine their own lives and futures.

- Behaviour change can be brought about using positive, person-centred approaches.

If you are currently working as part of an organization, for a start, the following questions need to be asked:

- Are you aware of the principles of your organization?

- Is it committed to inclusion?

- Is it committed to its clients being as independent as possible?

- Does it believe that its clients' views are valuable and should contribute to service planning?

- If SRE policies do exist within your organization, are all staff familiar with them? Are they understood? Are they being followed on a daily basis?

Policies should be living documents that grow and change with an organization, not left to gather dust in a filing cabinet, with staff unaware that they even exist.

Salient Policies and Procedures for Implementing Successful SRE

In addition to those directly linked to SRE, policies and procedures should also cover the related areas of child protection, acceptable sexual expression within the organization, privacy, behaviour management, and the training and treatment of staff.

Sexuality and Relationship Education

Some considerations for inclusion in SRE policies and procedures are the following:

- Who it will be provided to, what will be taught, when, for how long and by whom?

- Which materials are considered appropriate or inappropriate for use in the setting (e.g. photos or videos)?

- What will the staff ratio be during topics of a sensitive nature (e.g. masturbation)?

- Links to IEP planning should be formally made.

- Goals should be clearly stated, as should the criteria used to show that objectives and attainments have been met. What are the broader aims, objectives and goals of the curricula? Is it that the child will have a sexually fulfilling life? That they will be protected from danger? What is it that you expect the child to be able to do after completing the programme? How will success be judged? How will the child demonstrate that they have learned and understood the objectives of the lessons?

- The programme provided should be linked to up-to-date, best practice research and guidelines.

- Policies regarding staff training in SRE should be included.

- A child-centred approach focusing on individualized programming is best practice, even if this involves staff making considerable efforts to adapt materials, teaching methods or therapeutic models in order to make them accessible to the child.

- An emphasis on collaboration with, and building capacity within, families should be explicitly stated.

- There should be a community approach to any policy, with links to other organizations and agencies (e.g. social work services and local health clinics). Staff should easily be able to access information on relevant community resources for children and their families.

- Factsheets about SRE and the organization's SRE policies should be developed for both parents and children.

- Policies need to be in place for when disagreements occur. For example, what is the policy if the organization strongly feels that the child needs SRE, but the child's parents disagree?

Accepted Expressions of Sexuality

The fact that people with disabilities are sexually victimized is never an acceptable rationale to write policies that forbid the possibilities of consenting loving relationships. (Hingsburger 1995, p.8)

It is important to state explicitly in an organization's policies (which must be in accordance with the laws of the country or state) what kinds of sexual expression (e.g. masturbation, physical affection or romantic relationships) are or are not allowed between young people for whom it is responsible, within its boundaries. Policies that support peer relationship development and opportunities for healthy sexuality are best practice and have many benefits, including decreased need for secretive or inappropriate sexual expression. Without policies in this area, responses to the child will be inconsistent, as different staff respond to sexual behaviours by ignoring, punishing, allowing or rewarding. This will not only be confusing and potentially harmful for the child, but may also damage behaviour management goals. Individual beliefs should not control policy.

Increasingly, services are acknowledging that individuals with disabilities have rights regarding relationships and sexuality. However, translating this acknowledgement into proactive support is an ongoing challenge. One historical barrier may have been the predominance of religious patronage in organizations supporting individuals with disabilities. Another may have been legal issues, as in some countries certain laws exist which hinder organizations from allowing sexual relationships even between adults with learning disabilities.

However, when it is *children* who are being supported, there are of course different and significant legal (as well as ethical and moral) issues at work, and professionals need to be careful to balance the law, what they feel is right and what will keep themselves and the children in their care safe. It is clearly inappropriate, and may well be illegal in some countries, for schools to allow sexual contact between children, or indeed other expressions of sexuality (e.g. masturbation), as children need to learn that this should be done in the privacy of their own bedrooms. Organizations providing residential services must give more thought to accepted sexual expression within the child's bedroom. Also, it is important to note that 'accepted sexual expression' does not just cover 'allowing' a child to masturbate. It also entails how professionals *react* to these behaviours. For example, a child should not be allowed to masturbate in school. However, responses to masturbation in this setting should be consistent, planned and calm, including reminding the child that they can masturbate at home.

Privacy

Hingsburger (1995) advocates teaching privacy by doing privacy. Policies should be in place which show respect for children's privacy and personal space, seeking permission and involving people with disabilities in decisions regarding their own bodies. This includes staff encouraging as much independence as possible in self-care tasks, gaining permission before touch, restructuring environments so that privacy is maximized, averting gaze if the child is naked and teaching children the tools to communicate that they want privacy. For more information in this area, see Chapter 12, 'Teach Public and Private'.

Child Protection

Organizations must have up-to-date child protection policies and procedures in line with national child protection laws (including identifying and reporting abuse and managing disclosure). The children that these laws were designed to protect also need to be trained in how the system operates, and which boundaries should be in place between them and staff, as well as how to advocate on their own behalf.

EXAMPLES OF GOOD PRACTICE

- The management of one agency supporting people with disabilities organized for all frontline staff to develop a list of their clients' rights. Staff were then asked to create a list of restrictions on their own behaviour that their clients needed to know about. Simple illustrations were made for each of these rights and restrictions which were subsequently given to all clients in a booklet format. An external advocate regularly reviews how this system is operating.

- Some agencies have systems set up whereby outside agencies regularly meet with clients to discuss possible abuse, thereby communicating clearly to staff and clients that the system takes clients' rights seriously.

(Hingsburger 1995)

Following are some of the safeguarding issues that should be considered in an organization's policies and procedures, and which as a professional you need to be aware of:

- recognizing signs of abuse

- procedures to follow if abuse or exploitation is suspected

- procedures to follow if a child discloses information of a sexual nature or relating to abuse

- the process that is put in place following the reporting of abuse

- the process that is put in place if an allegation is made against a member of staff

- procedures to follow if a member of staff sees signs that another member of staff is behaving suspiciously

- when and how often staff training in child protection policies and procedures occurs. Due to the high turnover of staff that exists within special education, it is recommended that this is implemented more than once a year

- when and how often the children themselves will receive training in recognizing and reporting abuse. David Hingsburger, in *Home Safe: A Manual about Abuse: Preventing and Reporting in Community Services* (2010), emphasizes that an organization that trains its clients to report abuse and how to do so will have the added benefit of preventing potential abusers working within that organization. One agency that does just that has reported that some prospective staff decided not to take up a job there, as this approach 'upsets the natural relationship between a staff and client'. This agency was happy with this response as they felt that they had developed policies and procedure that protected their clients from staff who (while possibly not abusive) did not wish their behaviour to be discussed (Hingsburger 1994)

- there should be an ethos of always making time to listen to children, including those with no verbal language. Hingsburger (1994) highlights the 'tragedy' that many people with disabilities, despite having support staff around them all day, have no one to talk to in time of need.

Behaviour Management

Behaviour management policies and procedures should include specific information on dealing with sexual behaviours, with links to child protection policies and procedures, and should make clear which behaviours may need further investigation or reporting, why, how and to whom.

The Treatment and Training of Staff

A priority of any service or organization should be treating its staff with respect, which is the first step in treating clients with respect. This means that all staff need to be seen and treated as equal and respected members of the team. They should be involved at every step of a child's programme and aware of the child's history or any current issues. This seems to be stating the obvious, but often frontline staff (e.g. special needs assistants) are excluded from meetings and kept in the dark about many of the details of children's programmes.

Overall commitment to staff training should be explicitly covered within the policies of an organization. The ongoing training and support of frontline care staff (who will most likely be carrying out most tasks) will be critical to the success of any programme. Without it, their ability to support the children with whom they are working may be compromised. Training does not always need to involve formal 'lessons' from outside agencies. An ethos of ongoing learning, sharing of information, in-house training, observation, shadowing and sharing of information will benefit all professionals, as will sound policies on supervision (including peer supervision) and mentoring. An ethos of sharing and peer support will enhance confidence and have the added benefit of skills and knowledge being kept within the organization after professionals move on.

Developing SRE Policies

Working with children with ASD may involve individualized settings and communities, and therefore may need individualized policies and procedures. Although time-consuming, the development of policies by all stakeholders in a structured way will support ownership and 'buy in', which will be much needed when it comes to sensitive topics such as SRE.

Some Tips for Developing SRE Policies

- Look at national policies as starting points.

- Evaluate existing policies.

- Look at the principles of your organization. Do they need to be updated? Which are relevant to SRE?

- Involve all stakeholders in the process (including families, staff and children). Communicate with them regularly.

- Survey all stakeholders for their views on SRE (in particular parent committees).

- Evaluate what is actually happening on the ground within the organization in relation to sex education. Map this in a visual format and distribute to all stakeholders.

- Gather all related resources that the organization already possesses.

- Investigate new resources appropriate to your setting.

- Investigate whether any current members of staff have skills sets in the area.

- Future interest could be built through the establishment of an SRE forum for sharing information, research and good practice.

- Develop a committee to work on the policies, representing a mix of agencies and professionals and including parents and students.

- Investigate up-to-date, best practice guidelines and research in relation to SRE for children with ASD.

- Come to an agreement with all stakeholders regarding the policies.

- Ensure that policies are also produced in an accessible format for young people, parents and people with literacy difficulties.

See Appendix C for an Organization Checklist to support best practice in SRE within your organization.

Part II
Preventing

7

Teach Gender

Developing a gender identity is one of the developmental milestones of childhood. Although not traditionally thought of as relating to sexuality, it is an important stepping stone to developing a sense of self and a sexual identity. Knowing one's gender also supports the ability to make appropriate and safe responses in social situations. However, encouraging gender stereotypes is unhelpful at best. Boys and girls need to learn that despite their differences they are similar in many ways and should be given equal rights and responsibilities. For example, both women and men can be caring and loving parents, can do chores and can be employed in the same jobs. Boys can wear dresses (although they often don't), girls can have short hair, and girls can sometimes be stronger than boys. Boys and girls should also be encouraged to be friends. It is important that children are supported in learning to make their own choices as to how to behave, unconstrained by how society thinks they should because of their gender.

Typically developing children often learn to depend on subtle cues to determine gender, such as tone of voice, general appearance, body language and context. This is learned in such an unconscious and automatic manner that it is often hard for adults to imagine not being able to do so. However, children with ASD can find learning gender concepts difficult and confusing and often need extra support in this area.

Like all other areas of a child's SRE programme, what should be taught, when and how in relation to gender will depend on their age, developmental level, learning strengths and language skills. All children should be taught that they are a girl or a boy and be able to recognize and discriminate between the two genders. However, older or more able children should be taught about gender at a more advanced level, including gender stereotypes, gender roles and other gender concepts, for example, transgender issues. These will be important building blocks in other areas of the child's social skills and SRE programmes.

Gender: Teaching Activities and Recommendations

1. Access a wide variety of pictures of males and females of different ages using a variety of visual styles (e.g. photos, line drawings, cartoons and paintings). You can access many of these from magazines, or alternatively from the internet. Use these to cue in the child to concrete, observable features such as name, clothes, make-up and obvious

physical indications (e.g. facial hair or breasts). Remember to present a range of different races, cultures and body shapes. Lessons such as 'Girls wear dresses' or 'Boys have short hair' are not valid today. Therefore, make sure to include 'difficult' images, e.g. female body builders, girls with short hairstyles wearing trousers, and male rock stars with long hair wearing make-up. Also collect photos of the child's family and other people they know well, including people in the media and, if relevant, people related to the child's special interest. You may wish to laminate these images for durability, which can be then be used to:

- play games involving labelling, matching or sorting according to gender (e.g. 'Snap' or using separate gender sorting boxes)
- create separate gender folders
- create posters
- create collage pictures.

2. Make life-sized posters of bodies. You can make these yourself or have the child lie down on a piece of paper and draw around them. Ensure that you do not outline private body parts. These can be filled in later by yourself, or ideally by the child. Have the child fill in visual details for either male or female.

3. Make paper dolls and have the child guess whether they are male or female. The child can then undress them to see if they were correct.

4. Create papier mâché bodies.

5. Make a collection of different items of clothing. Ask the child questions such as 'Would a boy or a girl wear this?' Have the child sort the clothes into either male or female boxes (being careful to acknowledge that most could go in either).

6. Have the child search for gender images on the internet (supervised).

7. Other teaching materials could include anatomically correct dolls, skeletons, posters, books, stories, music and dressing-up clothes.

8. Remember to teach what is alike as well as what is different between the sexes.

9. You may choose to teach the slang words common for both sexes (e.g. 'bros' and 'chicks').

10. Encourage non-gender-stereotyped play and avoid assigning projects by gender (although it will be appropriate to divide some SRE activities by gender).

11. Remember not to tell children that any toys, colours, TV programmes, music, sports, hobbies or jobs are 'just for boys' or 'just for girls'.

12. Examine stereotypes with the child, e.g. 'Boys don't cry' and 'Women stay at home and mind the babies'.

13. Discuss different scenarios, e.g. 'What if Cinderella didn't want to get married?' and for older adolescents, 'If a man wants to wear women's clothes and make-up, is he still a man?'

8

Teach Body Parts and Fluids

In most western civilizations, it is expected that children be taught to label basic human body parts and bodily fluids. However, learning in this area should also encompass bodily *functions* (including sexual anatomy), as well as *internal* body parts (including reproductive organs). Children with ASD may have a fragmented understanding of their physical identity and need to be taught not only the names of their body parts, but also that they belong to and are part of them. Teaching a child to label body parts and fluids correctly will support them in learning other important concepts such as hygiene, health, toileting, reproduction and safety skills. Children need to know how a healthy body works and what it should look and feel like, so that if they are sick or hurt they can tell the difference.

Knowing the names of body parts and fluids forms the basis of teaching children which body parts should not be touched and by whom. They will also need to be able to label their body parts if they are to have the language to report abuse, already difficult for children with ASD who not only have issues with the language skills required, but also often have difficulty locating or describing pain.

Children need to learn that every one of their body parts (both external and internal) has a name and a purpose. They also need to learn that everybody's bodies do not look the same. In relation to SRE, it is particularly important that they learn that breasts, penises and vulvas all look different, and that it does not matter how big your penis or breasts are. They need to learn that men and women have body parts that are there to make (and feed) babies, as well as give pleasure. It is also important that they learn early that the appearance of body parts can change over a lifetime (e.g. because of age, weight, pregnancy or hormones).

Teaching body parts can also encompass teaching about the five senses and people's different sensory experiences – for example, learning how, even though everyone has a tongue that can taste, people don't always agree on what tastes good; or exploring how someone who is visually impaired experiences the world.

An important part of teaching a child about body parts will also be promoting a positive attitude about one's body. If you are embarrassed and avoid labelling certain body parts or fluids (e.g. semen), you may pass on the message that there are certain body parts or functions of the child's body that are either unimportant or shameful and not to be spoken about. This may make the child even more vulnerable to abuse and is unhelpful in contributing to a healthy body image. However, it *is* important to emphasize the private nature of the topic when talking about sexual organs or fluids.

Body Parts and Fluids: Teaching Activities and Recommendations

1. In general, start by teaching the child's own gender body parts first.

2. Link body parts to function regularly.

3. Incidental teaching should be particularly emphasized. For example, if tickling the child, say, 'Tickling the toes'. If the child touches your bracelet, say 'That's my bracelet, on my wrist'. Or after eating, pat your stomach and say, 'Tummy full'.

4. Encourage parents to label the body parts of even very young babies, including during bath time and nappy time or changing at the swimming pool. These incidental teaching moments are often not appropriate for professionals.

5. It is important to give the child the *correct* names for their sexual anatomy, including nipples, breasts, vagina, pubic hair, bottom, anus, clitoris and testicles (as developmentally appropriate).

6. Difficulties with language and abstract concepts can mean that the child with ASD will find multiple words for the same thing difficult to understand. Therefore, try to use one word for each body part and stick to it. Discuss this with the child's parents so that everyone is using the same words.

7. Depending on the child, decide whether to teach only correct terminology, or to include slang. A child with good language ability may need to be taught not only the correct words, but also the words that most adults use and the words that their peers will use when no adults are around. Insisting on the use of the 'correct' names may leave the child open to being teased or bullied by their peers. If working on this, have the child match slang terms and real terms. Create sorting boxes and have the child sort them into:

    • terms appropriate for friends, family, class time, yard time or doctors

    • terms which some people would find offensive or a lot of people don't like

    • terms that are suitable to use with most people.

8. Have the child point to their own and other people's body parts.

9. Teach songs with actions, e.g. 'Head, shoulders, knees and toes'.

10. Access a wide variety of pictures of clothed and unclothed males and females of different ages and races. Use a variety of visual styles (e.g. photos, line drawings, cartoons and paintings). Summer holiday pictures with people in bathing suits are particularly useful. You can access many of these from magazines, or alternatively search the internet – but be careful of what you find and be careful as to the

appropriateness of the material that you show the child. Consider whether you will need to include pictures of erect and non-erect penises in your teaching materials. Consult your organization's policies as to the materials acceptable for use, and always inform and obtain permission from parents if presenting explicit materials. It would be wise to do internet searches without the child present due to the inappropriate images that will be among the results. Images are available in Appendix G of naked men and women at different stages of the life cycle and incorporating different body shapes and sizes. Incorporate clothed pictures of the child and their family. Be careful to use pictures that include a range of realistic body shapes and ideals. If the child has a special interest, or likes a particular book or cartoon, use characters from it. Use all of these images to create flashcards, ideally laminated for durability, which can then be used in a number of ways, including:

- labelling
- grouping (e.g. 'female body parts', group 'legs' or 'private body parts')
- matching (e.g. games such as 'Snap').

11. Link activities to the child's own experiences, e.g. 'This is your mum; she has breasts just like you.'

12. Make life-sized posters of bodies. You can make them yourself or have the child lie down on a piece of paper and draw around them (being careful not to touch private body parts, which can be filled in afterwards). These posters can be used to:

- label body parts
- point to body parts
- draw body parts on
- throw a ball at a particular body part
- match flashcards to places on the body.

13. If relevant, make line drawings of characters from the child's special interest, and have them fill in their body parts.

14. Make a collection of different clothing items. Ask the child questions such as 'Would a boy or a girl wear this?' and 'What body part would this cover?' The child could also either sort the clothes into different baskets assigned by body part or match the clothing item to a picture of a body part, which they could then cover with the clothing item.

15. Make collage pictures of bodies or specific body parts.

16. Encourage the child to look at their naked body in a full-length mirror at home, in their bedroom. Encourage them to look specifically at their sexual anatomy. Encourage them to think about which parts they like and why.

17. There are many resources available online and in traditional SRE programmes for teaching children about the internal sexual reproduction organs, including diagrams of the penis and vagina.

18. You may need to counteract stereotypes about sexual anatomy, for example, that some people say that vulvas or penises are ugly. However, only do so if the child or somebody else in a group raises this first.

19. Some children with ASD may benefit from the analogy that the body is like a machine, with every part having an important 'job' to do (e.g. sweat cools down the body when it is hot).

20. Before teaching body fluids, the child should be familiar with the different body parts that produce fluids. Body fluids can then be taught using the same body part images (with additional fluid images) and activities (with minor adaptations). Some steps to teaching body fluids are the following.

    (a) Talk with the child about what happens when a man or woman cries. Explain that the liquid which comes from the eyes is called tears.

    (b) Follow the same process for all parts of the body that produce fluid, e.g. the nose produces mucus, the mouth produces saliva, armpits produce sweat and the penis produces urine and semen.

    (c) For females, say that urine comes from the urethra, and vaginal moisture and menstrual blood come from the vagina. Teaching a child about vaginal moisture will be an important step in learning about sexual health.

    (d) Now discuss when and why these fluids are produced, for example:

    - The body makes tears when someone is sad.

    - Urine is produced throughout the day to get rid of toxins.

    - Semen is produced to make babies. It comes out of a man's penis when he ejaculates.

    - Sweat is produced when someone is hot. It helps their body to cool down.

    - Menstrual blood is produced when a woman menstruates, usually once a month. It happens because her egg was not fertilized that month and is a sign that she is not pregnant.

    - Women produce more vaginal moisture when they are feeling sexually aroused.

9

Teach Growing and Changing

Learning about being human is learning that there are different stages in our lives, and that we are constantly growing and changing. It involves remembering our past, what we were like, what we were able to do and what we have learned, as well as thinking to the future, where we will live, what our bodies will look like and who will look after us when we are older. Typically, children with ASD have difficulty imagining the future and dealing with change, and therefore need to be prepared for the changes that will occur throughout their lives to their bodies, relationships, educational settings and living situations in order to enable them to handle these changes more confidently when they occur. They need to learn that a baby becomes a boy who becomes a man who becomes an old man. They need to learn that there are some things a man can do that a boy cannot, and some that a boy can do that a baby cannot. They also need to learn where *they* fit into the life cycle in relation to other people in order to support their relationship and social skills.

Growing and Changing: Teaching Activities and Recommendations

1. Emphasize the positive aspects of changing and growing.

2. Teach the child that all living things grow and change. You may use other animals (a caterpillar being a typical example) to make analogies, but remember that these may be too abstract for children with ASD.

3. Teach what living beings need to grow, e.g. water, sunshine, food and love.

4. Develop instructional stories (including pictures if needed) in a variety of areas related to growing and changing, for example:

    • My Family Changes

    • My Body Changes

    • Things I Liked when I was a Baby

    • New Things I Can Do Now that I am a Teenager.

These will need to be highly specific to the child.

5. Talk to the child about when they were a baby (what they did, what they liked, what they were able to do) and what they are able to do now. Also talk to them about what they would like for their future, where they would like to live, what they would like to be able to do. Try to be sensitive, optimistic yet realistic if they voice unrealistic expectations. Create visual timelines with this information.

6. Make full-length pictures of the child fully clothed at different stages of their life. These can be posted up on a wall.

7. If you can access them, anatomically correct dolls at different stages of the life cycle would be useful.

8. Watching long-running TV programmes in which the same child actor grows up can be a useful teaching tool.

9. It is important that the child doesn't develop an unrealistic view of what their own or other people's bodies should or will look like, e.g. from TV, movies or magazines.

10. Ask the child, at home, to stand next to an older family member (either in underwear or clothed) and discuss the similarities and differences between them.

11. Access a wide variety of images of clothed and unclothed males and females developing across the different stages of their life cycle, using a variety of visual styles. Be careful to include a range of realistic body shapes. Use these to teach about the change. Examples of these types of images are included at the end of this chapter and in Appendix G.

12. Also access a range of old and new photos of the child and the child's family, including as many people and generations as possible. Following are some activities that the child can do with these:

    • label in relation to themselves (e.g. younger sister)

    • arrange from youngest to oldest

    • place themselves in a line-up in terms of age

    • group into babies, toddlers, young people, teenagers, adults, older people or more sophisticated groupings based on tasks, e.g. 'People who are allowed to go out by themselves', 'People who are old enough to make babies', 'People who have periods' and 'People who live at home with their parents'

    • collect pictures of the *same* person throughout their life and have the child arrange them from when they were a baby onwards. Use these to show changes over time, e.g. hair loss, spots, breast changes, weight gain or height changes. Also use them to discuss things that the person liked or was able to do at the different stages – for example, 'When granddad was a teenager, he moved to London and lived in a bedsit. He loved dancing and going to parties'; 'That is granddad in the hospital when your dad was born' and 'Here is your granddad in his nursing home. He is old now and needs help to look after himself'.

Growing and Changing Man

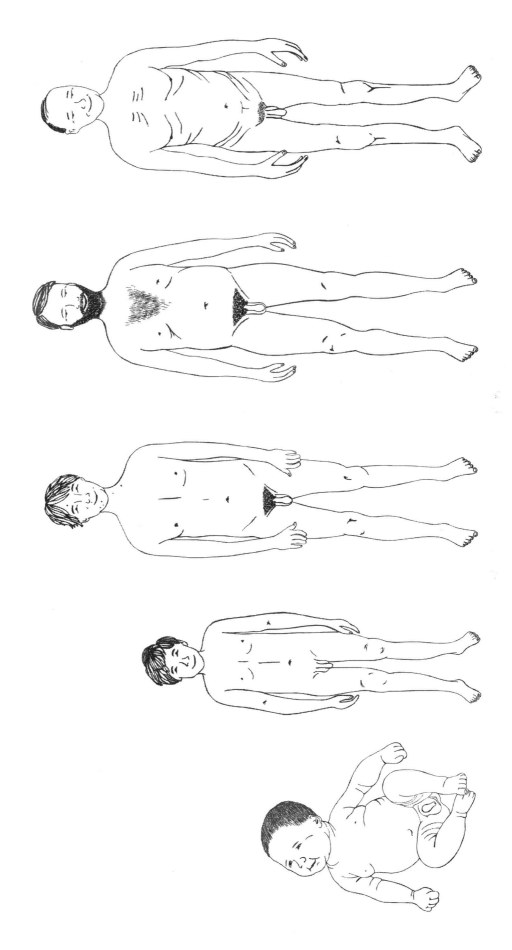

Growing and Changing Woman

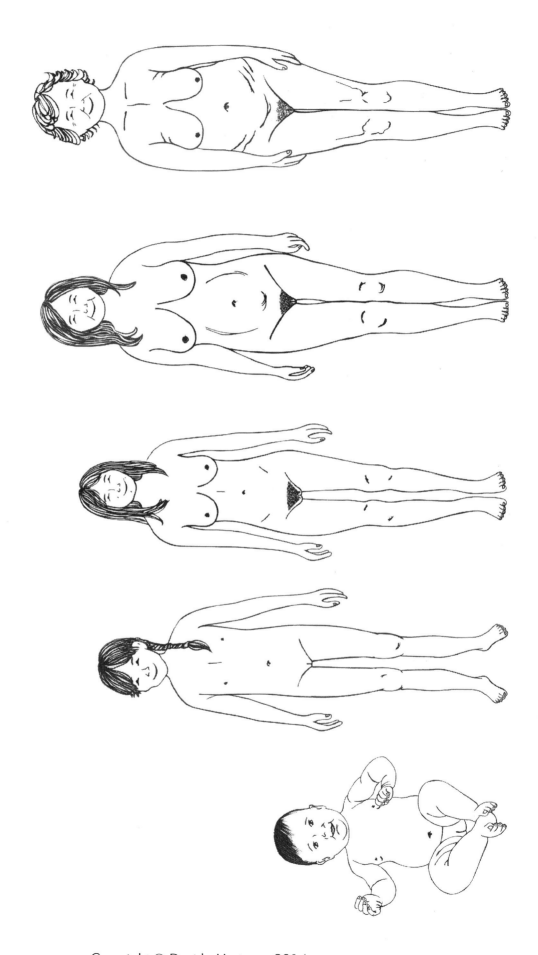

10
Teach Puberty

Although teaching children about growing and changing will naturally include puberty concepts, this stage in a child's life needs to be particularly emphasized and prepared for due to the volume and significance of the changes that occur. Temple Grandin, in her book *Thinking in Pictures* (2006), describes the onset of puberty as like living in a constant state of stage fright, akin to how it feels before a big job interview or a speaking engagement. She describes her nervous system during puberty as being constantly under stress, like a frightened animal. While this may be extreme, and not everyone with ASD will experience puberty in this way, it highlights some of the emotional changes and challenges of this time and will resonate with many adults, with or without ASD, when remembering their teenage years.

In addition to the emotional changes of puberty (e.g. feeling scrutinized, an increase in sexual feelings and the desire for autonomy and independence), a teenager's body also begins to change, and with these changes comes a range of new self-care tasks that need to be included in their daily routines, for example, applying deodorant, shaving, wearing a bra, cleaning after masturbation or a wet dream, wearing make-up, looking after their skin, choosing clothes to suit their new body shape and changing sanitary pads or tampons. Old self-care tasks such as showering now need to be done every day, and washing now must include hair, underarms and private body parts. For children who may have taken some time to learn to complete self-care tasks independently, or who may not even be independent in most, these increased responsibilities and tasks are a challenge. See Chapter 11, 'Teach Appearance and Personal Hygiene' for more practical information and advice in this area.

Puberty in Girls

> *I didn't notice the underarm hair growth or my breasts enlarging. Getting my first period at the age of ten was a huge shock. I thought I was going to bleed to death! I didn't understand why the other girls at school giggled when the boys passed by or why they wanted to go around in groups. (Lawson 2005, p.130)*

> *Puberty helped in some respects because I became sexy. I did everything to cultivate my looks. My peers' reaction began to change in the ninth grade. I was not ridiculed as much. However, puberty was hard because adults were having sex with my age. My 'popularity' was an illusion, and became one of the saddest parts of my life. (Mary Newport in Newport and Newport 2002, p.14)*

For girls, the physical changes of puberty usually begin between the ages of 7 and 14 when they begin to experience growth spurts and weight gain. They begin to develop breasts and pubic, leg and underarm hair. Menstruation usually follows within a year or two of these changes. Menstruation typically lasts between four and five days each month, but can range from two to eight days. The time between menstruations varies, but is typically 28 days. It can take two years for menstruation to become regular, and some girls may never experience menstruation at regular intervals. The average girl will first menstruate between 12 and 13 years of age, but possibly as early as 9 or as late as 17 years.

At this stage girls will experience a range of new feelings, including sexual feelings, and may experience mood swings, all of which they may find hard to understand or control. They produce more sweat, and therefore smell of body odour quickly. Their feet may start to smell, their hair becomes greasier and they may develop spots on their face, chests and back. Girls start to grow taller faster than boys. Their nipple area will become larger and darker and will become more sensitive, including feeling itchy at times. Their nipples will also start to become hard when cold or sexually aroused. Their breasts will enlarge and may feel sore or tender. An issue which particularly affects girls at this time is a change in response towards them due to their changing bodies.

> *I'm not sure why I never learned to take the precautions I obviously needed during my periods, but I surely wish I had. I think the executive functioning skills were just too weak to plan ahead or have contingency plans beyond turning to a friend or the school nurse. (Holliday Willey 2012, p.108)*

The onset of menstruation is one of the biggest challenges for girls to deal with at this time. In some cultures, the reaction to menstruation is positive. For example, in Hindu culture a girl's first menstrual cycle is celebrated with new clothes, feasting and ceremonial baths. In the west, however, menstruation is largely concealed and often has negative connotations. Although parents may dread its onset, anecdotally many girls with ASD have been known to accept it in a matter-of-fact manner. Where they may run into trouble, however, is in the self-care tasks that it entails and in dealing with PMT. Sanitary pads and tampons need to be changed regularly. However, difficulties with executive functioning, organization, sequencing, fine motor skills, sensory sensitivities and being either hypersensitive or under-responsive to the feeling of wetness can all lead to difficulties with self-care tasks.

Anecdotally, parents and teachers of girls with ASD have also reported an increase in behaviours (including self-injurious behaviours) prior to menstruation, as well as mood changes, including irritability and becoming withdrawn and less interested in previously enjoyed activities. These issues may be compounded by difficulties in locating, recognizing and reporting pain. PMT is a real occurrence, associated with fluid retention, increased acne, pain in the abdomen, headaches, irritability, weepiness, anger and an increased appetite, although not all women experience PMT and it may be experienced on a continuum from mild to severe. If you are working with girls with ASD who have reached puberty, it is important to take menstruation and PMT into account when undertaking any behavioural investigations.

Another important change for a girl during puberty will be the development of her breasts, and with it the need to wear an extra (and often irritating) clothing item, a bra. Finding the right bra that does not irritate sensory sensitivities can be a challenge for many women on the spectrum and they may take some time to get used to it. Although some women choose not to wear one (and this is of course a valid and individual choice), not wearing a bra may bring increased and unwanted attention to an adolescent whose breasts have noticeably developed.

Puberty in Boys

> *This puberty thing has made me recognize the world around me a bit more, especially certain members of the world. Whilst the adolescent rituals are unattainable and unattractive to me, I am getting better at fitting in. Well actually I must admit that these feelings change from day to day. Sometimes I even question my diagnosis and wonder if it is wrong, but then on other days I really do feel like the world's biggest freak! In fact, I have gone from thinking about computers ninety-nine per cent of the time to only thinking about only ninety-seven per cent of the time. Can you guess what I am thinking of the rest of the time? (Jackson 2002, p.191)*

Puberty usually begins for boys at 13 years of age, although some start at 12 and others may begin as late as 17 or 18. Boys typically lag behind girls developmentally by roughly two years at this stage. At this time they will experience growth spurts and increased muscle mass. They will also experience a range of new feelings, including sexual feelings, and may experience mood swings, all of which they may find hard to understand or control. Their voices will deepen, their hands and feet will get bigger and they will develop facial, pubic and underarm hair. They can develop smelly feet and their face, neck and back may become spotty. They will produce more sweat and therefore smell of body odour quickly. Their penises and testicles develop and they will begin to ejaculate semen (usually first while sleeping). This can be a frightening experience for some boys, especially those who initially struggled with toilet training. This has been known to lead to anxiety and emotional and behavioural issues in some boys with special needs, for example, refusing to go to sleep because they are afraid that they will 'wet' the bed. (To help adolescents with this, an instructional story about wet dreams is included at the end of this chapter.) Boys will also begin to have erections at odd or unplanned times. They need to learn that (despite any potential embarrassment) this is a normal part of puberty which should not cause alarm and will go away with time.

Puberty (General): Teaching Activities and Recommendations

1. Prepare in advance for the changes associated with puberty.

2. Emphasize the positive aspect of puberty. All changes need to be normalized and discussed and reacted to calmly and positively.

3. Many of the images already developed for use in Chapter 8, 'Teach Body Parts and Fluids' and Chapter 9, 'Teach Growing and Changing' can be used to teach about puberty. Relevant illustrations are also included in Appendix G.

4. First, concentrate on the more concrete aspects of puberty, such as observable physical changes. Introduce more abstract emotional changes later.

5. If possible, it is best if a female discusses puberty (including menstruation and wearing bras) with girls, and a male discusses puberty (including wet dreams and unexpected erections) with boys. It is also best if this information comes from a family member, at least for any initial teachings.

6. Start teaching the child about their own sex first, but remember to teach them also about the changes that the opposite sex will go through and experience. Emphasize the similarities as well as the differences between the two.

7. Use life-sized outlines of bodies. Either draw or add picture cards on the body where, for example, hair grows or spots can appear.

8. Teach the child about mood swings – for example, that they may feel a mixture of strong feelings all in one day. Link these feelings to hormones, which not only cause their bodies to change and grow but can cause them to feel a certain way. Support them in dealing with potential mood swings; for example, avoiding fights or taking a relaxing bath. See Chapter 17, 'Teach Emotional Understanding and Regulation' for more information in this area.

9. Create an 'I'm Growing Up' book, personal to each individual child.

10. Create instructional stories, e.g.:

    • What is Puberty?

    • Why is My Body Changing?

    • Getting Spots is Normal

    • My Breasts are Sore Sometimes

    • My Voice is Getting Deeper.

11. If the child likes reading, there are plenty of books available about puberty and the trials and tribulations of being a teenager. Nichols, Moravcik and Tetenbaum (2009) recommend adapting books that might not be wholly suitable by, for example:

    • using illustrations only

    • photocopying and enlarging specific pages

    • reading only specific pages or chapters

    • using certain pieces of information in the book as starting points, following which the child can look for more information on the internet

- reading a topic with the child before adding it to their 'I'm Growing Up' book
- giving the child a part of the book to read independently, which they then discuss with their parents at a later stage.

12. There are more and more websites and magazines (both online and in hard copy) specifically for teens all about puberty. Again, these will need to be pre-checked for suitability.

13. Use role play, social scripts and decisions worksheets to work through scenarios such as 'What if someone laughs at a spot on your face?'; 'Getting an erection in class'; 'What to do when you feel like everyone is looking at you?' and 'How to buy a bra'.

14. Watch video clips (found online) of teenagers talking about puberty.

Puberty in Girls: Teaching Activities and Recommendations

Bras

1. Encourage female relatives to show the girl bras when out shopping, even before she has started to develop breasts.

2. Encourage female relatives to model putting on bras in front of the girl.

3. Teach the reasons *why* girls need to wear bras.

4. Consider starting the girl wearing a bra before she needs to.

5. Discussion forums for parents of children with ASD can often be a valuable source of information for appropriate brands of bras (i.e. the bras that are least likely to trigger sensory sensitivities). Older children could be supported in posting topics on discussion forums specifically for individuals with ASD, asking questions about bras, as well as other puberty topics. This would need to be highly supervised.

6. Start off with soft sports bras that can be worn over the head and that do not include hooks that need to be fastened.

7. Find bras with no tags, or cut tags off.

Menstruation

1. Start teaching about menstruation before it begins. Red food colouring (or fake blood from the toy shop) can be used to show what a period might look like on a sanitary pad or underwear. These materials can also be used for other teaching activities when the girl has started to menstruate.

2. Emphasize the positive aspects of menstruation. Encourage female family members to talk about it with the girl, using a calm, positive outlook and open communication style. Ask them to tell her about when they first got their period, how old they were, how they felt and what type of feminine products they use and why. Discuss with them whether they would be willing to model the appropriate use of sanitary

pads or tampons for the girl (an important learning tool). When she does start menstruating, encourage the girl's female relatives to do something fun on the day; celebrate it! Have a 'Red' or a 'Girls Only' party, or get her nails done. Of course, if a girl lives with only her father, he can do all of these activities with her. Even for girls with no verbal language, doing enjoyable activities on the days she menstruates will lead to positive associations with it.

3. It is important that everyone involved with a girl communicates with each other. It is also important that there is a plan in place for each step of the journey. Questions that everyone will need to know the answer to (prior to first menstruation) include:

    • What happens if she first menstruates in school?

    • Who can she talk to about it?

    • Will she need assistance in the toilet?

    • How will she ask if she needs to change her pad?

    • If she needs help in the toilet, give the girl choice in who accompanies her, if possible.

4. Teach slang terms (e.g. 'the curse', 'the time of the month' and 'Aunt Flo').

5. Ensure that menstruation is included in teachings about gender, body parts and fluids, and growing and changes. For example, when looking at pictures of different people in the child's family, say things like, 'That is your mammy as a child. She doesn't her have period'; 'That is your mammy when she is older. See, her breasts are bigger and her hips are wider. She has gone through puberty. She is a teenager. She now has her period every month' and 'That is your dad; he does not have periods. Men do not get periods.'

6. More able learners will benefit from having the connection between menstruation and reproduction explained in a simple way and linked to other changes during puberty (e.g. the growth of hair and breasts).

7. Some ideas to help prepare girls with poor language skills for menstruation each month:

    • Use 'calendar boxes' or 'anticipation shelves' (i.e. boxes for each day with the items that they will need in them).

    • Start using pads a few days before menstruation is anticipated. This will help communicate that it is about to begin.

    • Make changes to the environment, e.g. with music, candles and massage.

    • Show a 'Menstruation' symbol (e.g. a picture of a pad with blood on it, or a pad with red dye on it) when it starts.

    • Always show a 'Change pad' symbol before changing a sanitary pad.

- Show the full packet of pads before menstruation and continue to show the pack becoming emptier. On the last day show the empty packet. Have the girl throw it in the wastebasket.

- When menstruation is finished, show a 'Menstruation finished' symbol (e.g. a picture of a clean pad or a picture of a pad with blood on it with an X through it). This step may not be necessary if she understands that throwing the empty pad packet in the bin marks the end of menstruation.

  A calendar will be a vital tool in teaching girls to self-manage their own menstruation. They should also be involved in their own charting, which will increase self-sufficiency and communication skills. More able girls can keep their own diary or personal calendar, recording changes throughout the month in their body, mood and menstrual cycle. Girls with poor language ability or who are less able can be supported to use adapted weekly or monthly calendars, which should be large and highly visual. Information can easily be recorded on them using stamps (e.g. happy or sad faces, different colours to indicate different moods, or red stamps to indicate menstruation). Visual pain scales can also be used to monitor PMT.

8. If appropriate (e.g. if the girl is experiencing behavioural difficulties), parents and professionals may also wish to keep their own record of the girl's monthly cycle. Relevant information to record could include mood, swollen abdomen, sore breasts, tiredness, blood flow, food changes, decreased language, cramps, irritability, as well as any potential positive changes.

9. Along with the child's parents, it will need to be decided whether changing her own sanitary pads is realistic (although independence should always be an ultimate goal). Questions to ask in making this decision should include:

   - What prompts would be needed?

   - How does she currently manage her underwear?

   - Is she independent in toileting?

   - Does she understand words, symbols, pictures or signs?

SANITARY PADS VS. TAMPONS

Before menstruation is due to start, teach the difference between pads and tampons and help the girl come to a decision as to which is more suitable or which she prefers. (There will of course be some situations where this decision may need to be made for her.)

1. In general, pads are easier for girls with ASD to use.

2. Tampons may be suitable if the girl has good fine motor and coordination skills, has no issues putting her finger inside her vagina and has an active lifestyle, e.g. she swims regularly. Some benefits of tampons are that they are small to carry and create no odour. However, they can be difficult to insert for lots of girls, and because they are easy to forget about after insertion they also carry the risk of toxic shock syndrome, relevant if someone is likely to forget to change them regularly.

3.   Go to the shop together (or encourage a female family member to do so) to buy different menstruation products, including ones that are scented and unscented. (Scented products may need to be avoided to prevent potential issues such as itching and thrush.) Include different thicknesses, shapes and sizes.

4.   Look at the packaging of different products with the girl. Which are easy to open? How many strips does each pad have? Will wings be too complicated to use? Will they fit in her bag?

5.   Do experiments – e.g. How much liquid do certain pads take before they leak?

6.   Let her take all of them apart. Discuss the purpose of each part.

7.   Weigh up all of this information. Make lists of pros and cons. Then choose one product with the girl to start off with.

8.   The girl can always decide to start with pads before moving on to tampons at a later stage.

Whether pads or tampons are decided on, teach how to wear, change and dispose of them appropriately. This may vary according to the setting. For example, in school she may need to dispose of a pad in a specific blue bin, whereas at home she needs to put them in a wicker bin under the washbasin. Therefore you will need to do task analyses specific to each of the child's settings. A picture-based instructional story is included at the end of this chapter to show some of the steps for changing a pad in certain situations. Photo sequence cards can also be useful. These, or other visual reminders, can be laminated and kept with the girl's other feminine products.

9.   When teaching the use of pads or tampons, start with the final step of taking them off and putting them into the bin, as this is an easier task than putting them on.

10.   Draw placement lines with a laundry pen on the girl's underwear if she is having difficulty with pad placement.

11.   A desensitization programme may be needed if the girl does not like the feel of either pads or tampons. To do this, start with thinner and smaller pads or tampons before moving on to thicker and larger varieties. Also, only require the girl to wear them for short (and defined) periods of time which can be increased gradually. Pair these steps with positive reinforcement.

12.   If tampons are chosen, a small amount of lubrication jelly may help with insertion initially. Decide between tampons with or without applicators. Practise opening and pushing out the tampon before teaching insertion into the vagina. Teach about relaxing vaginal muscles. The girl should understand that tampons are not meant to feel uncomfortable.

13.   Being able to make a judgement as to how often a sanitary pad or tampon needs to be changed can be very difficult for girls with ASD, and guidance will need to be given appropriate to the circumstances. Rather than the girl needing to remember or judge when she needs to do it, it may be easier to have a hard and fast rule that she

should change them every four hours. Reminders will most likely be needed. Use whatever format works for the girl, e.g. a discreet alarm on her phone or a special buzzer. A visual reminder could also be used, e.g. a cue card placed discreetly on her desk. Alternatively, matching the changing times to the natural breaks at school may be more practical and less conspicuous for the girl, although reminders may still be needed.

14. Always keep menstruation products in the same place, e.g. a special drawer at home or a special bag in school. Wearing a bag with a long strap across the body will make it less likely to be forgotten or lost. Spare pairs of clean underwear should also be kept here.

Premenstrual Tension

1. Teach the signs of PMT, preparing in advance through the use of a calendar. Encourage relaxation, exercise, light eating and lots of sleep during this time. Support the girl in finding ways to alleviate discomfort, e.g. a hot-water bottle, a microwavable 'wheat pillow', bubble bath or music. Note which of these tactics help her relax. Girls with less language can be given symbols or objects to represent these items so that they can request them independently (e.g. a bottle of massage oil to request a massage, a CD to request music, a piece of blanket to request a lie down, a piece of towel to request a bath). Make sure to have these items within the girl's reach when you anticipate that she will need them.

2. Recommend consultation with a doctor if she is experiencing severe pain (or behavioural concerns) alongside or prior to menstruation.

3. Taking pain killers may help alleviate PMT and, if a pattern emerges, could be taken as a preventative measure. Birth control can also help lessen PMT, as well as having the added benefit of making menstruation more predictable and therefore more manageable. Some women take a selective serotonin re-uptake inhibitor (SSRI) to manage emotional lows during menstruation. All of these would need to be discussed with the child's parents and family doctor before implementing.

4. Teach about appropriate clothing during menstruation, e.g. wearing dark clothes and underwear and avoiding white; wearing specific underwear to save all of her underwear from becoming stained; wearing clothes that are comfortable around the waist and breasts. Close-fitting clothes will help avoid odour. Clothes with pockets can also be useful to keep tampons, pads and spare underwear in. Also teach how to care for underwear by removing blood stains correctly.

5. Girls experience many unexpected difficult scenarios in relation to menstruation. Try to prepare for as many of these as possible, for example:
   - What if there is no wastebasket in the bathroom?
   - What if you get your period in a friend's house?

- What if you get your period unexpectedly and do not have any pads on you?
- What if you get blood on your clothes in school?

Puberty in Boys: Teaching Activities and Recommendations

Wet Dreams

Boys need to be prepared *in advance* for wet dreams by talking to them about them, reading books, looking at websites or using instructional stories.

Voice Breaking

A boy's voice breaking will also need to be prepared for in advance. However, do not use the terminology 'breaking' which may be taken literally. Instead, discuss how his voice will become deeper and become more like older men's (e.g. his father's).

1. Empathize with the embarrassment that it might cause the boy. Remind him that it happens to *all men*.

2. Show him video clips of young boys talking, boys when their voices are breaking and men's voices. Point out the differences.

3. Show him clips from long-running TV shows where the same child actor's voice changes from childhood through adolescence.

Handling Unexpected (and Unwanted) Erections

Boys need to learn that this is also a normal, although embarrassing, part of puberty. Remind them that they will be able to control erections better when they are older.

Teach the boy strategies for when he experiences unexpected erections, for example:

1. sitting down

2. covering his erection with a book

3. using specific excuses (social scripts) that he can use to leave the room

4. using simple phrases (social scripts) he can say if someone points out that he has an erection

5. wearing long shirts that cover his groin area

6. wearing trousers with stiff materials, such as jeans, which don't show up erections as much as loose fabrics

7. concentrating on 'unsexy' things.

Wet Dreams

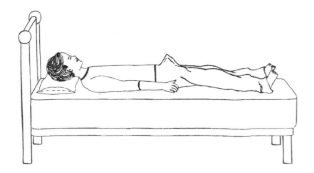

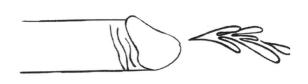

Both boys and girls dream about sexy things sometimes.

Sometimes when boys dream about sexy things they get erections.

This means that their penis goes hard.

Sometimes, boys ejaculate in their sleep.

This means that semen comes out of their penis.

This is called a 'wet dream'.

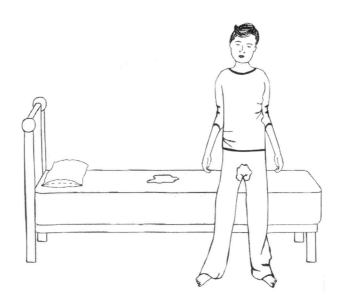

Wet dreams happen to all boys, usually when they are going through puberty.

When you have a wet dream, your sheets and pyjamas will get wet with semen. This will then dry. This is not pee.

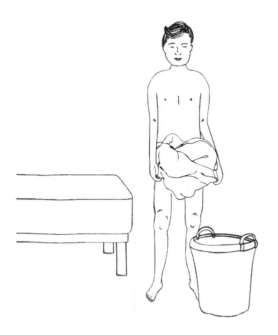 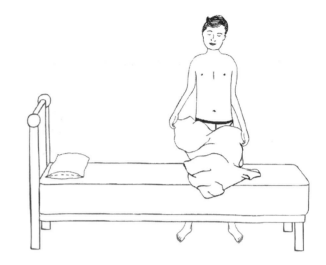

If you have a wet dream, you will need to put the dirty pyjamas and sheets in the wash basket.

You will need to put clean sheets on your bed.

You will need to have a shower.

Wet dreams is a private topic. It is OK to talk about wet dreams only with boys who you know are your friends, or your mum or dad.

Changing My Pad

Go to bathroom.

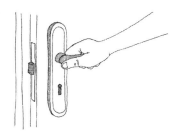

Close door.

Pull down underwear.

Take off old pad.

Put new pad on
underwear.

Pull up underwear.

Put old pad in the
wastebasket.

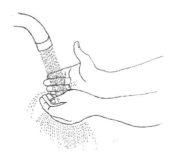

Wash hands.

Periods

Girls start their period at different ages.

'Having your period' means that blood comes from
inside your body and flows out of your vagina.

Period blood is clean, not dirty. It does not mean that you are cut, hurt or sick.

It can come at any time of the day or night.

Having periods means that your body is working right.
It means that you are becoming a woman.

You will usually bleed for a few days every month.

Over one period, only five or six tablespoons of
blood will come out of your vagina.

Sometimes you will feel the blood coming out. Sometimes you won't.

Pads stop the blood from getting onto your clothes. Pads need
to be changed regularly. If they are not, they will leak onto your
clothes. Also, other people will be able to smell them.

Sometimes you might feel a bit cranky before your period. Sometimes
your tummy and breasts might feel a bit sore. This is called PMT.
Lots of girls get PMT. Things that might help you feel better if you
have PMT are a hot-water bottle on your tummy or a bath.

Having your period is a private topic. It is OK to talk about it
only with girls that you know well or your mum or dad.

11

Teach Appearance and Personal Hygiene

Teaching children with ASD to care about and look after their appearance and personal hygiene can be a difficult, frustrating and time-consuming task. Difficulties with executive functioning (planning, organization and sequencing), higher order thinking and fine motor skills can all lead to difficulties in remembering and carrying out self-care tasks. Sensory sensitivities may result in feelings of genuine distress and pain. The author Stephen Shore (2003) has described how shaving feels like a power sander scraping his skin. Due to inherent difficulties understanding the social world around them, many individuals with ASD also struggle to understand *why* appearance and hygiene is so important to us 'neurotypicals', and so lack even the basic motivation to put all of that effort into carrying them out. Anecdotally, many parents have reported that their children first showed motivation to 'look after' themselves during puberty, that is, when they became interested in boys or girls romantically. However, many adults with ASD report that even though they have families, jobs and active social lives, they still need supports such as visual prompts and schedules to remind them to change their clothes, shave or wear deodorant. However, all of this effort (on everyone's part) to support independence in these tasks is worth it to increase a child's self-esteem and personal safety. Remember that every step you teach them to do by themselves will be one less thing that they will need somebody else to do for them in later life.

> *I have to admit that, even with specific instructions, washing and stuff like that are not a top priority in my life. I always feel as if I am doing it for the benefit of others because personally I don't care whether I am clean or dirty and don't care what other people think about me either. This is something that I am trying to change, purely and simply because I have read my own dating chapter!! (Jackson 2002, p.111)*

> *I was not very aware of the big hoo hoo over clothing until I was in my second year of college. In fact, I remember learning the 2000-year-old phrase* Vestus virum reddit *(clothes make the man) in my Latin class and thinking – really? Clothes are that important to society, so*

important I'm reading a phrase from eons ago dedicated to the concept? It was astonishing to me, the kind of astonishment that makes an ah-ha light bulb blink in the mind. (Holliday Willey 2012, p.106)

Caring for your appearance is not only about cleanliness and hygiene, but also about clothing and fashion, often important concepts for 'neurotypicals'. At a more advanced level, this topic also encompasses areas such as 'fitting in' and conformity, what it means to be attractive, stereotypes in relation to attractiveness and how the media perpetrates these stereotypes and why. Many adults (with and without ASD) make everyday choices *not* to conform to how society would wish them to look, and this is not only a valid lifestyle choice but also nobody else's business. However, it *is* important that for the individual with ASD this choice is *informed* and not arising from a lack of understanding, skills or knowledge (i.e. failure to learn the hidden curriculum that most of their typically developing peers pick up without effort). Part of this will involve teaching the child how their appearance will affect their future employment prospects and social and romantic lives.

On a related note, some professionals and parents feel that it is important that the self-stimulatory behaviours (e.g. wrist flicking or humming) associated with ASD be minimized, so that the child can better fit into a neurotypical world. Certainly there are times when self-stimulatory behaviours can be dangerous, or a child can become immersed in them to the detriment of their learning. However, often these behaviours serve an important function, and more and more ASD advocates are telling the world to back off and allow them to be themselves. Donna Williams, in *Nobody Nowhere: The Remarkable Autobiography of an Autistic Girl* (1992), tells how her own self-stimulatory behaviours provide security and release and help decrease built-up anxiety and tension, thereby decreasing fear. Often the child can be taught socially acceptable replacement behaviours that serve the same function as these behaviours and allow them to avoid unwanted attention. Certainly an intervention is good if it helps a child to navigate the world on their own terms. However, we need to remember that looking and acting 'normal' are not the only way to go about this. Our focus should be not on making individuals with ASD look less autistic, but on improving quality of life and changing societal attitudes.

Appearance and Hygiene Tasks: Some Learning Concepts

1. Differentiating between clean and dirty.

2. Looking after teeth (e.g. brushing, flossing, using mouthwash, having nice-smelling breath, making sure there is no food stuck in your teeth and going to the dentist).

3. Looking after your hair (washing, cutting, brushing and styling).

4. Showering or bathing (e.g. how to heat the water, changing the water temperature, knowing which body parts need particular attention and drying correctly).

5. Washing hands (e.g. after the toilet, after dirty play, before eating meals and before making food).

6. Washing your face.

7. Wearing deodorant.

8. Caring for nails (both hands and feet, cutting them and keeping them clean).

9. Caring for nose (e.g. wiping with tissue, refraining from picking your nose in public and trimming nose hair).

10. Shaving or waxing (e.g. face, legs, underarms or pubic hair).

11. Caring for your body (e.g. exercise, diet, weight management, and refraining from smoking or excessive drinking).

12. Looking after your skin, particularly during the teenage years (e.g. not touching your face often, refraining from picking at spots, washing regularly, having facials and visiting the dermatologist).

13. Wearing make-up.

14. Caring for your lips (e.g. if they are chapped).

15. Managing warts.

16. Managing facial hair (i.e. in girls).

17. Wearing clean clothes.

18. Knowing when to change your clothes.

19. Washing and drying dirty clothes.

20. Buying new clothes.

21. Checking your clothes before leaving the house (e.g. ensuring zippers are zipped, underwear not showing and shirts are tucked in).

22. Dressing for the occasion (e.g. interview, sports, beach, school and going to a friend's house).

23. Looking after your shoes (e.g. getting them repaired and knowing when to buy new ones).

24. Choosing appropriate clothing (e.g. not wearing black underwear underneath white trousers, avoiding sheer fabrics and avoiding clothes that are too tight or small).

25. Learning about fashion.

26. Developing a personal clothing style.

27. Choosing clothes to suit your body shape.

28. Choosing appropriate accessories.

Appearance and Hygiene: Teaching Activities and Recommendations

As in all areas of a child's curriculum, aiming for as much independence as possible in all tasks is a priority. Teach *why* each task is important, empathize with any issues and praise all efforts.

Self-care and Hygiene

1. Help the child locate a specific friend, peer or family member who cares about them, whom they can ask embarrassing questions (e.g. 'Does my breath smell?') and who will tell them the truth in a kind way.

2. Arrange it so that the child can regularly observe tasks such as shaving and putting on deodorant being carried out.

3. Decide with the child and their parents which self-care tasks they need to be carrying out now, and also in the future. Some may not be necessary or appropriate, given their age (e.g. girls shaving their legs).

4. Write out personal routines and make schedules for all tasks. Consider which have to happen in the morning and which at night. Plan for success! Work tasks around existing timetables. Be specific and also realistic. How many times a day or week does a certain task *really* need to be done? (Skills in doing task analyses, prompting, teaching through backward and forward chaining and visual schedules will be vital here.)

5. If working on a particular task (e.g. washing hair), ensure that people around the child notice and compliment them.

6. Don't be afraid to be blunt – in fact it is advised! Make consequences clear, for example, 'If you go for an interview smelling of urine, with your belly showing and your hair greasy you *will not get* the job, even if you are overqualified for it'.

7. Teach rules such as 'Always check your clothes and teeth before leaving the house'.

8. Create an individualized 'My Hygiene Book'.

9. Create sequence cards (either in photos, pictures or written words) for different tasks. Have the child arrange them in their correct order.

10. Teach the child to differentiate between dirty and clean (e.g. by sorting pictures or items of clothing). Teach about germs but be careful not to overemphasize this. Teach the child to be critical of the scaremongering tone of many advertisements for cleaning products.

11. Visual reminders about self-care tasks can be placed around the house (e.g. the steps to complete while showering could be laminated and kept in the shower).

12. Create instructional stories, e.g.:
    - How to Put on Deodorant
    - Why I Need to Shower Every Day
    - Why Everyone Looks Thin and Good-looking in Magazine Ads
    - Wearing the Right Make-up for Me

    (Instructional stories relating to being clean and smelling nice are included at the end of this chapter for both girls and boys.)

13. Explore with the child all the different ways to keep a body clean (e.g. bathing, showering, washing hands, washing face, using hand wipes).

14. Explore the products that help to clean bodies (e.g. shower gel, face-wash, deodorant, soap, shampoo and toothpaste).

15. Have the child match products to body parts, using either pictures or actual items placed on the outline of a body.

16. Due to sensory sensitivities, children with ASD may have some difficulty finding hygiene products (e.g. deodorant or moisturizer) which they like the smell or feel of. Be understanding about this and give them as much ownership over choosing products as possible. Bring them to the shop and allow them to test different products. Then choose different kinds to try out at home (e.g. spray or roll-on deodorant).

17. Some parents have reported that using an electric toothbrush is easier for children with ASD as it requires significantly less time and effort to use correctly.

18. The internet is full of online tutorials in the areas of clothing, make-up, shaving and fashion.

Dress Code

In the area of clothing, the following is recommended:

1. Encourage looking in a full-length mirror regularly. Ask parents if one could be placed inside the front door as a reminder to the child to check themselves before leaving the house.

2. Consider how often clothes need to be changed. Come up with a rule and stick to it, e.g. 'Socks and underwear need to be changed every day. Other clothes can be worn two to three times, unless they are stained or dirty. Then they need to be washed.'

3. Teach how to wash and dry clothes independently if possible.

4. Alter clothes to make them more comfortable for the child.

5. Never force a child to wear clothes that they find uncomfortable for any reason.

6. Teach why clothes are so important to so many people.

7. Look to their same age peers to see what clothes are in fashion at the moment.

8. Teach about the different dress codes for different social situations and why they exist.

9. Do activities such as matching pictures of clothes to occasions.

10. Point out people's clothes in real life or on TV and in books.

11. Dress up dolls. Pretend, for example, that they are going to the park. What should they wear?

12. Use mannequins (easily bought secondhand online) to teach dressing.

13. Watch video clips (e.g. of a beach scene, a job interview, skiing or a basketball game) and have the child pick clothes from a pile that are appropriate for the scene.

14. Use pictures from magazines to start discussions about clothes, e.g. 'What is your first impression of this person based on how they are dressed?'

15. Teach how to look for clothes online or through catalogues if the child dislikes clothes shopping. They will then also need to be taught how to size themselves and return items online.

Discuss and debate what it means to be attractive. What are the stereotypes? Discuss the role of airbrushing. (There are airbrushing tutorials available online which show how magazine images are altered, and which are particularly enlightening.) Discuss the under-representation of 'normal' looking people in the media, including people with disabilities. Teach that being different is good and that it is not necessary to be the same as everyone else. Emphasize that being different is often more valued once the teenage years are over. Look at how the perception of attractiveness differs in different cultures and over time. Talk about what influences this.

Being Clean and Smelling Nice is Good!

Sometimes I get
smelly and dirty.

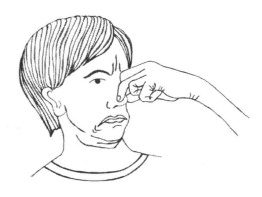

Most people think it's gross
when I am smelly and dirty.

I will try to have a shower every day.

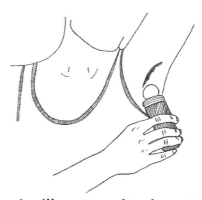

I will put on deodorant
every morning.

I will put on clean clothes every day.

People like it when I am
clean and smell nice.

Being Clean and Smelling Nice is Good!

Sometimes I get
smelly and dirty.

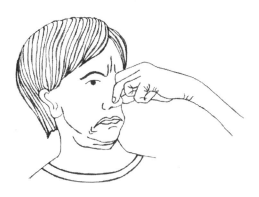

Most people think it's gross
when I am smelly and dirty.

I will try to have a shower every day.

I will put on deodorant
every morning.

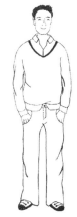

I will put on clean clothes every day.

People like it when I am
clean and smell nice.

It is Good to Feel Good about Your Body!

All bodies are special.

All bodies are different.

Bodies can do amazing things.

Differences make us unique.

How you feel about your body affects your feelings and behaviours.

If you like how you look, you will feel and act happier. This is a good thing.

If you do not like how you look, you might feel sad or angry. You might avoid other people. This means that you miss out on lots of fun stuff!

People often feel pressure from other people or TV, movies or magazines to lose weight or to change how they look.

Most people DO NOT look like the people on the TV or in movies or magazines.

Many teenagers think a lot about how they look. This changes when they become older and more mature.

How you look is NOT the most important part of you. What is most important is on the INSIDE, your personality and how you treat other people.

Different people are attracted to different things about a person, in their personality and how they look.

People of all shapes and sizes have good feelings about how they look.

Someone who likes themselves and likes their body will be more attractive and likeable to other people.

It is good to feel good about your body!

12

Teach Public and Private

Privacy is an extremely difficult and abstract concept to teach to many children with ASD. Such children have most likely needed extra support in self-care activities, are used to having little to no control over who sees their body, and may subsequently have become desensitized to being seen naked. Constant supervision and surveillance can be par for the course. Parents and professionals are reported routinely to walk in during self-care activities without asking permission. Personal self-care details can be openly discussed. It is therefore not that surprising that children with ASD often have significant difficulties in differentiating between public and private concepts, in addition to possessing a skewed understanding of privacy, which presupposes that their life, their spaces and their bodies are open to public view and consumption (Hingsburger 1994).

> *For many years we're teaching our children to go with everyone and hold everyone's hand for safety issues and it's OK to have someone help you get dressed and go to the bathroom, to shower you. Now they are older, and still need personal assistance. I try to tell them when it's not OK to pull down your pants and it's OK for this and not OK for that but there are too many rules. (Parent of a child with ASD, in Ballan 2012, p.681)*

> *Privacy awareness is fundamental in abuse reporting. Sex education may give language with which to report abuse but privacy awareness gives the concept with which to understand it. (Hingsburger 1994, p.73)*

All children need to learn the difference between what is public and what is private, including places, parts of the body, conversations, behaviours and even online communications. Understanding these concepts is not only a factor in protection from abuse, but will also help them to behave in more socially appropriate ways. However, teaching this area is difficult, and not only for the reasons outlined above. There are also a vast number of different rules in this area, with a vast number of grey areas and exceptions to these rules depending on age, sex, family, culture and setting. For example, it makes sense to teach children that masturbation is a private topic, but what are they then to do when it is the main topic of conversation in the school yard?

> ## PRIVATE BODY PARTS
>
> When teaching the concept of private body parts, it is important not to teach that your private parts alone should not be touched and not to label the rest of a child's body parts 'public'. They are not public, as they belong to them. Other body parts may also be considered private, as well as important and special, and if you don't want someone touching your knee on the bus, you have every right to tell them 'No' and report it. See Chapter 13, 'Teach Safety Skills', for more information in this area.

Public and Private: Some Learning Concepts

1. A private place is *somewhere noone can see you, or just walk in*. A public place is one where *anyone can go*.

2. Some places can be both public and private, e.g., a door marked 'Private' in a shop might mean that the room is only for use by the people who work in the shop.

3. Bedrooms are (or should be) private.

4. Most toilets in people's homes are private. However, public toilets are not really private because people can still hear you or they might be able to see you through the bottom or top of the door.

5. Cars are not private, as people can see in at the windows.

6. If you want to enter a private room, you need to knock first and wait for permission before you enter.

7. If a behaviour is to do with private body parts, then it should be done in a private place.

8. If a behaviour involves private body parts and somebody else, you need to seek the other person's permission or consent.

9. Outside of your bedroom, private parts need to be covered with clothes. There are some exceptions to this, e.g. if you are getting changed after swimming, if you are in somebody else's bedroom and they have given you permission to be naked, if you are going to the toilet or if you are on a nudist beach.

10. If you are changing your clothes outside of your own bedroom, you should be naked only long enough to change your clothes. There are some exceptions to this, e.g. if you are in somebody else's bedroom and they have given you permission to be naked for longer.

11. It is not OK to stare at or talk about other people's private body parts unless they have given you permission to do so.

12. Communicating online (using Twitter, Facebook, email, Skype or other methods) is never private. Your messages (whether in words or pictures) can always be forwarded

on to someone else, or to many people. They are also saved on the hard-drive of your computer, even if you delete them.

13. Some topics of conversation are private, e.g. sex, masturbation, wet dreams and menstruation.

14. Underwear is private.

15. Scratching your private body parts and picking your nose are private behaviours.

Public and Private: Teaching Activities and Recommendations

Show Respect for the Child's Privacy

This ethos should be reflected in an organization's policies and procedures.

1. Encourage as much independence in self-care tasks as possible.

2. Restructure environments so that privacy is maximized, e.g. use of half doors or screens. Always ask and at least attempt to get permission before touching a child (including those with no verbal language and significant ID).

3. Don't watch children in the shower, naked, changing clothes or going to the toilet, even if you are innocently conversing with them or someone else. If they don't need help, leave the room.

4. If a child needs help during self-care tasks, avert your gaze as much as possible.

5. If you need to touch them during self-care tasks, always ask permission first, even if it is a task that you help them with daily.

6. Always describe what you are doing and why during self-care tasks, even if the child has no verbal language, e.g. 'I am now wiping your bum. I am doing this to make sure that it is clean.'

7. The child should be given the tools to tell you 'No', that they are finished or that they want you to leave. For nonverbal children this may be a picture symbol.

Use the Words 'Public' and 'Private' as Much as Possible

1. In everyday life comment, for example:
   - 'You need to be private, so shut the toilet door.'
   - 'This is public; anyone can be here.'
   - 'Do you think this bus is private?'

2. Use real-life opportunities to teach public and private concepts, for example:
   - during swimming classes
   - going to a shop and asking to use the toilet
   - going shopping for clothes and changing in the changing room.

Teaching about Privacy Begins in the Home

1. Some recommendations for the child's parents:

    - Think about the parts of your home that are public and private.

    - Decide how family members' privacy is to be respected.

    - Introduce a family rule that bedrooms are private and that bedroom doors must be knocked on before entering.

    - Have a family discussion to introduce these ideas to all siblings.

    - Make 'Private' signs (with the help of the children) to put on all private rooms in the home.

    - If a child shares a bedroom, ensure that they are given specific scheduled times in their room that are private to them. Specific private signs for each child could be created. If a certain child's 'Private' sign is on their door, nobody is allowed to enter without permission, even if they share the room with the child.

2. Bedrooms should be used for sleeping and relaxing and regarded as the child's private place. They should not be used for 'time out' or as a punishment area.

3. Teach the child through role play and instructional stories how to knock on doors and ask and wait for permission to enter. Also teach them to respond to somebody knocking on the door to their private area. Teach them to respond appropriately, either by saying phrases such as 'Come in'; 'I am not ready yet'; 'Please come back in five minutes'; or by showing a sign for 'Wait' or 'Private time'.

SOME PUBLIC AND PRIVATE SCENARIOS TO CONSIDER TEACHING THE CHILD

1. Come up with personalized lists, specific to the child's situation, of private and public places, behaviours, conversations and body parts.

    - Where can I be naked (or in my underwear)?

    - When can I be naked?

    - Who can see me naked?

    - Where can I be in my underwear?

    - Where can I get dressed and undressed?

    - Where can I touch my private parts?

    - Where is it OK to touch someone else's body parts?

    - Where is it OK to talk about sex?

    - Who is it OK to talk about sex with?

    - Where is it OK to hug a friend?

    - What are the private areas of my home/school/community?

- What are public places in my home/school/community?
- What are the privacy rules in home and school (e.g. knocking before entering the room or wearing a towel when going from room to room)?

Take the time to think about the exceptions to any rules you come up with. Ask other people if they see any 'loopholes' in your rules. Most importantly, spend time watching the child's peers. How relaxed are they with regard to nudity? What kind of topics do they talk about when they think nobody is listening? How often do they touch, hug or kiss each other?

2. For some children, it will be most appropriate to come up with a few simple rules and stick to them. However, other, more able children should be taught exceptions, and how to problem solve for themselves in the situations that they find themselves in.

3. Be very careful that you are respectful of the child's individual rights and sexuality when creating privacy rules. Remember the power and control that you have over their lives. Individuals with ASD can be literal and once having learned rules they can be rigid in sticking to them. For example, if you teach a child the rule 'No one should touch you except to clean you or to check for your health', what happens if somebody brushes off them in a shop or gives them a consoling pat on the back when they are crying?

Teaching Private Body Parts

Most children will need to learn that touching rules can change over time. While it may be appropriate to teach a five-year-old girl that only her mum, dad or doctor can touch her vagina, it is not appropriate to teach this to an 18-year-old young woman who wishes to have a romantic and sexual life.

1. Private body parts include the mouth, nipples, chest, buttocks, breasts, penis, scrotum, vagina and vulva.

2. Teach why certain body parts are private through the use of instructional stories.

3. Revise body parts and fluids.

4. Colour code different parts of the body.

5. Give the child drawings of bodies and have them colour in the private parts.

6. Cut out pictures of clothes and underwear from magazines (or access them online) and have the child cover pictures of naked bodies with these.

7. Use the materials and activities developed to teach body parts, this time with an emphasis on labelling, sorting and drawing private body parts specifically.

8. Create flashcards and play 'Snap' when two private body parts are shown in succession.

9. Use mannequins and have the child cover the private parts with clothes.

10. Discuss with the child *why* it is important to wear clothes over their private body parts. Discuss how these rules are different in different cultures and countries.

11. Collect pictures of different body parts and pictures of different people or places (in addition to conversation cards). Pair them randomly (e.g. a teacher with a private part) and have the child say whether it is 'OK' or 'not OK'.

Teaching Public and Private Places

Collect pictures of different settings and rooms (e.g. the child's bedroom, the street where they live, the supermarket, an airplane, a toilet and a public park). Ideally, children could take many of these pictures themselves. Use these materials to:

1. label as 'Public' or 'Private'

2. sort into 'Public', 'Private' or other groupings such as 'Places it is OK to have sex', 'Places it is OK to change your clothes' and 'Places it is OK to do your homework'

3. play games such as 'Snap'

4. create collages

5. have the child place pictures representing a naked body on private settings alone

6. colour code the public and private places. Or alternatively colour code the places it is OK to be naked and not to be naked (e.g. green for 'OK' and red for 'not OK')

7. ask questions about private parts in public places, such as: 'Can you touch your vagina there?'

8. ask other questions, such as: 'Is it OK to dance there?' 'Can you pick your nose there?' 'What if you are there and you see that your sanitary pad is leaking?'

9. make small laminated picture of private places, which can be kept on a key chain to remind the child. If the child does something that should be done in private, they can be shown the correct picture

10. create personalized 'My Public and Private Places' books, folders or posters.

Teaching Public and Private Topics of Conversation

1. When discussing private topics, use a sign to indicate that it is private. This sign can then be used as a discreet visual reminder if the child talks about a topic at an inappropriate time (e.g. in class). This sign could be put on the door during SRE sessions.

2. Put different conversation topics on cards, e.g. 'What you had for dinner last night'; 'Who you think is pretty in your class'; 'Who you want to win the cup final' and 'Santa Claus does not exist'. Group these with the child into 'Public' and 'Private', explaining why.

3. Make cue cards of different topics, including personal information, e.g. my name, address, email, age, my bra size, which movie star I like, my sister's name, who I

kissed yesterday, my pubic hair, my favourite band. Make a second list of all the people in the child's life, e.g. strangers, friends, teachers, my grandmother, the bus driver, my best friend, my cousin, carers, shop assistants, neighbours. Have the child match the information that it is OK to share with the right people. Also teach exceptions – e.g., they are lost and need to give their parent's phone number or address to a stranger.

4.   Teach common public and private signs (e.g. public toilet signs). Teach the rules to follow in these places.

5.   Teach the child what to do if someone asks them a question that they do not want to answer.

Private Body Parts

Most private parts are covered by underwear.

Men's private body parts include their bum, mouth, penis and scrotum.

Women's private body parts include their nipples,
bum, mouth, breasts, vulva and vagina.

It is important to learn to take care of your own body parts so
that other people do not need to touch them to help you.

Sometimes people touch their own private body parts
when they are alone and in private. This is OK.

Very few people should see or touch your private body parts.

Parents might need to touch or see them if you are
hurt, or to make sure that you are clean.

Doctors or nurses might need to touch or see them if
you are hurt, or during a medical examination.

Boyfriends or girlfriends might look at them or touch them,
but *only* if you want them to and if you say it is OK.

You should only touch another person's private
body parts if they first say it is OK.

Private body parts should only be touched in private places.

Private body parts is a private topic. This means that you should only talk or
joke about them with your friends and family. You should also talk about
them in private places, where nobody else can overhear the conversation.

Sometimes people joke about private parts in public. These might
be OK jokes. If you are unsure, you can ask someone you trust. It is
not OK to joke about private parts if you are in your classroom.

Other people need to ask permission first before
touching your private body parts.

13
Teach Safety Skills

We have already discussed in the Introduction how and why children with ASD are vulnerable to abuse, and have begun discussing how to keep them safe by teaching public and private concepts. In this chapter we will further explore how we, as professionals and parents, may actually be unhelpful in this area, and how to counteract this issue by teaching children lifelong safety skills.

While compliance is highly valued in special education, it does little to support a child's safety skills. Remember that if you teach a child to do everything that you tell them to do, you have also taught them to do everything an abuser tells them to do. The first step in being able to protect yourself is to know that your body belongs to you, and that you have control over it and what you do with it (e.g. touching other people). It is the basis of learning that you do not have to perform any sexual act that you do not want to (Hingsburger 1994). Non-compliance training (i.e. learning how to say 'no', when, and under which circumstances) goes some way to teaching children these concepts and reducing vulnerability. When a child says 'no' to abuse, it clearly demonstrates that they understand the rules of touching and sexual behaviour. If they can clearly demonstrate that they know these rules, they are also demonstrating to any potential abuser that they are able to report it.

> I was at a complete loss when it came to speaking up about my own sexual abuse. A significant part of this was because no one ever encouraged me to talk about it. As a result, it took me over 10 years after the fact to identify what I experienced was sexual abuse. I always knew something was not right about what happened, but I didn't know how to verbalize it. (Lindsey A. Nebeker, in Ashkenazy and Yergeau 2013, p.119)

> When working with people with disabilities one regularly meets people who are proud, strong and able self-advocates. This communicates that it is possible to be disabled, proud and strong all at the same time. Learning to see people with disabilities as being able to care for themselves, given the right training and the right messages, allows us to transfer the power and responsibility for self-protection to them. It is only when people who are developmentally disabled can discriminate abuse, say no to it and report what happened that abuse will stop. (Hingsburger 1994, p.4)

'Allowing' the child options for a healthy sexuality, as well as defending a human right, is also part of helping keep children safe. Take the example of a child being taught that only her parents and teachers can tell her who can touch her body. What if one of her teachers is the abuser? If we teach a child that all things sexual are 'wrong', then if anything related to sex happens to them (either with or without their consent), they will see themselves as having done something bad and may not admit to it or tell anyone. In addition, if they feel that their relationships or certain behaviours are not allowed, they may be forced into secrecy, leaving them even more vulnerable to abuse.

> *In an atmosphere of equity and respect, people with disabilities can learn how best to deal with those who disrespect or those who abuse. (Hingsburger 2010, p.29)*

David Hingsburger (1995), a lead author in the area of sexuality and disability, has warned that the people who surround individuals with disabilities, by taking on the responsibility for keeping them safe, leave them instead vulnerable and with no skills to protect themselves.

He describes this as a 'Prison of Protection', in which people with developmental disabilities are protected from:

- relationships
- sexual information
- decision making
- society.

To counteract this 'Prison of Protection', Hingsburger (1995) proposes the model of a 'Ring of Safety', which not only protects individuals with developmental disabilities from abuse but also supports them in developing healthy, loving relationships. Included in the Ring of Safety are:

- someone who listens
- an understanding of personal rights
- a healthy self-concept and self-confidence
- options for a healthy sexuality
- sex education
- privacy awareness
- the ability to non-comply.

The two concepts of the 'Prison of Protection' and the 'Ring of Safety' are excellent starting points for reflecting on our own practices in relation to child protection, as well as preparing to teach appropriate safety skills to children with ASD. For simple visual representations of each, see David Hingsburger's highly recommended book *Just Say Know! Understanding and Reducing the Risk of Sexual Victimization of People with Developmental Disabilities* (1995).

STRANGER DANGER

Stranger danger is an outdated and potentially dangerous concept which has the unfortunate consequence of further separating people with disabilities from the society in which we aim to involve them (Hingsburger 1995). How does a child use public transport without at times needing to talk to a stranger? If something happens to the child on the street and all they see around them are strangers, who are they to ask for help? Is a police officer a stranger? Should we not talk to a friendly older woman who remarks on how nice our dog is as we pass by? What if a teenager sees a girl he thinks is pretty sitting next to him in the library? Abuse is more likely to occur with somebody that the child knows, yet the 'stranger danger' concept teaches them that abuse cannot happen with someone they are familiar with. Talking with strangers is in fact an excellent life skill to develop.

GOOD TOUCH/BAD TOUCH

The concept of 'good' and 'bad' touch can be easily misinterpreted and should be approached with caution. Never teach that 'bad touch' is touching the genitals, which sends the message that genitals are bad; that anyone (even your wife) touching your genitals is bad; and that the child is bad if they touch themselves, even if they are only going to the toilet or putting on clothes. It can also give the impression that touching in general is somehow wrong. There are other, better ways to teach children similar concepts, many of which are included in the Teaching Activities and Recommendations section of this chapter.

Sure there were some things I learned. I learned not to take candy from a stranger. I learned not to talk to anyone I didn't know by name. I learned not to give out my real phone number to the random pimp who approaches you on the street… I didn't learn you had to watch out for anyone you are familiar with… I didn't know a survivor can take any pleasure in an experience and still be abused. I didn't know that a survivor could act as a 'willing participant' and still be abused. I didn't know a survivor could refrain from saying 'NO' and still be abused. I didn't know a survivor could still love the person who abused them and still be considered abused. This is why it has taken me so long to realize what happened to me. (Lindsey A. Nebeker, in Ashkenazy and Yergeau 2013, pp.123–124)

After learning how to embrace your own sexuality and define your own sexual and consensual boundaries, the most fundamental part of engaging in a happy and fulfilling sex life is learning to recognize and respect the boundaries and consent of others. Nobody is born knowing how to recognize good consent, but it doesn't have to be difficult to learn, even for somebody on the autism spectrum. I used to struggle with respecting personal space, consent, and people's boundaries, but I learned, through exercises in active listening, asking questions, checking in with others, and being aware of my personal space, how to recognize consent, differentiate good consent from false consent, and have healthy, respectful relationships with my friends and sexual partners. (Leah Jane Grantham, in Ashkenazy and Yergeau 2013, p.53)

Although it is a natural instinct to protect children from many of the ugly concepts in the following list, information is power when it comes to protecting children from abuse. As always, information should be chosen and presented in the way that is developmentally appropriate.

Safety Skills: Some Learning Concepts

1. Assertiveness.

2. Consent.

3. Saying 'No!'

4. 'No means No.'

5. Different types of touch.

6. Non-compliance.

7. Recognizing the characteristics of healthy and unhealthy relationships.

8. Recognizing, dealing with and responding to bullying, including cyber-bullying.

9. Learning the differences between surprises, privacy and secrets. Learning about good secrets (e.g. surprise parties, which are OK because they are not kept secret for long) and bad secrets (e.g. those that the child is supposed to keep secret forever).

10. Learning the ways that people may try to control you or make you do something you don't want to do, e.g. tell you it's a secret, bribe you, hurt you, tell you that they will tell everyone that you wanted to do it, or tell you that nobody will believe you (because you are a child, because you are stupid or because you have a disability).

11. Sexual harassment, i.e. bullying, teasing, touching, but with a sexual element.

12. Stalking.

13. Sexual abuse:

    • What is it? (Pornography, talking about sex, showing sexually explicit websites, taking photos or videos of the child or making the child watch someone touch themselves)

    • Who can abuse? (A child, an adult, male or female, stranger or someone you know)

    • How do you recognize it?

    • How do you report it?

    • Who do you report it to?

- What do you do if you tell someone and they don't believe you or it continues happening?
- Sexual abuse and the law.

14. Rape:
    - What is it?
    - Date rape.
    - Statutory rape.

15. Abuse within relationships:
    - Sexual abuse.
    - Physical or emotional abuse.
    - The characteristics of healthy and unhealthy relationships.
    - Signs of abuse within a relationship, e.g. being bullied, not being allowed to see your friends, being told what to wear and constantly worrying that the other person will lose their temper.
    - What to do if you are being abused in a relationship.

16. Dealing with pressure to have sex within a relationship, e.g. if your boyfriend tells you that he will break up with you if you don't, or your girlfriend tells you that if you really loved her you would do it.

17. Safety when answering the phone and door.

18. Safe dating (including internet dating).

19. Internet safety (See Chapter 16, 'SRE in a Modern Age' for more information).

20. Prostitution.

21. Child pornography.

Safety Skills: Teaching Activities and Recommendations

The same issues that lead children with ASD to being vulnerable to bullying lead to them being vulnerable to abuse. If someone is taught to 'just ignore' bullying, are they learning to 'just ignore' more serious abuse? Keeping children safe involves teaching them how to recognize, prevent, deal with and report bullying. All organizations should have active anti-bullying policies and procedures, including actively teaching children to become 'bully safe'.

Sit down with the child's parents and the other professionals involved with the child and look at the two concepts of the 'Prison of Protection' and the 'Ring of Safety'. First, think critically about each section of the Prison of Protection. Are they a reality for the child? Have they been overly protected in any or all of the sections? Next, look at the Ring of Safety. How can the child be supported/what do they need to learn in each of these areas to keep themselves safe? Some of these concepts are explored below. Others (such as sex education, options for a healthy sexuality and privacy awareness) are covered elsewhere in this book.

Someone Who Listens

Make a 'safe list' of people the child knows that they can talk to about any topic. The child should be told specifically that these are the people to discuss abuse with. The list needs to include more than one person and should include somebody from outside of the child's family. The people on the list need to be able to understand the child when they communicate. They also need to be accessible and to see them regularly. If living in a residential community, the child will need regular scheduled time with at least one person from the list so that they do not have to request it from staff who may be abusing them. This 'safe list' can be made into poster format with photos of each person, or a written list kept in the child's wallet. The people on the list need to know that they are on it, so that if the child comes to them at any time over any issue they make the time to listen to them and take all concerns seriously.

It is important not only to listen to what the child is saying but also to observe their nonverbal behaviours. Professionals and parents need to be able to see and understand even subtle changes in mood, behaviour and personality. For children with no verbal language, Hingsburger (1995) recommends making a 'language dictionary' detailing all of the subtle ways they may communicate. This will be especially useful if the child experiences a high staff turnover. It means that new staff can learn about the child more quickly, and it also means that all staff have this information, not just one, who may as a result hold all of the power. Using tactics such as language dictionaries creates a hostile environment for abusers (Hingsburger 1995).

An Understanding of Personal Rights

Policies should be in place within organizations regarding respecting clients' privacy and personal space, seeking permission before touching, and involving them in decisions regarding their bodies. (See Chapter 6, 'Developing SRE Policies and Procedures' for more information in this area.)

Children need to be trained regarding their rights within the organization's operational system (e.g. appropriate client–staff boundaries). These could be put in a simple visual format and given to each child. (See Chapter 6, 'Developing SRE Policies and Procedures' for more information in this area.)

Never force a child to kiss, hug or touch somebody if they don't want to. It is disrespectful of their wishes and also teaches inappropriate messages about the power that other people have over their bodies and whom they touch. Let children know that they have the right to make decisions about their bodies. Empower them to say 'no' when they do not want to be touched, even in non-sexual ways (e.g. politely refusing hugs).

A Healthy Self-concept and Self-confidence

Children who have good self-esteem, who believe in themselves, their abilities, their decisions, their choices and the love of those close to them are poor potential victims.

Unfortunately, self-esteem is not an easy concept to teach, as it is learned through messages from your environment and set into motion from a very young age. As much as possible, try to set up the child's environment so that they learn lessons of competency. Communicate to them regularly that they are special, that they are powerful. A child with good self-esteem, self-confidence and belief in their own competency is more likely to say 'No!' to abuse. (See Chapter 22, 'Teach a Sense of Self' for more information in this area.)

The Ability to Non-comply

1. Everyone around the child needs to discriminate linguistically between giving choices and demands. This distinction needs to be made clear so that the child can learn to assert themselves when there is in fact a choice. Otherwise you are teaching the child that 'No' does not mean 'No'. Set up safe situations where the child has the opportunities to say 'No'. If you offer the child a choice (even mistakenly), you will need to stick to the answer they give.

2. Teach how to say 'No!' (see the instructional stories at the end of this chapter). However, be careful to teach the child how to say 'no' as appropriate to the situation – e.g. it would be inappropriate for them to hold their palm up and shout 'no!' if a peer is merely asking them if they want a cigarette.

3. If the child cannot speak, they need to be taught a symbol or sign to say 'no'. If they are using a picture card (for example) this will need to be accessible to the child at all times (e.g. laminated on a key ring attached to their trousers).

4. You may wish to teach the child with little language two different types of 'no' by using different signs, symbols and colours, thereby differentiating between 'No, I don't want to watch a DVD right now' and 'No! Stop doing that!'

5. Teach the child how to act assertively in different scenarios, using role play, video modelling and social scripts – e.g. being asked to smoke, drink alcohol, take drugs, have sex, being bullied, or being told to do something that they don't want to do. An instructional story about assertiveness is included at the end of this chapter. Flashcards could be made up with different persuading statements on them, e.g.:

   - Your parents said it was OK.

   - All the other children are doing it.

   - Just this once and I'll never ask again.

   - I'll tell everyone that you are a slut if you don't do it.

6. Encourage the child to take self-defence classes.

7. Be very careful not to teach the child that they should *always* say 'no' to the things you think they should (e.g. drinking, smoking and sex). They will one day reach a legal age for these and will have the right to choose to say 'yes' at this time. Instead, teach them how to make informed decisions for themselves.

Touch

Utilize visual strategies as much as possible, e.g. colour coding and organizing information visually into circles and timelines.

1. Teach the reasons why people touch each other, e.g. to flirt, get attention, please or comfort.

2. Teach the different types of touch, e.g. rub, kiss, hit, snuggle, scratch and wrestle.

3. Consider teaching the concept of 'comfortable' and 'uncomfortable' touch.

4. Consider teaching the concept of 'business touch' for touch given by doctors, helpers or other related professionals, i.e. it is their 'business' to touch you in order to help you.

5. Help the child make a list of their own personal touching rules. Find out the kinds of touch they like and don't like, e.g., how they feel when somebody stands too close or touches them lightly.

6. Have the child ask other people what kind of touch they like and don't like.

7. Teach appropriate body distance in different situations using role play, string or hula hoops.

8. Create an individualized 'Circles of Intimacy' poster with the child. This is a visual strategy which groups all of the people in a child's life into concentric circles. The innermost circle should include the people the child is closest to, the next circle contains people in their class or doctors/helpers, and the outer circle contains people they know in the community (e.g. the girl who works at the local newsagent). Of course, you may choose to create different circles, depending on the child. Using these circles as a starting point, the child can be taught who it is safe to trust and the different types of touch that are acceptable within each circle. Actual photos of people could be placed in each circle. Using Velcro will allow flexibility to change the people over time. Children can be taught that outside of these Circles of Intimacy there should be no touching, except in certain circumstances, e.g. if it is accidental, if they are being introduced to someone, or they fall over and someone helps them up.

9. Make separate individualized posters for the kinds of touch that are OK for different people or in different settings, e.g.:

    • a poster with photos of the child's family at the top. Underneath, pictures of the kinds of touch they use, e.g. hugging, kissing on cheeks and cuddling

    • a poster with 'Everyone!' at the top. Underneath, pictures of handshakes, high fives, a tap on the shoulder, etc.

    • a poster with a photo of a park at the top. Underneath, pictures of holding hands, a kiss on the cheek, etc.

- a poster with a photo of the child's bedroom at the top. Underneath, pictures of OK touch depending on age and developmental level. This poster will need to be kept in a private place. If needed (i.e. the child is experiencing behavioural issues in this area) photos or illustrations of 'private touching' could be used here.

10. Make a visual timeline for the stages of a friendship or intimate relationship. Different stages could include 'Getting to know someone', 'The first few months of a relationship', 'When you have been in a relationship for a year' and 'When you are married'. Work out with the child the different kinds of touch that may be appropriate at the different stages.

11. Make examples of different types of touch, put them on cue cards and problem solve with the child whether they are 'OK' or 'not OK' (in addition to working on how they should respond to each), e.g.:

    - Someone bumps into me during a game by accident.

    - My little sister hugs me.

    - A friend of my mother's touches my penis.

    - The doctor touches my chin.

12. Access pictures of different types of touch from the internet or magazines. Discuss them with the child. Have the child cue in to the different features of the pictures including people's facial expressions, body language and how close they are to each other.

13. Rather than hard and fast rules, it is better to teach children to problem solve themselves about whether situations are wrong or bad. Create decision making worksheets to support the child in making up their own mind about different touches. Sections to fill in could include 'Am I happy for them to touch me?' and 'Is it an OK place to touch?' Also teach them about equality in sexual experimentation (i.e. that there should be no significant difference in age, IQ, physical strength, popularity, size or position of trust). Teach them to be careful not to be taken advantage of due to their disability. The ability to make up their own minds about what is right and what is wrong is the first step to their own autonomy, a good self-esteem and the ability to say 'No!'

Safety Skills and Precautions

Liane Holliday Willey, in her book *Safety Skills for Asperger Women* (2012), recommends that people with ASD should have a plan, a safe place and a safe person to turn to if they are going to a social event, in case something goes wrong. She recommends knowing where the police and fire stations are and having an emergency contact on speed dial. She describes a safe place as somewhere where people know and understand you and you can have a meltdown. She also recommends leaving the social event the minute you feel unsure about where you are and what you are doing. Help the child come up with their own individualized safety plan.

Holliday Willey also recommends having a 'neurotypical' whom you trust to ask about people that you are unsure of, and:

> *If you don't have anyone to help you judge a person's feelings towards you, make a list of all the things you really want and need in a friend and make sure the other person does not violate one of them. No friends are better than friends who abuse. (Holliday Willey 2012, p.44)*

Helping a child keep safe also involves protecting them from allegations of abuse themselves. They will need to learn which behaviours they are not allowed to display in certain situations, with certain people and why (e.g. staring, groping, stalking and talking about sexual topics). They need to be aware of the severity of their behaviours and the natural consequences of them, including legal consequences and restrictions on their freedom and community access. They also need to learn about the laws regarding statutory rape, and who it is not appropriate for them to have sex with and why. Learning to ask people's age if they are considering a sexual relationship with them is an important future life skill to learn, especially for those who find it difficult to discern details of people's physical appearance.

All of these safety skills will need to be practised and rehearsed, using tactics such as role play. However, as in other areas of the child's curriculum, they are unlikely to carry over into real life without practice in real-life situations. Given the subject matter, this will pose some safety problems. Practice situations will need to be highly organized and set up in such a way as not to distress the child. Examples could include having a family friend drive up and ask the child to help them look for a lost dog, or having a person unknown to the child (but known to you) ask them for a hug.

I Can Say 'No!'

I own my own body. Nobody can touch my body if I don't want them to. If I don't want someone to touch me, I will say 'No!' I will keep my head up. I will use a loud and clear voice. I will not smile. I will try to look very serious. I will try to look them in the eye. I will put my palm up towards their face.

I Can Say 'No!'

I own my own body. Nobody can touch my body if I don't want them to. If I don't want someone to touch me, I will say 'No!' I will keep my head up. I will use a loud and clear voice. I will not smile. I will try to look very serious. I will try to look them in the eye. I will put my palm up towards their face.

Being Assertive

Being assertive is a good thing.

Being assertive means letting other people know
what you want, and saying how you feel.

Being assertive does not mean shouting, hurting or scaring other people.

It does not mean that you will always get what you want.

Being assertive means knowing that you have the
right to disagree with other people.

Being assertive means knowing that you have
the right to refuse to do something.

It means being honest, direct, speaking up for yourself
and using assertive body language.

Being assertive involves asking directly for what you want.

Being assertive can sometimes be difficult.

Lots of adults aren't good at being assertive.

Some people get nervous that if they are assertive, people
will not like them or people will get angry with them.

People who care about you will like it if you are assertive.

It is good to practise being assertive with someone you
trust. They can tell you what you are doing right and what
you still need to work on so you can get it right!

Some Touching Rules

1. Someone should have a good reason for wanting to touch you.

2. Other people can touch you if you are happy for them to do so.

3. Touch should make you feel good.

4. Touch should not make you feel uncomfortable, or give you an 'uh oh' feeling inside.

5. Touch should not hurt, or make it hard for you to breathe.

6. Tickling can be OK, but only if you like it.

7. Doctors sometimes need to touch you. Sometimes this can hurt.

8. Just because you like someone, it doesn't mean that they are allowed to touch you if you don't want them to.

9. You do not have to touch somebody else's body if you don't want to.

10. It is OK to change your mind about touch.

11. It is never a child's fault if someone touches them in a way that they don't like.

12. Touching should never be secret.

13. You should never be bribed for touching.

14. Everyone has the right to tell someone not to touch their body.

14
Teach Sexual Health

Teaching children about sexual health traditionally encompasses topics such as STIs and their consequences, and contraception, but the World Health Organization (WHO) defines sexual health as:

> *A state of physical, emotional, mental and social wellbeing in relation to sexuality;* it is not merely the absence of disease, dysfunction or infirmity. *Sexual health requires a positive and respectful approach to sexuality and sexual relationships, as well as the possibility of having pleasurable and safe sexual experiences, free of coercion, discrimination and violence. For sexual health to be attained and maintained, the sexual rights of all persons must be respected, protected and fulfilled. (WHO 2012; emphasis added)*

Although preparation for these concepts should begin early (e.g. by learning about healthy bodies and hygiene), this chapter will focus mostly on the adolescent years.

For individuals with ASD, there are multiple barriers to accessing sexual health teachings and services, including societal attitudes towards their sexuality and sexual relationships, lack of appropriate resources and accessible information, and poor coordination between services and agencies. They are likely to have very low awareness of the issues involved in one's sexual health, and of the sexual health services available to them. There are also a number of reasons why they find health care appointments in general particularly stressful, including crowded and noisy waiting rooms, long wait times, bright lighting, difficulties understanding what they are being asked, difficulties locating or describing pain, and the unfamiliarity of the setting and professionals involved.

> *Addressing sexual health at the individual, family, community or health system level requires integrated interventions by trained health providers and a functioning referral system. It requires a legal, policy and regulatory environment where the sexual rights of all people are upheld. Addressing sexual health also requires understanding and appreciation of sexuality, gender roles and power in designing and providing services. (WHO 2012)*

In providing SRE, professionals should therefore aim not only to increase adolescents' awareness of their sexual health needs, but also to advocate for attitudinal changes at a societal level in relation to the sexuality and sexual relationships of individuals with

ASD, and advocate for disability-friendly services at a systems level, and improve this client group's ability to access these services independently or with support. This will be particularly relevant during transition planning to adult services. Some factors that need to be taken into account with regard to accessing services include the following:

1. How will they access sexual health services in the future?

2. How will they know that they need to access services?

3. Are they able to access services confidentially – e.g. if they do not want to tell anyone they know about a rash, or they want to ask for advice about contraceptives?

4. Which services should they access – e.g. their GP or a women's health centre?

5. How will they make appointments?

6. How will they travel to and from appointments?

7. What are the costs of the various services?

8. Which are the free services (potentially the most relevant)?

9. Do they know how to use a pharmacy?

10. Can they organize payment for medical appointments and medication?

11. Are they aware of other avenues for accessing advice on sexual health, e.g. helplines or reputable websites?

Learning concepts and teaching activities and recommendations in this chapter will focus on the more traditional aspects of sexual health (e.g. contraception and STIs) in addition to improving access to services. Other important sexual health topics, such as sexual rights, are covered elsewhere in this book.

Women's Sexual Health: Some Learning Concepts

1. The appearance of normal vaginal discharge.

2. Changes in vaginal discharge throughout the menstrual cycle.

3. Recognizing abnormal discharge.

4. The importance of gently washing your vulva every day.

5. Not using douches, deodorant or scented products on the vulva (in order to prevent infection).

6. The importance of wiping from front to back after using the toilet.

7. Wearing cotton underwear that 'breathes' in order to prevent infection.

8. Knowing that the vulva should not be painful or excessively itchy.

9. Knowing that you should only bleed from your vagina if you are menstruating.

10. Knowing that if you experience pain in the genital or pelvic area, it is necessary to see a doctor.

11. Conducting breast examinations and the importance of doing them regularly. Knowing that the presence of lumps indicates that a doctor's appointment is necessary, but is not always a sign of cancer.

12. Contraception: knowing the different methods, the pros and cons of each, how they work, how to use them and why they are important.

13. STIs: what they are, how to recognize them and how to prevent them.

14. The consequences of unprotected sex.

15. Knowing your right to say 'no' to unprotected sex.

16. Preparing for regular gynaecological exams and smear tests.

17. Organizing your own medical appointments.

Men's Sexual Health: Some Learning Concepts

1. The importance of keeping your penis clean.

2. If uncircumcised, the importance of washing under your foreskin and how to do this gently.

3. Wearing cotton underwear that 'breathes'.

4. Not using perfume on your penis.

5. If you are not having sex, knowing that, if they are not painful, small white bumps on the penis shaft or scrotum are normal.

6. If you *are* having sex, knowing that painful bumps in the genital area could be a sign of an STI.

7. Knowing that if you experience pain or excessive itching in the genital area, it is necessary to see a doctor.

8. Conducting testicular examinations and the importance of doing them regularly. Knowing that the presence of lumps indicates that a doctor's appointment is necessary, but is not always a sign of cancer.

9. Contraception: knowing the different methods, the pros and cons of each, how they work, how to use them and why they are important.

10. STIs: what they are, how to recognize them and how to prevent them.

11. The consequences of unprotected sex.

12. Knowing your right to say 'no' to unprotected sex.

13. Preparing for medical check-ups, including testicular or rectal exams.

14. Organizing your own medical appointments.

Sexual Health: Teaching Activities and Recommendations

STIs

There is a wide range of teaching materials about STIs available online, in health clinics and in traditional SRE books and programmes for adolescents that can be adapted for use with those with ASD by emphasizing the visuals and reducing the language component.

Showing pictures of genitals affected by STIs will not be enough to teach the adolescent with ASD (who has difficulty making links between concepts) to be wary of them. The book *Let's Talk about Sex: Changing Bodies, Growing Up, Sex and Sexual Health* (2009) by Robbie Harris and Michael Emberley includes a nice summary of the different STIs and how to prevent them, suitable for older children with good reading skills.

1. Emphasize the importance of doctor's visits in order to prevent issues with STIs becoming more serious.

2. The adolescent will need to be taught the physical signs of an STI but also needs to understand that many STIs have no visible symptoms.

3. Emphasize that you cannot get STIs by kissing, sitting beside someone, sitting on a toilet seat, masturbating, sharing a swimming pool, holding hands or touching – *only* by having sex without a condom.

4. Create a visual 'tree' representation of a couple who have had sex, along with all of the people that they have had sex with in the past. Create stories for each of these people as to why they did or did not use contraceptives. Show the progression of an STI if a condom was not used during sexual intercourse (i.e. how many and who are likely to have contracted it). Following this, show the STI's lack of progression if protection was used (i.e. the STI would not have moved on beyond the first 'carrier'). Have the adolescent circle who would need to get checked for an STI if one specific person found out they had contracted one and contraceptives were either used or not used.

Contraception

There are also plenty of materials available to teach about contraceptives which can easily be adapted for use with adolescents with ASD. Again, for those with good reading skills, *Let's Talk about Sex* includes an easy-to-read summary of the topic with pictures of various contraceptives.

1. Have the adolescent do research online about contraception. Create worksheets for them to fill in information on how effective each one is, where they it can be obtained, and the pros and cons of each.

2. Bring in contraceptives to show, but be careful about prescriptive contraceptives such as the pill, which only health professionals are allowed to carry.

3. Teach the effects of drugs and alcohol on decision making with regard to sex, contraceptive use and the ability to use contraceptives effectively.

USING CONDOMS

1. Teach condom use with a model and not, for example, a cucumber, which will only confuse further. Be specific and explicit in your teaching. Troubleshoot potential issues that may occur. For example, with regard to condoms, young people need to know:

   - how to pick the right-sized condom

   - where to buy condoms

   - that it will be hard to put on the condom with the lights out, and they may need to turn on lights or go to the bathroom to do it

   - that they should keep their nails short so as not to rip condoms

   - that if the condom tears, they need to use a new one.

   - the man's penis needs to be hard for the condom to go on

   - it is normal to make several attempts to get a condom on correctly, so there need to be lots of condoms available

   - if all of the condoms break, they will need to wait until they are able to get more before having sex

   - they need to use a different condom every time they have sex

   - they cannot use something else, such as a plastic bag, instead of a condom

   - what to do if the condom breaks or stays inside of the woman.

   It may be beneficial to create a visual schedule for the steps to putting on a condom.

2. Teach some common excuses that might be given for not wearing a condom, (e.g. that they smell horrible, that you won't be able to feel anything, that it takes the fun out of sex, that they don't really work or that the woman is on the pill, so they don't have to). Teach responses to these excuses. Use role play to support learning. Information on teaching assertiveness can be found in Chapter 13, 'Teach Safety Skills'.

3. Along with learning information about the various contraceptives, some older adolescents will need to be taught about making choices about contraception, where to go for advice about it, and how to go about getting contraception if they wish to do so. Factors such as which method they will be able to use consistently and effectively will need to be taken into account. A planned visit to the local family planning clinic could help with this.

ABORTION

Teach about abortion, the legalities and people's beliefs about it based on religious, cultural or family values. Teach that nobody can be forced to have an abortion if they do not want one. Also teach that emergency contraception is not a method of abortion.

Seeking Advice on Sexual Health Issues

1. Make a list of 'safe', non-judgemental people that they can ask about sexual health issues.

2. Create a plan of who to talk to and what to do if they want sexual health information or if something happens that they need support for.

3. Create a map of local health services, including how they can get to them and how much each one costs.

4. Create visual instructional stories of breast and testicular self-examinations. There are also videos available online to demonstrate these.

PREPARING FOR SEXUAL HEALTH CARE APPOINTMENTS

1. Have the adolescent ask family members about their medical appointments, why they went, what happened, why they were important and how they felt during and afterwards.

2. Teach the importance of being honest with your doctor, who should be non-judgemental and who needs to know all of the relevant information in order to help.

3. Some tips on preparing for sexual health care appointments (which will apply to all health care appointments):

   • Appointments can be put in advance on a large calendar.

   • Visit the setting prior to any appointment so that they can familiarize themselves with it (and meet staff) in a non-threatening way.

   • Teach the roles of the different professionals that they will meet (e.g. receptionists, doctors and nurses).

   • Let them know in advance how long the appointment is going to last, and how often they may have to return.

   • Bring distractions and relaxing activities.

   • If the adolescent has difficulty describing and locating pain, teach these skills ahead of time using visual body maps and rating scales. Then ensure that these visual tools are brought to appointments and that the doctor is aware of and understands them.

   • Request ahead of time for a quiet room to wait in.

   • Ring ahead and ask the doctor what will happen during the appointment (e.g. a rectal, pelvic or breast exam) and what the adolescent will be asked. Then prepare thoroughly, using factsheets, visual schedules, instructional stories or video clips. Bring these to the appointment. The non-intrusive sections (e.g. the questions and answers section) can be prepared for by using role play.

- Prepare for the type of private questions that will be asked, e.g. if they have had sex or whether they are on birth control.

- The adolescent should know which medication they are on and be able to tell the doctor (if they have the language skills).

- Prepare them for the possibility that they might need to take off their clothes.

- Prepare them for where they will be touched and how it will feel.

- Teach relaxation techniques (e.g. deep breathing and visualizations) that they can use during appointments.

- Notify health care professionals ahead of time about the adolescent's needs and communication skills. For example, you could make a request for the lights to be dimmed, for sentences to be kept short and for open-ended questions to be avoided.

- Request that appointments are kept short and to specific lengths.

- Bring along a visual countdown timer to count down time during appointments. (If using one, the end time will need to be kept to.)

- Request that appointments are held at specific times, e.g. first thing in the morning, so that waiting is reduced.

- Do something nice after appointments to build up positive associations.

As far as possible, teach adolescents to advocate for their own sexual health needs, including managing their own appointments, answering doctor's questions themselves and deciding who they want in the room with them (i.e. who they give permission to hear confidential information about themselves).

15

Teach Conception, Pregnancy and Birth

Like the sexual health topics of contraception and STIs, conception, pregnancy and birth are an established part of many traditional SRE programmes and so there is a wealth of information available about them, either online or in SRE books or programmes. This can easily be adapted for use with children with ASD by emphasizing the visuals and reducing the language component.

While all children need to learn about these topics, they can be especially important for children with ASD, who may learn the 'facts and figures' easily enough, but often hold incorrect beliefs which, unlike their typically developing peers, they may continue to hold into adulthood and as a result have negative experience of intimate relationships.

> *I knew all about sperm, eggs, gestation and birth by the second grade. But I thought the sperms just floated from the father to the mother while they were asleep together. I knew never to fall asleep too close to a male, because sleeping together caused pregnancy. (Mary Newport, in Newport and Newport 2002, p.33)*

Conception, Pregnancy and Birth: Some Learning Concepts

1. Fertilization and conception.

2. Myths about conception (e.g. that you can't get pregnant if you have sex standing up, the first time you have sex or if you use the withdrawal method).

3. Development from zygote to baby.

4. Staying healthy (and keeping your baby healthy) during pregnancy.

5. The signs of pregnancy.

6. Steps to take if you think you are pregnant – buying and taking a pregnancy test, talking to someone you trust, phoning a helpline, or making an appointment at a women's health centre.

7. The law in relation to underage pregnancy.

8. Labour and caesarean delivery.

9. New body parts related to birth: the placenta and the umbilical cord.

10. Breastfeeding and bottle-feeding.

11. Premature births.

12. Miscarriage.

13. Fertility.

14. Abortion.

15. IVF.

16. Surrogacy.

17. Menopause.

18. Sterilization.

19. Adoption.

20. Genes and chromosomes and how these are passed down.

Conception, Pregnancy and Birth: Teaching Activities and Recommendations

1. Revise Chapter 9, on 'Growing and Changing', Chapter 8, on 'Body Parts and Fluids' and Chapter 10, on 'Puberty'.

2. Create instructional stories in the learning concept areas.

3. Keep all information factual and language concrete.

4. Be wary of potential issues with language being taken literally, e.g. thinking that the woman's egg is hard like a chicken's egg.

5. Create illustrations to size, e.g. sperm and women's eggs.

6. Do not assume any knowledge on the child's part, even if they appear to be informed.

7. Be explicit about the links between menstruation, fertility, sperm, sex, contraception, conception, pregnancy and childbirth. Create visual representations to help with this, e.g. flow charts.

8. Anecdotally, some pregnant teachers of children with ASD have reported that their students react badly to their growing 'bumps'. This could be as a result of either confusion on the child's part, or dislike of change in general. Either way, make sure to teach the child about why their teacher's tummy is getting large – e.g. that it is not because she is getting fat! Prepare them for the changes that will occur,

including their teacher going on maternity leave, why she is going and how long she will be gone.

9. Show videos of a foetus developing in the uterus, along with videos of the progression of a pregnancy from the outside of the woman's body. (Both are freely available online.) Videos of childbirth may also be helpful, but use them with caution.

10. Teach medical terms, and also any slang alternatives for them.

11. Utilize teachable moments, e.g. pregnant teachers or pets.

Making Babies

Men and women have body parts that are there just to make babies.

When two people love each other, they might decide to have a baby.

To do this, they hug and kiss each other in private. The woman helps the man put his penis inside her vagina. Then the man ejaculates semen into the woman's vagina. A baby is made when the man's sperm and the woman's egg join inside her.

If the woman becomes pregnant, the baby will grow inside her uterus for about nine months.

The uterus is separate from the stomach.

The woman's tummy looks bigger and bigger as the baby grows inside her uterus.

It is important to be gentle with a woman's pregnancy bump so that the baby inside it is kept happy and safe.

Babies usually come out of the woman's vagina when the baby is big enough.

The woman's vagina stretches to let the baby out.

The woman's breasts produce milk for the baby. Some people feed their babies with bottles.

Not all men and women can have babies.

Babies aren't made every time a man and a woman have sex.

If a man and woman do not want to have a baby, they need to use contraception every time they have sex.

16

SRE in a Modern Age

I've had two girlfriends – two internet girlfriends. My first girlfriend was Marie who is French-Canadian and lived in Montreal. We used to talk every night via a net meeting. Obviously it wasn't a physical relationship and we didn't go out, but it was emotional. (Lee, aged 18, in Molloy and Vasil 2004, p.42)

Sometimes people can be nasty on the internet. Someone at school secretly copied my email address when I was giving it to a friend and she must have given it to some other kids and they've been chatting with me on MSN Messenger. It was like lots of rude stuff like saying that I'm a witch and '39 per cent angel, 50 per cent evil…' and strange things like that. In the end I had to block them so they wouldn't chat to me again. (Sarah, aged 12, in Molloy and Vasil 2004, p.68)

There is no question that SRE needs to adapt and update to the modern world. Children today are growing up in an age of freely available information on any topic they wish to search for, and not just from their computers, but also from their phones and games consoles. Online, and in their own developing language, they share information, views and experiences, create content, watch movies, chat, play games and meet people through blogs, video sites, email, gaming groups, instant messaging, texting, chatrooms, social network sites and much more. It is commonplace today for children to have online friends, boyfriends and girlfriends whom they have never met and possibly never intend to meet.

There may be positive aspects to this, in particular for children and adults with ASD, including making learning highly visual, meaningful and interesting, supporting communication through the use of apps, being able to investigate information independently in relation to sexuality, 'talking' to others without having to worry about body language or eye contact and connecting with groups of people with the same interests (no matter how obscure). It can be a valuable trove of knowledge to feed many children's special interests, not just for distraction or entertainment purposes, but also to provide intellectual stimulation. Online dating is now a widely accepted practice and has been beneficial for many people with disabilities who find it difficult to meet the right people. The internet is unique in its ability to share people's creative outputs (e.g. in art, photography, crafts, music or fashion) with vast numbers of people. It is also a place where people who are considered 'different' can find acceptance and understanding from all over the world, thereby reducing feelings of isolation. It has been invaluable in the disability rights and advocacy movements.

However, there also exist many disadvantages. Children are now regularly exposed to pornography and other sexualized images, even if they do not actively search for them (e.g. through 'pop up' ads and site links). Girls may be pressurized into exposing themselves online and are subsequently the subject of exploitation. Anecdotally, it would appear that it has become normal even for pre-teens to text explicit photographs of themselves (termed 'sexting'), and boys may be learning many of the 'facts' of sex through hard core pornography. In general, children with ASD appear to be more susceptible than most to spending too much time on their computer.

The internet is full of elaborate (and not so elaborate) hoaxes and money scams, many of which arrive directly to children's email accounts. Identity theft is commonplace, as are adults pretending to be children, with motives ranging from monetary scams to luring children towards abusive situations. There exist many unsafe 'support groups' such as pro-anorexia and pro-suicide sites. Cyber-bullying is rife, and has been associated with suicidal behaviour (Litwiller and Brausch 2013). Cyber-bullying is particularly dangerous because it is faceless. Unfortunately, children with ASD are particularly vulnerable to the dangers of the internet due to the difficulties they have in evaluating information, including other people's motives. Even when parents or teachers make attempts to block content, they may find themselves (often unknowingly) outwitted by children with superior computer skills.

SEXUALITY, SOCIETY AND CULTURE

It is important for children to learn the impact of the media (as well as their family and friends) on their thoughts, feelings, behaviours and values in relation to sexuality. Children need to be supported in critically examining the world around them for biases based on sexual orientation, ethnicity, race or gender. This includes learning about sexuality in relation to the media, law, religion and arts and interpreting overt and covert sexual information (e.g. in pornography and commercials). Children need to learn to make their own decisions, as unbiased as possible by media influences. They also need to know that it is OK to hold a different opinion from the majority or even from their own friends and family (and that these relationships will continue to be loving and supportive).

Despite the dangers of the internet, banning children from the use of computers and mobile phones entirely is probably going too far. The internet is here to stay, and blocking a child from using it alienates them from their peers and deprives them of valuable learning experiences. What needs to be taught is a healthy and critical attitude towards the internet and modern methods of communication, in addition to lifelong safety skills in relation to them.

CASE EXAMPLE

Michael is a 13-year-old, popular and friendly boy with ASD who attends a mainstream school. During class one day, he loudly asked a female peer would she 'touch his willy to see if it would grow?' resulting in Michael being suspended from school. The girl's parents were notified, and made a request that Michael be transferred to a special school. While the school was reluctant to force this issue, his mother was advised to seek 'professional help' for Michael and it appeared to her that he was now being seen as a potential 'sexual predator' due to his actions.

Michael himself appeared genuinely confused by the commotion. When asked, he said that he had heard that when a girl touched a boy's penis it grew bigger and was interested to see if this was true.

His mother sought professional advice from a psychiatrist. She told the psychiatrist that following the incident she had looked through Michael's phone and found numerous images of girls in his class with their tops off as well as sexually explicit texts detailing how they wanted to give him oral sex. Some of these texts and images were from the girl whom he had asked to touch him. Worried that Michael was being targeted in some way due to his ASD, his mother asked him, was he the only one being sent these texts. Michael informed her that, on the contrary, 'everyone in school' did it and that he had seen the texts himself on other boys' phones. Michael's mother notified the school, who told her that there was nothing they could do about it as the texts were sent outside of school time (due to technology in place which blocked the use of mobile phones in the school).

Clearly, there is a school-wide (indeed society-wide) issue at work here. In this context, in addition to difficulties understanding social rules and norms due to his ASD, it is no wonder that Michael became confused by the messages from his female peers and subsequently behaved inappropriately. In the absence of the text messages, a comprehensive SRE programme for Michael would have been suitable, including work on appropriate public and private behaviours and conversations and insight training regarding why people might have been offended by his comment. A 'traffic light' system whereby comments and behaviours are colour coded according to appropriateness might also have been useful. However, in the context of text messages such as those he was receiving, while a programme such as this is still extremely valuable, it does not address the systemic issues, and presumably Michael's peers would continue to act as they had done previously. These continued mixed messages would probably not only confuse Michael further and compromise the success of any programme, but also alienate him from his peers. Applicable here is something that many ASD advocates talk about: the injustice that they often need to act 'more normal than normal people'.

Despite the school's protests, what is needed here is a school-wide intervention in relation to texting (and 'sexting'), SRE and learning respect for one's body and sexuality. Parents' associations in particular need to become actively involved. In addition, a number of child protection issues are raised in relation to the nature of the images (viewed by Michael's mother and subsequently reported to both the principal and the psychiatrist), which would need to be investigated. As the girls in the photographs are underage and naked, depending on local laws it may be the duty of the professionals involved to report the images to the relevant authorities.

Safety in a Modern Age: Teaching Activities and Recommendations

1. Remain as up to date as possible with modern technology, in particular in relation to the internet. It is also advisable to keep up to date with 'text speak' in order to help keep children safe. A parent seeing 'WMIRL' on their child's phone may think nothing of it, but 'translated' it means 'Would you like to meet in real life?', i.e. the child is being asked to meet up with somebody they have as yet only met online.

2. Teach that NOTHING on the internet is private.

3. Teach skills in recognizing credible websites.

4. Teach about internet scams.

5. Teach about 'bugs', 'viruses' and how they don't just damage computers but are often designed to collect personal information.

6. Teach what can be done with a person's collected personal information, e.g. identity theft.

7. Teach not to give any personal information to anyone looking for money, information or help, but instead to ignore these messages.

8. Teach not to share any information online that you wouldn't share with a stranger.

9. Teach about the dangers of unsafe support groups, e.g. pro-suicide or pro-anorexia sites. Teach that they are often run and populated by very troubled individuals.

10. Teach not to download information (in particular, images) onto your computer, as they may be explicit or contain viruses.

11. Teach that people online are often not who they appear to be, and that it is common for adults to pretend to be children or a different gender.

12. Teach how to 'block' people and sites from sending you content.

13. Revise Chapter 13 on 'Safety Skills', such as the concepts that nobody should ask you to run away with them, or to keep their existence a secret.

14. Teach rules about meeting up with 'online friends' in real life – e.g. that they must bring along a parent, tell other people where they are going, bring a fully charged mobile phone and only meet in a public place.

15. Teach about cyber-bullying and how to deal with it, by not replying, telling a trusted adult and blocking people. Also teach how to prevent it, by not posting naked or potentially embarrassing photos and not sharing too much personal information online. Cyber-bullying should be covered in organizations' anti-bullying policies.

16. Teach to recognize online harassment and stalking.

17. Teach about appropriate behaviour online, e.g. how many messages it is appropriate to send someone if they haven't messaged you back.

18. Teach texting skills.

19. Teach about 'sexting', its dangers and its legality. Make and teach rules, such as 'No showing body parts online, even to friends'.

20. Use software to block adult content and pop ups on computers.

21. Teach facts about pornography, including the legalities, and also that it does not include realistic portrayals of sex.

Parents can be advised to go online with their children and supervise email accounts. Some parents may only allow their younger children to open social networking sites if they are added as a friend and know their passwords. However, parents need to be aware that it is easy for children to block specific people from seeing specific information on these sites. Learning skills in looking up browser histories (although these can be deleted) will also be useful. Some families also have rules that computers are kept in public spaces.

Although the child may be too young now, they may wish to take part in online dating in the future. Teaching them online safety skills will support this. They should also be encouraged to investigate the goals of dating or social media sites, and learn that if they only mention sex or 'hook ups' they are best avoided, and why.

Enlist the help of older peers and siblings (who will most likely have more credibility in the child's eyes) to teach about safety online.

Some Internet Safety Rules

1. If a site makes you feel uncomfortable, you do not need to look at it. Tell a trusted adult.
2. If you get a message online that worries you, don't reply to it. Tell a trusted adult.
3. Don't answer any question online that you don't want to answer.
4. Ignore any message asking you for help or personal information, even if they say you have won something. It is always a lie.
5. Block anyone who sends you information or asks you questions that you don't like.
6. You do not have to be friends with someone online just because they ask you. If you do not know them, block them.
7. Remember that online friends may not be real friends.
8. Online friends should not be a substitute for real-life friends.
9. Don't post details about yourself such as your name, date of birth, telephone number or where you are going. Keep personal details PRIVATE.
10. Never give anyone (except your parents) your passwords.
11. Don't use your real name as a username.
12. Close all pop ups without opening them.
13. Never post pictures or videos of any part of your body, even to friends.
14. Don't tell anyone that you are a child.
15. Don't arrange to meet someone without bringing along a trusted adult.
16. If anyone asks you to keep something secret, tell a trusted adult.
17. Never send photos or videos online that you would not want your friends, family or teacher to see.
18. Don't say anything to anyone online that you would not say to the person's face.
19. Don't say anything to anyone online that you would mind being on a 40-foot billboard outside your parents' house.
20. Don't be mean to people.
21. Don't spread gossip.
22. Don't believe everything that you read or see.
23. Remember that people are usually not as popular or good-looking as they appear to be online.

Part III
Supporting

17

Teach Emotional Understanding and Regulation

Difficulties with emotional understanding and regulation affect the majority of people with ASD, and there are many books and programmes available to support children in this area. Teaching children to understand and regulate their emotions supports communication skills, mental health, coping skills and positive relationships, and therefore helps prevent behavioural issues. Children need to learn that their emotions affect their thoughts, which affect their behaviour, which in turn affects other people's reactions to them. They need to learn to identify and avoid situations that can lead to certain emotions, and to understand that other people have different emotions from them. Developing and learning in all of these areas, even for typically developing people, is a lifelong and difficult process.

While this topic is a common feature of many ASD programmes, unfortunately what are often left out are the romantic and sexual feelings of love, tenderness, attraction and desire, as are the mood swings and 'crushes' so common during puberty and adolescence. Also hugely important here is learning about homosexual feelings and what it means to feel them. It can be difficult for many parents to acknowledge their children's sexual feelings and it is a tricky subject for professionals to teach. However, the importance of feelings related to sexuality in our lives cannot be underestimated, nor indeed how prevalent messages about them are in modern media outlets. Gay characters are now standard in most television programmes and sex is used to sell everything from carpet cleaner to cars. Love, lust and attraction are all part of what it is to be human, and failure to teach them leads to incomplete understanding of both ourselves and other people.

Instructional stories at the end of this chapter focus on love and sexual feelings (including homosexual sexual feelings), but it is recommended that an SRE programme should cover all emotions. These instructional stories are quite detailed, as they are designed to be adapted for use with individual children depending on their age and developmental level. More information about sexual feelings, attraction, dating and relationships is included in later chapters.

Emotional Understanding and Regulation: Some Key Skills

1. Being aware of and understanding your feelings.

2. Being aware of and understanding other people's feelings.

3. Expressing a range of emotions.

4. Being able to express strong emotions appropriately.

5. Being able to communicate your needs and wishes.

Emotional Understanding and Regulation: Teaching Activities and Recommendations

1. It is important to teach not just happy, sad and angry, but a full range of emotions and feelings, including feeling envious, compassionate, silly, sexy, brave, hopeful, pleased, moody, guilty, shy, careless, hate, love, respectful, ambitious, wonderful and proud.

2. Talking about sexual feelings is a private topic and therefore privacy rules apply. Of course, sensitivity also needs to be given to the subject matter when developing materials (e.g. the use of photos or video clips), and it would not be appropriate to role-play sexual feelings. However, for older adolescents, role-playing love or flirting, if appropriately managed, would be very useful.

3. Teach why it is important to learn about your own and other people's emotions.

4. Teach why it is important to express your feelings to other people.

5. Teach when and where it is appropriate to display or talk about certain emotions, e.g. 'It is not appropriate to tell every girl that you like that you are attracted to her', or 'It is not appropriate to shout out in the middle of math class that you are angry at your mother for not giving you breakfast cereal that morning'. Remember to teach why.

6. Teach the good ways to tell or show the different people in your life how you feel.

7. Teach that you can ask how somebody is feeling, if you do not know. Teach skills to go about this.

8. Teach body awareness, which will help support the child in understanding the physical and emotional changes to their body when they experience different emotions.

9. Teach about the body's reaction to different emotions, e.g. knees shaking, heart beating fast and sweaty palms. Teach the reasons why the body reacts these ways, including the 'fight or flight' response. Teach about the 'anger cycle'. Create a 'body chart' to teach these concepts.

10. Teach how to identify different emotions, e.g.:

    - Access a wide variety of pictures of people showing different emotions. Use these to match, label, sort and discuss.

    - Show video clips of people experiencing different emotions and have the child identify them.

    - Use role play and video modelling. Have other people express emotions for the child to identify but also have the child express different emotions and receive constructive feedback.

    - Create instructional stories about different emotions and how people usually look or behave when they are feeling them.

    - Have the child identify how they are feeling throughout the day by choosing from a list or pointing to a picture.

    - Create an individualized 'My Feelings Book', including things that make them feel a certain way and how their body reacts to different emotions. This can be expanded and added to over time.

11. Never assume that you know the emotion that a child is feeling. Make sure to check in.

12. The use of emotional thermometers and other visual rating scales will be extremely useful, in particular when working on anger or anxiety.

13. Teach the difference between sexual and romantic feelings.

14. Teach that feelings can change rapidly or slowly over time.

15. Teach that it is possible to feel lots of different feelings all at the same time.

16. Teach that different people can feel different emotions about the exact same things.

17. Teach that people can show the same emotion in different ways.

18. Have the child ask a friend or someone they trust for help with their nonverbal body language when conveying different emotions (i.e. help them make sure that they are expressing how they are feeling in the right way). For example, if they want to convey annoyance, the friend could notice their tone of voice or facial expression to tell whether they are looking or sounding angrier than they mean to.

19. Teach good listening and coping skills for when other people are showing strong emotions.

20. Teach how to regulate emotions, e.g.:

    - Give the child some personalized options for when they are feeling a certain way, using tools such as 'When I feel…I can…,' e.g. 'When I am sad, I can tell my mum, hug my bear, cry or ask dad for a cuddle' or 'When I am frustrated, I can ask for a break, go for a short walk, kick a ball against the wall or shout into a pillow'. These could be put into picture or poster format.

- Teach relaxation strategies such as deep breathing, music, exercise, yoga and progressive muscle relaxation exercises.

- Teach about positive self-talk.

- Teach strategies to deal with negative self-talk, such as visualizing a 'Stop!' sign and always checking for the truth.

- Encourage the child to write about their emotions in a diary.

- Create an individualized 'My Relaxation Book' with pictures of all the things that help them relax, such as doing yoga, their bedroom, their dog and a nice mountain scene.

- Teach about preventative measures to look after your emotions, such as getting enough sleep, eating well, talking to someone and exercising.

Love

When you LOVE someone you feel warm, happy and deep feelings for them.

You can love friends, family, pets, your boyfriend or girlfriend, your husband or wife or your children.

There are different kinds of love. The love that you feel for your family is one kind. The love that you feel for your husband or wife is another kind. This kind is sometimes called being IN LOVE.

Being in love means that you feel very deeply about someone and are also attracted to them (have sexual feelings about them). But it is even more than this. Being in love is very hard to describe!

People call the time when you first start being in love with someone FALLING in love. Of course, you do not really fall anywhere! Falling in love can be an intense, exciting and scary feeling.

If you love yourself and feel good about yourself, it will help you to love other people.

Sometimes love can change and you can stop loving someone or they can stop loving you. This will not happen with your family. They will ALWAYS love you and you will always love them.

Love is difficult to understand. Sometimes it is hard to know if you are really in love with someone. Sometimes people mix up really liking someone, thinking about them a lot or having sexual feelings for them, as being in love. Sometimes people only realize that they were not really in love after some time has passed.

If you have never met the person (for example, if they are a celebrity) it is NOT likely that you are really in love with them, although it might really, REALLY feel that way.

Some people fall in love many times in their lives. Some people only do it once. Some people never fall in love, but have lots of people that they love in their lives.

Sometimes people love someone, but the person doesn't love them back. This is hard.

You CANNOT make someone fall in love with you.

If you are in love with someone and they are not in love with you, it is better to try to forget about being in a romantic relationship with them. It is a waste of time and energy to try to persuade someone to like you. It is much better to wait until you love somebody who LOVES YOU BACK. This will help you to be much happier.

You show love differently to different people. A boyfriend and girlfriend might show they love each other by kissing on the lips. A friend might show that he loves his friend by making him a really great birthday card. A mother might show that she loves her son by making him dinner every night. There are lots of great ways to show someone that you love them!

Being in Love

Most people fall in love with people from the opposite gender to themselves.

Some people fall in love with people who are the same gender as themselves.

All of these people love each other JUST THE SAME.

Sexual Feelings

People have different names for sexual feelings, such as feeling 'horny', feeling 'sexy', being 'turned on' or being 'sexually aroused'. Sexual feelings are also sometimes called 'sexual desire', 'attraction' or 'lust'. Both boys and girls feel sexual feelings.

Sexual feelings are special. They are different from the feelings of love or friendship that you have for your family and friends. Almost everyone feels sexual feelings at some time. They are normal.

Sexual feelings are a private topic. You should only talk about them with people you trust.

Sexual feelings feel different for different people. Some people say that when they have sexual feelings they feel giggly, excited, weird, warm, happy, or just different. Their heart might start beating really fast. Their tummy might feel different. They might not be able to concentrate on anything else. Men might get an erection. Women's vaginas might become wetter, swollen and throb (but in a nice way).

People usually feel sexual feelings about another person. This person could be someone in real life or someone they see on the TV, in a movie or on the internet. People sometimes feel sexual feelings when they touch their own body, rub off something nice or are touched by someone they like. They might also feel sexual feelings if they see sexy pictures, such as pictures of people kissing or having sex.

If you feel sexual feelings when you look at someone, it means that you are sexually attracted to them or have a crush on them. The person could be of the same sex or the opposite sex, but is usually the opposite sex. Both are OK. You might feel nervous, uncomfortable or excited around the person. You might act giddily or impulsively. You might want to touch that person. You might want to kiss them. You might want them to touch you. You might want to tell them how you feel. But it is important to remember that they might not feel the same way about you.

Sexual feelings can be fun and exciting but sometimes they can be scary.

It is normal for teenagers to feel sexual feelings a lot of the time, although not all teenagers do. Older people also have sexual feelings, but they might feel them less than teenagers.

All feelings are OK once they are not against the law, upsetting you, upsetting anyone else, or stopping you from doing anything. For example, it is not good if you are spending all day every day in your bedroom having sexual feelings.

It is important to be careful about what you do with your sexual feelings. You cannot talk about them with everyone. Lots of people feel sexual feelings every day and just enjoy the feelings. You can feel them and do nothing. You can talk about them with a good friend who also wants to talk about them. You can touch yourself when you are in your private place. If you are old enough, they have said it is OK and you are in a private place, you can be sexual with another person.

✓

18

Teach Sensory Sensitivities

Although sensory issues are not part of the diagnostic criteria for ASD, most authors with ASD report that they have had a *significant* impact on their lives, at times leading to feelings of severe physical pain and distress. Issues with processing sensory information can lead to difficulties understanding the world around us, what we see, hear, smell, feel and taste. How we interpret and learn from our environment subsequently affects our behaviour. This means that the impact of sensory sensitivities on a child's ability to learn from and interact with others is significant. The sensory needs of an individual with ASD can range from mild to severe, and can at times lead to sensory overload or meltdown. However, awareness and subsequent environmental changes can often lead to improvements in coping.

Sensory sensitivities can occur across all of the senses, that is, sight, sound, smell, touch, taste and movement. Our inner movement senses are termed vestibular (sense of balance) and proprioceptive (perception of movement and spatial orientation). All of these senses can be experienced either as intensified (hypersensitivity) or underdeveloped (hyposensitivity). If someone is *hyper*sensitive to touch, they may not like the feel of certain hygiene products such as shaving foam or deodorant, light kissing, holding hands or being kissed by someone with a beard. If someone is *hypo*sensitive to touch, they may seek out strong hugs or touch and prefer tight clothing, spicy foods and extreme temperatures. Sensory sensitivities can become worse if a child is sick, tired or has no control over the stimulation.

Authors with ASD have reported that even a romantic partner wearing a specific aftershave, a necklace that jangles, or a particular colour or texture of clothes can leave them feeling scared, physically unwell or irritated. Sensory issues related to understanding and interpreting touch can lead to significant issues within relationships for individuals with ASD. Sexual stimulation may cause discomfort or even pain leading to avoidance of intimate relationships. Wendy Lawson (2005) has known some couples who wear gloves to reduce the overload of direct contact, and others who spend time in a bath with candlelight so that direct touch is minimized but intimacy is maximized.

Regardless of their ability level, children with ASD need to be aware of and understand their own sensory profile, so that they can advocate for their own needs.

Sex didn't scare me, but being touched made me extremely anxious. I have always been aware of my sensory sensitivities; they are what led me into the field of occupational therapy, and shortly thereafter, to specialize in sensory integration disorders. I found that the only place I could tolerate being initially touched was on my back, the least sensitive part of my body. My touch sensitivity also made kissing a problem for me, and a source of confusion and hurt for my husband... Touch sensitivity affected the playful forms of touch in our relationship as well. Playfully being grabbed by the arm, having my hand patted or held when my husband felt romantic were responded to by my pulling away or yelling that it 'hurt.' Even worse was when he would, in play, try to surprise me. My reflex reaction was to hit or kick him or fall screaming to the floor shaking in fear and rage. My nervous system simply couldn't handle sudden movements or unexpected sounds. It became clear that my unpredictable and excessive reactions were a perplexing and upsetting roadblock to the development of a mutually trusting and comforting relationship, at least until I understood my own sensory processing issues enough to explain them to him and better figure out how to accommodate our mutual needs. (Golubock 2009, p.56)

As a toddler, I would not kiss my father. The smell of coffee on his breath and the scratchiness of his moustache was too much for me to bear. (Shore 2003, p.19)

SENSORY INTEGRATION THERAPY

Sensory Integration Therapy is widely used with children with ASD and there is a lot of anecdotal evidence as to its effectiveness. Children may be given a 'sensory diet', with individualized treatments including sensory stimulation or inhibition techniques (such as deep pressure through massage or the use of weighted blankets), auditory integration techniques and physical exercise. However, the current evidence base does not support the use of sensory integration therapy in the education and treatment of children with ASD (Lang *et al.* 2012).

Sensory Sensitivities: Teaching Activities and Recommendations

1. Consult an occupational therapist who specializes in supporting sensory needs.

2. Everyone involved with the child needs to understand how sensory sensitivities affect them and to make preventative measures to their environment to lessen their impact.

3. Help the child learn about their own sensory needs – e.g. by creating posters of things in their environment that they find distracting or painful. Help them identify and avoid situations which affect them badly, although not if this means that they are missing out on vital experiences (e.g. meeting friends). Help them learn how their sensory needs affect their behaviour. Help them figure out which things are OK to avoid, and which should be tackled and worked on and why.

4. The typically developing people around the child will need to be understanding about sensory sensitivities and not take offence if a child expresses their thoughts (e.g. if the child tells you that your breath smells). However, there is a balance to be taught here between the child learning to express their thoughts and advocate for their needs and following the 'rules' of polite conversation.

5. Teach the child to look after themselves physically and emotionally in order to prevent any sensitivity issues becoming worse.

6. Develop an individualized 'sensory coping plan' for when the child is feeling overwhelmed, i.e. what exactly they will do, where they will go, what they will say. For example, if a child knows that he does not like visiting the local supermarket, his personal plan could include:

    • taking his music and headphones with him while shopping

    • staying for only 20 minutes

    • making a list beforehand to minimize the amount of time spent in the shop

    • having a script of what to say to people who might want to talk to him in the shop (e.g. 'Sorry, I'm in a bit of a rush today')

    • if he does become sensory-overloaded and upset, go to the park bench outside of the shop and do deep breathing exercises until calm.

7. Sometimes, sensitivities can be overcome (or at least made manageable) if a child is exposed to what they dislike gradually and in a safe and managed way. For example, if the child hates the sound of hand dryers (which is affecting their ability to go to the toilet in public places) a desensitization programme could be implemented in which the child is initially shown pictures of hand dryers, then shown video clips of hand dryers with no sound, before the sound is incrementally turned up. The next phase could be visiting a public toilet but staying outside the door before gradually moving inside, and so on. The child should receive a lot of praise and reinforcement for taking part in the programme. Any sign that the child is in distress, and the programme should be taken back a step, or a number of steps, until the child is comfortable again.

8. Give the child literature written by authors with ASD about their sensory sensitivities and how they overcame them.

9. Teach advocating for their own sensory needs, such as being able to ask could they move seats in a restaurant to somewhere quiet, or explaining to a girlfriend that they find soft touch difficult and why.

10. Make lists of the different ways in which sensory sensitivities can affect a person. Go through these with the child and have them tick the ones that relate to them. Or have the child choose whether they affect them mildly or strongly on a visual rating scale.

11. For older partners in intimate relationships, Wendy Lawson has created some statements to use as discussion prompts in order to increase mutual understanding:

- I need you to slow down and take more time with me; kissing me and stroking me help me to relax.

- Because you spend so much time kissing and cuddling me I get overloaded and I switch off from you.

- I can concentrate better with the radio on.

- I can relate more easily to you when you stop talking and allow me to focus.

- I miss the feeling of 'skin'.

- I need to keep my pyjamas on because I can't cope with the feeling of skin on skin.

- I can feel you better when we don't face each other.

- I can't cope with having you too close to me; lying on our sides back to back gives me the closeness I can cope with.

- I need you to touch me firmly; light touch is uncomfortable for me.

(Lawson 2005, p.166)

This approach could be adapted for use with younger children sharing information about their sensory sensitivities with friends, parents or teachers.

19

Masturbation

Behavioural issues in relation to masturbation (i.e. children masturbating at inappropriate times or places) are commonly reported in special education. This is wholly understandable, given that it is developmentally a typical behaviour resulting in immediate feelings which are intensely pleasurable, and therefore far more strongly reinforcing and immediate than other types of reinforcement (e.g. praise or edibles). Couple that with the difficulties that children with ASD have in understanding the social rules that govern their behaviour, and issues will naturally arise. However, unfortunately, the topic of masturbation is not an easy one for open discussion due to strong social taboos, and often it is parents' and professionals' personal values in relation to masturbation that determines whether these behavioural issues are addressed. Common concerns cited include, if a child is taught to masturbate appropriately, will it lead to them spending large amounts of time masturbating, to the exclusion of other activities? However, there is little evidence of this in the research literature with regard to ASD or ID (Cambridge, Carnaby and McCarthy 2003).

It is important to note here that what is being advised is not to teach a child to masturbate *if they are not already doing so, or are doing so appropriately in their own bedroom.* However, where intervention may be necessary is if a child with ASD is masturbating either inappropriately or ineffectively and it is having a negative impact on their quality of life.

> *There is no point in doing sex education…if people with disabilities are prohibited from engaging in appropriate sexual behaviour. (Hingsburger 1995, p.67)*

Masturbation in one form or another is common and developmentally appropriate for both boys and girls. It is an adaptive rather than maladaptive behaviour which allows children to experience pleasure and self-sufficiency with their bodies. It is often used as a method of relaxation or to release sexual tension and is a good way to learn about one's body. It is also a sexual act that brings with it no danger of pregnancy or STIs, and for a person who lacks the ability to discuss or negotiate sexual intercourse, it may be the only safe sex option available. It is possible that with more experience with masturbation, a person is less likely to become 'carried away' during sexual contact, and to this extent it affects responsible sexual decision making. It is also normal for teenage

162

boys to masturbate several times a day (mentioned because it is therefore not abnormal for a teenage boy with ASD to want to touch himself regularly throughout the day). However, while it is developmentally appropriate, children with ASD, like all children, need to learn appropriate behaviours for the society in which they live in. They need to learn that while masturbation is normal, it is also a private behaviour.

For some children with ASD, learning to cope with their sexual feelings can be difficult. They may not fully understand why they feel aroused and, for males, getting an erection may be frightening and physically uncomfortable. Ejaculation may be upsetting for some boys who have struggled with toilet training in the past, and they can become confused or ashamed if their clothes get wet with semen. Girls with ASD should not be ignored or forgotten in discussing this topic. While they may display less overt behavioural issues in relation to masturbation, this does not mean that they do not have the same sexual needs as boys, or that they do not struggle with similar issues concerning lack of pride in their bodies, or social taboos about discussing their sexual feelings.

In residential communities the physical spaces that the children share are often communal, and privacy may be restricted. While a child may have a bedroom of their own, time alone can be discouraged and there may be no way for the child to lock their door or ask for privacy. For children with multiple or profound disabilities private spaces may be even scarcer, leading to self-stimulation happening during personal care tasks (i.e. the only opportunities the child may have to touch themselves while naked). This, of course, often raises concerns about staff protection.

It is important to be aware that in addition to typical sexual feelings, there are a range of reasons why a child may be masturbating or displaying masturbatory behaviours that need to be investigated and addressed if they are causing issues. Some of these may include:

- boredom, inactivity and under-stimulation

- seeking attention

- genital discomfort or medical problems, e.g. due to irritation, tight clothing, yeast infections, urinary tract infections or an allergic reaction to detergents or fabric softeners

- response to traumatic sexual experiences

- difficulties masturbating, effectively leading to frustration or aggression, e.g. due to poor technique, using inappropriate objects, feelings of guilt, the effects of medication or lack of privacy.

If behavioural concerns in relation to masturbation are ignored, a child will subsequently learn to masturbate whenever and wherever they wish, with significant implications for community inclusion and involvement. However, it is *crucial* that the response to masturbation is not one of elimination. These approaches do not respect children's human rights, and besides are often unsuccessful and result in new challenging behaviours. 'Time out' is also inappropriate as a reactive strategy, as well as being most likely ineffective, as all it does is provide the child with alone time with nothing else to do.

MASTURBATION SHOULD ONLY BE CONSIDERED A PROBLEM IF:

1. it is done in public

2. it is excessive (i.e. it is causing pain or interfering with the child's other daily living activities)

3. the child is finding it upsetting or it is causing other behavioural issues (e.g. due to the child being unable to masturbate to satisfaction or to cope with the intensity of the feelings).

Responses to masturbation should not be punitive. Children should never be given the message (either verbally or through body language or tone of voice) that masturbation is bad. We need to be supportive of children's sexuality, not create shame or secrecy. In *Just Say Know!* (1995), David Hingsburger discusses a client who, as a result of being punished for touching his penis, had for years been mutilating himself by only touching his penis with objects (which included knives) even when he needed to urinate.

> *This is the other abuse. The punishment of appropriate sexual expression is as abusive as any other form of assault. When an individual is taught that they, their feelings, their bodies, their hearts, their genitals are dirty, wrong, immoral, evil, profane or wicked and when this message is taught through pain and punishment, then they have been sexually assaulted. It is as if their soul is pulled in the bushes and raped. (Hingsburger 1995, p.8)*

On the contrary, it is essential to accept, and even promote, *appropriate* masturbation. Thus, the aim is not to stop the child masturbating, but to help them learn where, when and how it is done appropriately. The ultimate goal is for the child to be able to self-regulate their own sexual feelings and behaviours in a way that is socially acceptable, but still meets their own sexual needs.

INAPPROPRIATE MASTURBATION AND ID: THE REASEARCH

Some lessons from the research base regarding supporting clients with ID displaying inappropriate masturbation behaviours are as follows.

1. Teach appropriate socio-sexual skills.

2. Do not tolerate inappropriate touching.

3. Do not overprotect.

4. Do not contribute to clients being seen as perpetual minors.

5. Neither anticipate nor overreact to inappropriate masturbatory behaviours during puberty.

6. Rule out organic and medical causes, in addition to medical effects which may be interfering with sexual drive.

7. Meet clients' personal and interpersonal needs.

8. Teach positive attitudes towards one's body and sexuality.

9. Aim for self-regulation in managing inappropriate behaviours.

10. When working with individuals with severe ID, use positive reinforcement and supporting methods in addition to explicit SRE programmes as opposed to aversive stimulus control.

11. Avoid unconsented, intrusive interventions such as medication or surgery to suppress sex drive, e.g. the removal of testes for non-medical reasons.

12. Be aware of the legal circumstances around intimate interactions with clients.

13. Teach steps towards self-restraint to ensure ethical treatment and protection of clients.

(Tarnai 2006)

Masturbation: Teaching Activities and Recommendations

1. Remember that this is a sensitive and difficult topic to address for most parents. Be empathic.

2. If a child is displaying *problematic* masturbation behaviours it will be necessary to do an FBA to gain a clear picture of *why* the behaviour is occurring and to rule out medical causes. This is important, as responses to the behaviour should be somewhat different depending, for example, on whether the child is engaging in them for self-stimulation or to gain attention.

3. Children need to learn that if they want to masturbate, they must do it in their bedroom in private. They could be encouraged to masturbate in the shower (which eliminates clean-up), but the child would need to be able to differentiate between the shower at home and other showers, e.g. at the swimming pool. Regarding

allowing masturbation in school toilets, remember that this would be considered inappropriate for a typically developing child and, once again, the child would need to understand for their own safety that they cannot masturbate in other public toilets.

4. Make sure that the child has a private bedroom to go to. This means somewhere where they can close the door and people do not just walk in without asking permission. Revise 'public and private' rules with the child, and everyone around them.

5. If a child is masturbating in their private room and somebody walks in, the person needs to remain calm, apologize for interrupting and leave.

6. Children with multiple and profound needs experience particular difficulties accessing privacy and will need to be given time consistently in a comfortable, warm and safe place (without restrictive clothing or pads) to allow time for body exploration. This could be in their bed or in the shower. Communicate with the child both verbally or nonverbally that this 'private touching time' is allowed and respected.

7. Have a specific term for masturbation that everyone around the child uses (in addition to visual supports if necessary), e.g. 'private touching'.

8. Everyone involved with the child will need to show positive attitudes towards *appropriate* masturbation (i.e. at appropriate times and places).

9. Everyone involved with the child will need to be consistent in their approach to masturbation, including their nonverbal language. Consistency requires that all carers respond to masturbation in the same way 100 per cent of the time.

Supporting a Child Who is Masturbating 'Excessively'

1. Revise 'public and private' concepts.

2. Rule out medical causes.

3. Reflect on whether developmentally they *are* in fact masturbating 'excessively'.

4. Make sure that they are being provided with meaningful and engaging experiences throughout the day.

5. Keep unstructured times to a minimum.

6. Ensure that the child is wearing comfortable, loose-fitting clothes that 'breathe'.

7. Teach alternative self-soothing techniques.

8. Increase pleasant, non-sexual sensory input, such as music, massage, swimming and bubble baths.

9. As part of a full FBA, eliminate factors in the environment that may be acting as 'triggers'. For example, a child may only masturbate in public when they are

wearing clothes that are very loose (or tight), or are in the presence of a particular object.

10. If the child is touching their private parts a lot when in public, a simple strategy could be to dress them in complicated clothing that makes accessing private parts more difficult, e.g. pants that are zipped and belted.

11. Consider whether the child is masturbating 'excessively' due to inappropriate technique or difficulty masturbating to satisfaction.

Supporting a Child who is Masturbating in Public

1. Revise 'public and private' concepts.

2. Do not accept masturbation at inappropriate times or places. Remember that a learned behaviour takes time to unlearn.

3. Match pictures of a boy or a girl masturbating with pictures of appropriate private places to masturbate.

4. Have the child put crosses through pictures of public places where they should not masturbate.

5. Consider teaching a masturbation routine with a condom, which can then become a stimulus cue for masturbation (i.e. the person may only masturbate when a condom is available) (Dalrymple, Gray and Ruble 1991). This allows masturbation to be restricted to appropriate times and places, as well as preparing for safe sex. For females, a vibrator could serve the same function.

6. Create symbols for 'private touching', 'sexy feelings', 'bedroom' and 'wait' (symbols will of course vary depending on the child and individual circumstances). Be careful that the symbols used are not too abstract; the most important thing is that the child understands them. Try to think creatively, e.g. using black and white drawings of an erection paired with a photograph of the child's bedroom (Tissot 2009).

7. When a state of arousal is noted, show the child their symbols and bring them gently and calmly to their bedroom where they should be given privacy.

8. The child can be left in their bedroom with the symbols or other visual supports, such as instructional stories.

9. Once a connection is established – this may take several months – the child can be taught to request private time by using these symbols.

10. Next, introduce the concept of *waiting* for 'private time', inserting symbols into the child's visual schedules so that they learn that they can access this time after school or a community activity.

Supporting a Child who is Finding Masturbation Upsetting

If masturbating is upsetting the child, or causing other behavioural issues (e.g. if they are not able to masturbate to satisfaction):

1. Some children will need the steps of masturbation to be broken down (i.e. using a task analysis) and taught to them with visuals in the same way as other daily living skills, such as brushing teeth. These steps can be formatted as an instructional story or visual schedule. As with other skills, the child should be 'taught' these steps during calm times to support learning. Don't try to teach these concepts only when the child is visibly aroused.

2. There is some evidence in the research literature regarding adults with profound ID as to the benefits of physically directing the person's hand (i.e. 'hand over hand') as an intervention in order to teach masturbation (Kaeser and O'Neil 1987). However, this method brings with it significant issues related to consent as well as staff and child protection. Professionals contemplating using or recommending this method will need to be very careful to protect both themselves and the child by acting in accordance with the laws of their country or state, their organization's policies and their professional codes of practice. Parental consent and involvement will of course also be vital.

3. When teaching the steps to masturbation, use the least intrusive methods first. Following are some examples of teaching methods organized roughly from least to most intrusive:

   - directing the child to an appropriate place
   - black-and-white line drawings
   - colour illustrations
   - puppets (which may introduce a conceptual barrier)
   - demonstration on a model vagina or penis
   - vibrators or other sex aids
   - photographs
   - videos
   - physically directing the person's hand (i.e. hand over hand).

4. For women experiencing frustration with masturbation, in particular if they experience motor coordination difficulties, the use of vibrators may be useful.

5. *Hand Made Love: A Guide for Teaching about Male Masturbation* produced by David Hingsburger (1998) and *Finger Tips: A Guide for Teaching about Female Masturbation* produced by David Hingsburger and Sandra Haar (2003) are videos available through Diverse City Press and include a 'step by step photographic essay about masturbation and the joy of private time'. These may be beneficial for adolescents with significant related behavioural issues who are failing to learn from visual schedules or instructional stories, and when hand over hand teaching has been ruled out. Naturally, the content of these videos is explicit. As with the method of 'hand over hand', professionals contemplating the use of these with a child will

need to act in accordance with parental consent, local law, their organization's policies and professional codes of conduct.

6. If a child is using an inappropriate object to masturbate with, and is persistent in wanting to use an object, consider replacing it with a similar shaped sex aid. (There are many different types available online.)

7. Consider providing lubrication if friction is an issue.

CASE EXAMPLE

Luke is a gentle 13-year-old boy with ASD and a severe ID who attends a residential special school. He stays at his home every weekend with his parents and two younger sisters, aged three and five. Luke has no verbal language but understands and uses a limited number of signs and symbols (mostly for requesting food and TV programmes).

Luke had been touching his penis at inappropriate times for a number of years and everyone around him had thus far taken the approach of ignoring the behaviour, hoping that it would go away. However, recently this behaviour had escalated and Luke began touching his penis for significant portions of the day and across all environments. His rubbing became more vigorous day by day and it appeared that he might be hurting himself. He also began rubbing himself off furniture and became agitated and lashed out if attempts were made to move or distract him. This progressively led to Luke being excluded from more and more previously enjoyed community activities, and certain members of school staff began to refuse to work with him. Crisis stage was reached when during one weekend visit his mother walked in on Luke rubbing his three-year-old sister's foot into his genital area. Luke's parents made the decision that he could not stay at home again until these behaviours were eliminated. During his first weekend away from his family, Luke's behaviours, overall mood and general appearance worsened considerably.

Staff at Luke's special school undertook a thorough FBA in relation to Luke touching and rubbing his genital area. They learned that Luke displayed these behaviours by himself and also in a number of different contexts and in front of a number of different people. He was observed rubbing a number of different objects into his crotch area, including a teddybear. He was observed becoming visibly distressed and agitated after almost every incident of rubbing himself. It appeared that he was not ejaculating. Staff hypothesized the following:

1. Luke's self-stimulation was developmentally appropriate for his age.

2. He was unaware of how to masturbate to ejaculation.

3. This was causing him frustration and leading to an increase in self-stimulation behaviours.

4. He was unaware of the social rules with regard to masturbation.

5. By ignoring these behaviours in the past, the adults around Luke had unintentionally taught him that it was OK to masturbate in public.

6.   It was likely that Luke had used his sister's foot as an 'object' to gain self-stimulation which had nothing to do with sexual feelings directed towards her.

School staff started a programme in which every time Luke touched his penis, a staff member said 'private' in a calm voice, showed Luke a photograph of his bedroom and gently directed him there. Luke was then left in his bedroom with a visual schedule made up of line drawings of a masturbation sequence (pants down, hold penis, rub up and down, liquid comes out). This programme was followed for a number of weeks. Although it appeared that Luke was beginning to learn that when he wanted to touch himself he needed to go to his bedroom, when there he continued to rub himself off furniture and become increasingly agitated.

School staff hypothesized that the visual schedule provided to Luke might be conceptually too abstract and therefore not effective in teaching him the steps he needed to masturbate to satisfaction. School staff met with Luke's parents to discuss the further options of either showing Luke pictures or a video of a man masturbating, or his father coming in to teach him how to masturbate, either by modelling or using 'hand over hand'. His parents decided that they would prefer Luke to learn from his father.

In the next phase of intervention, every time Luke touched himself outside of his bedroom, he was shown his bedroom symbol and brought there, where his father (who had taken time off work to stay in the school temporarily) privately taught him the steps to masturbate. His father also had the idea of giving Luke magazines with pictures of pretty women in them which could be kept in a special place in his room. Within two days Luke learned to masturbate effectively and independently. Over the next couple of months he was taught to request 'private time' by pointing to a picture of his bedroom (which was kept on a keychain on his trousers), which led to a gradual reduction in masturbation behaviours in public. Although at first Luke requested 'private time' often, this gradually decreased. Within three months, Luke no longer masturbated in public. All community activities were reinstated and his relationships with school staff improved. As Luke was no longer using objects inappropriately, his parents felt that a gradual reintroduction to home could be trialled, and this was ultimately successful. At home Luke requests 'private time' using a photograph of his home bedroom, which is also kept on his keychain. His sisters have been taught that if Luke's door is closed, this means that it is his private time and they are not to enter. Luke has been taught the same about their bedrooms.

Private Touching

When I have sexy feelings…

I go to my bedroom.

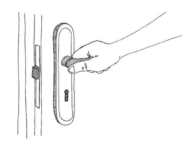

I close the door.

I pull down my clothes.

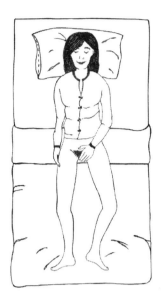

I do private touching. It feels nice.

I put my clothes back on.

I wash my hands.

Private Touching

When I have sexy feelings...

I go to my bedroom.

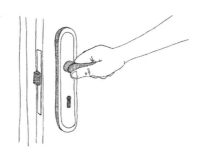

I close the door.

I take off my underwear and trousers.

I do private touching. It feels nice.

Liquid comes out of my penis.

I clean my penis with tissues.

I put the tissues in the bin.

I put on my underwear and trousers.

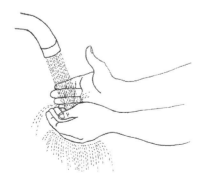

I wash my hands.

✓

Private Touching is a Private Behaviour

Sometimes I feel sexy feelings in public places.

These make me want to touch my private parts.

Lots of girls and boys feel this way.

Private touching is a private behaviour. Nobody should see me do it.

People get upset when I touch my private parts in front of them.

If I feel sexy feelings in public, I can:

1. tell myself that I can touch my private parts later when I am at home in my bedroom
2. fold my arms and count to ten
3. try to think about something else
4. squeeze my stress ball.

Masturbation

Masturbation means rubbing or touching your own private body parts. People do it because it feels good and exciting.

Boys usually rub and touch their penis. Girls usually rub and touch their clitoris.

Not everyone masturbates, but lots of people do. Masturbation is normal.

How often someone masturbates is different for every person. People sometimes masturbate more when they are teenagers and then less as they get older.

Even though lots of people do it, masturbation is a private topic.

Most people think about sexy things when they masturbate. Different people think about different things. Sometimes people look at sexy pictures. What you think about or look at when you masturbate is a private topic.

Masturbation should be done in private. This means closing the door and also any curtains. It is important to make sure that no one is watching or can hear you.

Some people like to masturbate with their hands. Other people like to do it in other ways, such as rubbing their private body parts off something safe and clean, or squeezing their legs together. Your private parts should not hurt after masturbation. If they do, you might be rubbing too hard or have an infection.

It is important to wash your hands after masturbation. Boys need to clean up any semen that might have got onto their clothes or other places.

Some religions and cultures have beliefs that people shouldn't masturbate. Some people were told stories about masturbation being bad for you, that are not true.

If you are not hurting or upsetting yourself or someone else, and you are doing it in private, then masturbation is OK.

When someone masturbates, they get warm, tingly and excited feelings. These feelings get stronger and stronger. Lots of times, this will lead to the person having an orgasm.

An orgasm is an intense burst of sexual feelings at the peak of sexual arousal. They feel different for different people and can feel different every time you have one. Orgasms should feel great.

For boys, an orgasm means that they ejaculate (sperm comes out of their penis).

For girls, an orgasm leads to the muscles around their vagina moving in what feels like waves. Their vagina can become wetter after an orgasm.

Most people masturbate alone, but sometimes people do it with a partner (their boyfriend, girlfriend, husband or wife). Masturbation with a partner is one way of being sexual while avoiding pregnancy or a STI. Both partners have to give permission and be happy for masturbation to happen together.

20

Teach Relationships

Teaching children about relationships involves concepts such as friendship, marriage, what makes a family and what it means to be a parent. It also includes teaching the unwritten rules and boundaries of different relationships, such as the difference between being someone's friend and their girlfriend, and why a helper is not a friend. Relationships can be particularly confusing for people on the autism spectrum due to the core deficits of ASD, as well as for environmental reasons such as experiencing high levels of supervision from school or other staff. These particular relationships may be based on an imbalance of power, which may in turn affect the child's views of relationships in the outside world.

Children need to learn how to express love and intimacy appropriately within their different relationships. They need to identify and avoid relationships based on exploitation and manipulation. They need to understand the law in relation to relationships. They need to be taught the intrinsic value of having positive relationships in their lives. They also need to be taught that relationships change and end, and why. Understanding these relationship concepts gives children a sense of who they are and the systems within which they operate. It also gives them information to help choose socially appropriate behaviours according to context, further helps to keep them safe and supports them in developing supportive, non-coercive, caring relationships, whether they be friendships or intimate.

When I was a child, time and time again, I failed to form any kind of long-term friendship. I didn't want lots of friends, but it would have been nice to have just one. (Lawson 2005, p.41)

College life really opened my eyes to many possibilities. People date, people have friends and best friends, people have classmates. Relationships can be as simple or complicated as people want. I have found myself free to pursue relationships I want to have with others... I may have gone about it in a slightly odd way, but I have found people that I can have genuine caring relationships with. I am a friend. I am also a colleague to many of my classmates. I am a student to my teachers... I am a tutor for some of my friends... I am NOT a girlfriend to anybody and that is fine with me. (Elizabeth Boresow, in Ashkenazy and Yergeau 2013, p.76)

I don't know about wanting to be like other people. I just wanted to have friends. (Jerry Newport, in Newport and Newport 2002, p.176)

Remember that just because a child can define various relationships, it does not mean that they know how to go about creating new ones or maintaining the relationships that they have. Therefore, in addition to learning about relationship *concepts,* children with ASD need to be taught *skills* (i.e. social skills) and to be supported in becoming active members of the communities in which they live, thereby increasing their relationship circles. Many authors with ASD have written about how, as children, they chose to spend large amounts of time on their own and found socializing difficult, but still felt lonely and craved friendship in a way that was meaningful for them. The value and importance of having true, meaningful relationships in our lives cannot be overstated, even for those children on the spectrum who may struggle in this area. In these cases, while it is important to respect the child's wishes and preferences, they should also be encouraged and given the opportunities and skills to develop relationships in ways which *they* find comfortable and beneficial.

Relationships: Some Learning Concepts

1. Family.
2. Friendship.
3. Relationships with helpers, carers, teachers, doctors and other professionals.
4. Marriage.
5. Romantic relationships.
6. Soulmates.
7. Homosexual relationships.
8. Sexual relationships.
9. Online relationships.
10. Work relationships.
11. Dating.
12. Parenting.
13. Change within relationships (e.g. through divorce or bereavement).
14. Characteristics of healthy and unhealthy relationships.

As discussed in the Introduction, there are many programmes available to teach children with ASD social skills. The following teaching recommendations and activities will therefore focus on teaching relationship *concepts*. Once again, the instructional stories in this chapter are detailed and designed to be adapted for individual use. For more information on sexual and intimate relationships see Chapter 21, 'Dating, Intimate Relationships and Sex'.

Relationships: Teaching Activities and Recommendations

1. Many of the materials developed for teaching the topics 'Growing and Changing', 'Safety Skills' and 'Public and Private' can be used here – e.g. photos and illustrations of different people within the child's family and social circles.

- Arrange the family photos in the shape of a family tree and talk about the relationships within it, e.g. 'Who is your granddad's daughter? Yes, your mum.'

- Put a picture of the child on the table. Pick another picture at random and discuss the child's relationship to that person.

- Pick two random pictures from the pile and discuss the individuals' relationship to each other, as well as the child, e.g. 'That person is Jack. He is your helper, but he is a stranger to Michael.'

2. Collect pictures of people unknown to the child, using a range of ages and ethnic groups. Give the people names and identities, abilities/disabilities and a sexual orientation. Start with one picture, say, a female, middle-aged, white, heterosexual teacher. Discuss the various relationships that she could have with the other people, e.g. 'This could be her son, boyfriend or doctor. Which one do you think he is?' 'Could she be friends with this person?' 'How do you think she feels about this baby?' 'Who do you think she sees the most?' 'Who is she closest to and why?'

3. Revise the child's 'Circles of Intimacy'.

4. Read books with the child about different family set-ups.

5. Teach the difference between 'knowing' a celebrity and 'knowing' a friend or acquaintance.

6. Have different children's parents come in and show pictures or videos of their own families and how they have changed over the years. They can also discuss topics such as 'What it is like to be a parent'.

7. Have children list the relationships in their lives, e.g.:

- Who is in my family?

- Who is my friend?

- Who am I closest to?

- Who have I been friends with in the past?

- What kind of relationships would I like to have in the future?

8. Make lists of things that families and friends often do together.

9. Have the child draw a friend of theirs and discuss what they like about them.

10. Use a staircase or ladder analogy to show the progression of relationships.

11. Talk to the child about their helpers/carers. Be sensitive, but open and honest about their role in the child's life.

12. Make lists with the child of appropriate ways to show you love someone in your family, a friend, or someone with whom you are in a romantic relationship.

13. Create instructional stories in the learning concept areas.

Families

Families are two or more people who love and care for each other.

There are different kinds of families.

You do not have to be related to your family.

Children can live with both parents, one parent, adoptive parents, grandparents, friends, foster parents or older brothers or sisters.

Some children have more than one family.

Families change all the time for different reasons.

Families might not all live in the same place.

Different people have different ideas of how families should be.

Families have fun together. Sometimes families fight or disagree.

Sometimes close friends are part of a family.

In lots of families, the brothers and sisters become good friends when they are adults, even if they weren't friends when they were children.

Different families have different meals, holidays, jokes and rules. They watch different TV programmes and movies and celebrate different holidays.

It is important to try to be kind to your family. It is important to try to talk to the people in your family and let them know how you feel.

Friendship

A friend is someone you like to spend time with,
who also likes to spend time with you.

Some people have lots of friends. Some people only
have one. Some people have no friends.

There are different types of friends. Friends can be older or younger,
male or female. They can have different religions and come from
different countries. They can have different colour skin.

Friends care about each other and are kind to each other. Friends
help you when you have a problem. Friends help you feel good about
yourself. If someone makes you feel bad, they are not your friend.

Friends share their feelings with each other.

Friends can sometimes fight or disagree. Friends aren't perfect.
Friends make mistakes. It is good for friends to apologize
to each other when they have made a mistake.

Online friends are not always real friends.

Sometimes friendships change. Sometimes friendships end. This is sad.
It happens to everybody. Making new friends can help with this.

It hurts when someone does not want to be your friend. This happens to
everyone. It does not mean that there is something wrong with you.

It is good to think about how a good friend should act towards you. It is
also good to think about how you can be a good friend to other people.

The main difference between being someone's friend and being their
boyfriend or girlfriend is that a boyfriend and girlfriend both feel romantic
(or sexual) feelings about each other, and might also want to spend more
time alone together than most friends (although lots of friends also like to
spend time alone together). In all other ways it is very similar to friendship.

Sometimes friendships turn into romantic relationships.
But lots of the time they don't.

Being a Parent

Many people want to have children.

Having children can be wonderful, but it can also be very difficult.

If you have a child, you need to put what the child
needs and wants before yourself.

Parents need to be able to give their children a home, love, education,
toys, money, food, hugs, trips to places such as the park, and clothes.
Having children takes a lot of time, money and patience.

A parent's job is to love, look after and teach their children. It is an adult job.

Babies wake up a lot during the night. They cry a lot. They need
their nappies changed lots of times during the day. They need
to be watched all of the time in case they hurt themselves. They
need to be fed a lot. All of this can be very tiring for parents.

It takes a lot of hard work to be a good parent.

Some people become parents by having babies. Some people
become parents by marrying or living with someone who already
has children. Some people adopt children or look after them
for short times because the child's parents need help.

Men and women can look after children equally.

People with disabilities can have and care for children.

Some people choose not to have children, for different
reasons. People can have happy lives without children.

21

Dating, Intimate Relationships and Sex

The most important aim of any SRE programme is to support people to develop meaningful relationships (which may or may not have a sexual element) in which they can experience love and intimacy and identify and avoid relationships based on manipulation and exploitation. This includes learning about attraction, flirting, choosing a suitable partner, healthy and unhealthy relationships, relationship skills, dating and intimate relationships. Any teachings on the 'mechanics' of sex will be just a minor element of this curriculum. Much more important will be teaching the 'hidden curriculum' with regard to intimate relationships, without which many individuals with ASD are left vulnerable to facing embarrassing and hurtful situations and being accused of inappropriate or even illegal behaviours, such as stalking (Stokes *et al.* 2007).

I thought I flunked at relationships because my fat body didn't cut the mustard…, my skin tone was unlovably blotchy, my polycystic ovarian syndrome-ravaged scalp unforgivably unfeminine and gross despite all the work I did to hide it. Of course the men I liked didn't want to be seen with me, I was hideous! What I didn't know, in all those years I went undiagnosed, was this: it was what was going on behind my scalp that was the real barrier between the men I pursued and me. Men…were just plain weirded out by me: my raggedy speech patterns, my staring spells, my almost costume-like wardrobe, my idiosyncratic interests and unladylike sense of humor, even the herky-jerky left-sided way I moved and walked. I could read all the books and magazines I wanted, have all the therapy I could scrounge around in the couch cushions to pay for, work on myself until the cows opened a McDonald's franchise, and there was no way, no way at all that these nice, 'normal' men I was drawn to for their seeming niceness and 'normalcy' would ever even have considered giving me anything more than a fast roll in the hay (if that). (Andee Joyce, in Ashkenazy and Yergeau 2013, p.3)

I went out with a girl from my math class and I thought we had a good time, so I asked her out about 13 or 14 times. I asked her out so many times that she quit the math class to get

185

away from me… I felt badly that apparently she dropped out of class to avoid me. It was pretty humiliating to feel I'd done that to somebody. (Jerry Newport, in Newport and Newport 2002, p.195)

Probably because of our perseverating nature, we find a bond, we grow to it like ivy to a tree. It isn't an evil obsessive perseveration. It's more like a cherished luxury, a solid sense of honest-to-goodness wonder, to know there is someone out there with whom we can share our true selves in ways that are accepted and, if we are lucky, cherished. Too often we are told we are too challenging or difficult to be around. Perhaps this is what makes a good relationship into so much more than it should ever be?… Clearly, personal relationships are the most difficult to let go of, but I don't see any break in what I am attached to as a good thing. I don't like change. Find me an Aspie who does! (Holliday Willey 2012, p.52)

I have been married for more than half of my life. My wife has been such an integral part of who I am and how I navigate life that I can't really imagine a world without her. I hear that people on the spectrum don't know how to have or maintain relationships with others. We are told regularly that we lack empathy, theory of mind, and the ability or desire to maintain social relationships. For me this just doesn't hold true, and it certainly has not been my experience. (Michael Higginbotham, in Ashkenazy and Yergeau 2013, p.99)

If teenagers are to develop the skills needed to enter meaningful, adult relationships, they will need practice and support to get there, and part of this will be learning to date. Adolescents with ASD in particular need as many different socialization opportunities as possible, and shielding will not support them either to learn appropriate behaviours or to develop realistic views of dating or relationships. Although this is a frightening area for parents, they could be pleasantly surprised to learn that what dating means for their child is (for example) to go in a group for a hamburger and a milkshake.

In relation to *settings* for dates, for older adolescents, places normally associated with meeting people (e.g. bars or parties) are often unsuitable due to noise, unpredictability and crowding. These settings also rely heavily on unstructured, nonverbal communication. Many adults with ASD have reported that activity-based dating works best for them. Many also report that dating through the internet is a viable alternative (in particular dating through websites specifically for individuals with ASD), with benefits that include talking without having to deal with stressful face-to-face interactions, and knowing from the start that the person has no problem dating someone with ASD. While online dating is, of course, not suitable for children, it *is* common nowadays for them to meet friends and 'romantic' partners through social networking sites. This was further discussed in Chapter 16, 'SRE in a Modern Age'.

Dating and intimate relationships will, of course, be extremely challenging for those individuals with ASD and additional significant and profound learning needs. Even for more able children, parents and professionals may worry that encouraging dating or other related behaviours will lead to frustration, hurt and disappointment, in particular for those who may not possess even one friend due to repeated failures at socialization with peers. As in all areas of their SRE programme, the child's parents and professional team (while taking the rights and wishes of the child into consideration) will need to decide which concepts are age and developmentally appropriate, and work from there.

DATING

If the adolescent's peers are dating, it is developmentally appropriate for them to do so also, and if their family is willing to support it, the following information may be considered with regard to dating 'readiness' and what can and should be taught:

- If they are *unaware*, no active intervention is needed at this time but attention should be paid to emerging signs of interest.

- If they are *uninterested*, work on perspective taking, e.g. would others be interested in a relationship? Without pressure, try to find out why they are not interested in order to better understand their thoughts and feelings on the subject.

- If they are *ambivalent*, work on dating and relationship skills as well as developing self-insight, self-esteem and confidence. Combine group and individual work.

- If they are *interested*, actively teach dating and relationship skills. Group and individual work is recommended.

- If they are *desperate* (i.e. have a heightened awareness of others' dating, are obsessed, angry and jealous, or coping with rejection badly) it is likely that they lack insight into their own needs and the kind of person they want to date. Individual work is essential, as personal safety may be at risk and mental health concerns could arise. Intensive work on social understanding and skills building is needed.

(Adapted from Nichols *et al.* 2009)

Dating, Intimate Relationships and Sex: Some Learning Concepts

1. Attraction.
2. Flirting.
3. Partner choice.
4. Dating readiness.
5. Dating rules.
6. Date planning.
7. Dating skills.
8. Dating safety.
9. Online dating.
10. Phone and email skills.
11. Relationship skills, e.g. listening, sharing and compromising.

12. Categories of relationships, e.g. strangers, casual dating, serious dating (but not having sex), dating (having sex) and deep intimacy – boyfriend/girlfriend, husband/wife.

13. Relationship stages.

14. Sexual orientation.

15. Homosexual relationships.

16. The characteristics of healthy and unhealthy relationships.

17. Dealing with rejection and coping with unrequited romantic or sexual feelings.

18. Ending relationships.

19. Disclosure about diagnosis within relationships.

20. Virginity.

21. Consent.

22. Readiness for a sexual relationship.

23. Stages of physical intimacy, e.g. holding hands, kissing, hugging and massage.

24. Sexual intercourse, e.g. the 'mechanics' of sexual intercourse, the phases of sexual response, oral sex, foreplay and homosexual sex.

25. The unrealistic and unrepresentative portrayals of sex and relationships in the media.

26. Pornography.

27. Contraception.

28. Stalking, sexual intimidation, abuse and harassment.

29. Sexual dysfunction.

30. Sex and religion.

31. Sex and the law.

Dating, Intimate Relationships and Sex: Teaching Activities and Recommendations

Attraction and Flirting

1. Show video clips of people flirting. Analyse their behaviour. Discuss whether they were successful or not and why.

2. Use video self-modelling and role play to teach flirting behaviours. Also consider having the adolescent act out bad flirting behaviours (e.g. talking too much about one thing), before analysing the reaction of other people to these behaviours.

3. Use clips from TV song contests such as *American Idol* in which facial expressions are exaggerated to show people's like or dislike for contestants. Often, the judges'

reactions are exaggerated and go unnoticed or misinterpreted by the singer, which can also provide good discussion points (Davies and Dubie 2012).

4. Discuss the concept of sexy. What is sexy? Who is sexy? Does the adolescent know someone who they think is sexy? What is it about the person that makes them appear sexy? Does everyone think that this person is sexy?

5. Draw scenarios using thought bubbles of different 'couples' who like each other (or not). For example, draw out a scenario of a male sitting on a bench beside a female. In the male's thought bubble, write something like 'I like this girl so I sit next to her every day, hoping she will talk to me.' In the female's thought bubble, write something like 'There is this boy in school who sits too close to me. It makes me uncomfortable.' Use these scenarios to discuss various flirting and attraction concepts.

6. Organize role plays of different characters meeting in a shop, such as strangers, lovers and friends. Work on eye contact, appropriate body distance and how much touch would typically occur. Have the adolescent act these details out, and also watch other people 'blind' to the roles they are acting out. Discuss which type of relationship the people are in, and why.

7. Teach the signs that someone likes you (although teach that this may not mean that they are attracted to you), e.g. smiling, eye contact, laughing at your jokes, sitting close to you and asking questions about yourself.

8. Teach the signs that someone is not interested in you, e.g. not laughing when you tell a joke, looking around the room at other people, yawning, looking at their watch and making excuses to leave you. Teach how to deal with these occasions in the moment.

Dating

The adolescent's parents should have clear definitions for what dating means and what is accepted in their home. If dating rules are different for siblings, this will need to be explained clearly and sensitively to the child. Help parents create personalized dating rules according to age and circumstance. Siblings or peers of the child could be asked for advice as to what is current dating practice in the child's world.

1. Dating rules could include 'Only at the weekends', 'Only if you are driven to and from the date', 'No sexting' and 'Only if it is in a group or if there is a chaperone'. Dating opportunities could be organized by parents in group settings, such as after school programmes or a church event.

2. Wendy Lawson (2005) advises that sometimes an individual with ASD might need to listen to the advice of family and friends in relation to whether they are ready to date. She also advises asking the individual how they will know that the time is right to pursue a relationship, e.g. what signs they should be looking out for. She recommends creating a chart with this information so that the person can see themselves developing towards the goal of being ready for relationships.

3. Davies and Dubie (2012) have created a worksheet which includes sentences designed to help the individual with ASD analyse for themselves whether they are ready for adult relationships and dating. The sentences, which are categorized into topics such as 'Being available', 'Tolerance' and 'Openness', create excellent discussion points and include:

   - I am willing to change my plans for a friend.

   - I accept that my friend is not like me.

   - I am able to look at conflict from someone else's point of view.

   - There is something I like about my friend other than the fact that they like me.

   - I am willing to be my true self.

   - I am willing to share my feelings.

   This format could be adapted in a number of ways for individual children.

4. Practising dating skills means practising social skills, such as doing nice things for other people, making small talk and being a good listener. Support learning these skills.

5. Encourage the adolescent to have hobbies and join groups which interest them, so that they are more likely to meet people with similar interests.

6. Teach about the importance of being friends first and dating a few times before deciding on being in a relationship, and why this is important.

7. Watch video clips of people being asked on dates. Analyse what was said and how successful or unsuccessful it was. Also analyse the person's reactions to being asked.

8. Teach that they need to wait to see if the other person feels the same way before letting them know that they are attracted to them or want to date them.

9. Teach how to react if rejected when asking someone on a date or to be in a relationship – e.g. not getting angry, arguing or trying to persuade the person, and going to a private place if you want to cry. Have prepared social scripts ready. Role-play potential scenarios.

10. Teach what to expect on a first date – e.g. that they are often awkward.

11. Create lists of appropriate topics for first and then subsequent dates. Role-play and practise these.

12. Teach how to deal with questions on a date (typically difficult for people on the ASD spectrum).

13. Work on choosing settings for dates. Make lists of personalized good and bad places and why they fit that category. Encourage picking a location that is familiar to them, so that they don't need to worry about other tasks (such as ordering food

or knowing where to sit), in order to minimize sensory sensitivities. Also encourage them to do 'practice run' dates in this location with a trusted person.

14. Teach appropriate and polite ways to end a date, depending on whether they want to see the person again, are not sure, or do not want to see them again.

15. Make date preparation lists, including things such as hygiene and grooming, dressing, money, phone and who to call in an emergency (Nichols *et al.* 2009).

16. Prepare the adolescent for the feelings they may experience on a date and how to handle them, such as feeling over-anxious at the start and finding it hard to speak as a result. Preparation with role play, video modelling and social scripts can help with this.

17. Have the adolescent survey different people about what dating means to them.

18. Support them in analysing a date after it has occurred, making a list of positives, negatives and things that they would do differently next time (Davies and Dubie 2012).

19. Consider supporting the child to organize a 'peer helper' during social gatherings who can be on 'standby' in a non-intrusive way to help figure out jokes and comments and to check whether they are OK (Holliday Willey 2012).

Choosing a Partner, Healthy Relationships and Relationship Skills

Work consistently on social skills across settings and in real-life situations; revise 'Relationship Skills', 'Safety Skills' and 'Sense of Self'. Work with the adolescent on thinking critically about what it means to be a good friend and the qualities they want from a friend or romantic partner, possibly ranking these in terms of importance. However, be careful to emphasize the importance of being somewhat flexible – for example, not insisting that a romantic partner *has* to like the same kind of music as they do. Teach that the majority of qualities that are important in a friend will be even more important in a romantic partner.

1. Discuss how some of the best relationships are those in which the people have similar values. Discuss what this means. Encourage valuing internal qualities whilst remembering that it is very typical for teenagers to have crushes on people for looks alone.

2. Work sensitively around unrealistic expectations with regards to partners, and teach that if someone does not want to be a friend on a social networking site (but they are active online), it is unlikely that they are interested in the adolescent as a friend or romantic partner.

3. Have the adolescent interview people about what it means to be in a long-term relationship – how they met, how they knew they wanted to marry, what they love about their partner and what the hard parts are of being in a relationship.

4. Write on cue cards some positive and negative characteristics of relationships (e.g. 'Give each other freedom', 'Have other friends', 'Trust each other', 'Tell secrets', 'Feel safe', 'Feel scared to leave', 'Try to change each other', 'Tell everyone personal things about their partner', 'Have fights which last for days'). These can be sorted into 'Caring Relationship' and 'Uncaring Relationship' boxes.

5. Draw timelines for relationships, including average lengths of time for each stage (while noting that not all relationships will be the same). Start with a good friendship. How long until they knew that they were friends? How long before they trusted each other? How long before they slept over in each other's houses?

6. Watch movies based on relationships. Pause at different stages, and assign stages of relationships (strangers, friends, lovers, ex-partners).

7. Highlight how relationships in movies, and soap operas in particular, are unrealistic and over-dramatized.

8. Teach the importance of communication and sharing your feelings and wishes within relationships.

9. Encourage the adolescent to seek advice from a trusted friend or family member with regard to a potential partner, if they feel unsure about them or their motives.

10. Teach about the realities of feelings in long-term relationships and how they can change, flow and become less intense.

11. Teach skills in 'checking in' with people, such as learning to say 'Sometimes I have problems knowing what other people are thinking. Did you have fun last night?' or 'Is it OK if I hold your hand?'

12. Work on the adolescent's own views about when or whether to tell a romantic partner about their ASD diagnosis. Wendy Lawson (2005) advises asking the following questions of yourself: How is this relationship doing? Have we spent time together getting to know each other? Do we both want to continue in the relationship? If the answers to these questions are 'yes', and they are already happy to share information about their family, background and learning style, then it may be a good time to talk about their diagnosis. Ms Lawson recommends giving the person clear, simple information, and possibly recommending a specific book on the subject.

13. Teach the signs that somebody does not want to be in a relationship any more (not returning calls, not calling, texting or emailing, refusing to meet several times in a row and making excuses not to meet). Teach how to deal with rejection.

Intimate Relationships and Sex

Revise 'Emotional Understanding and Regulation', 'Sexual Health' and 'Conception, Pregnancy and Birth'; prepare developmentally appropriate instructional stories about sexual intercourse.

DECISION MAKING AROUND SEXUAL RELATIONSHIPS

1. Teach, also, metacognition around these decisions, i.e. to recognize how they come to their decisions. Teach them to ask themselves questions such as:

    - What age am I?

    - What age is the person?

    - Do I like this person?

    - Do I trust this person?

    - Is this person pressurizing me into having sex?

    - Do I have somewhere private to have sex?

    - Do I feel happy about having sex with them?

    - Do I have contraception?

    - Is my partner happy to use contraception?

    - Does this person want to have sex with me?

    - Will this person still like me if I decide not to have sex with them?

    - Can I talk to this person about worries I might have?

    - Am I sure this person wants to have sex with me?

    These could be put into worksheet format.

2. Teach that it is OK to say 'no' and it is OK to change your mind.

3. Teach that sometimes people don't feel ready for sex but that after knowing the person better and trust has developed they may change their mind.

4. Teach that they need to do what feels right for them.

5. Teach how and why different religions hold different values around sex before marriage and homosexuality. Teach how some people still continue to follow a particular religion but make a choice that some parts are not relevant to them. Teach that partners may hold different views about sexuality and sexual behaviours because of their religion. Teach ways that they could go about problem solving these issues with a partner.

6. Create scenarios with different couples meeting and deciding whether to have sex or not, e.g. a couple meet in the park for the first time and the man asks the woman to have sex. Go through each scenario with the child, analysing how to go about deciding whether sex is a good idea or not.

7. Teach the law with regard to sex.

8. Teach why children are not emotionally or physically ready for sex.

9. Teach the slang words for sex.

BEING SEXUAL DOES NOT ALWAYS MEAN HAVING SEX

1. Teach some typical occurrences within intimate relationships – whilst emphasizing that all relationships are different – e.g. 'Go on a few dates', 'Introduce to family and friends' and 'Stay over at each other's houses'.

2. Make cards with different stages of an intimate relationship or behaviours within relationships written on them. These cards could be either backed with Velcro or placed sequentially on a shopping line with clothes pegs (i.e. methods which allow them to be moved around easily). Examples could include 'Holding hands', 'Cuddling without clothes', 'Giving someone your home address', 'Breaking wind in front of someone', 'Meeting their friends', 'Having children' and 'Going on a date'. Discuss topics such as: Do all things happen in every relationship? Would your mother or your best friend put these in the same sequence? How would someone's religion affect the sequencing? This same technique is good to use to teach about friendships and non-sexual relationships also (omitting the behaviours related to sex).

3. Explain that people in relationships have lots of different ways of being intimate and sharing sexual pleasure, e.g. hugging, kissing, massage, having a bath and listening to music together.

4. Teach social scripts that can be used in situations which involve choices about sexual activity, e.g.:

   - I do not feel ready yet.
   - Why do you want to have sex with me?
   - I am worried about getting pregnant (or an STI).
   - No, I do not want to have sex.
   - No, I do not want to have sex right now. Maybe when I am ready. I do not know when I will be ready.
   - I do not know what I want to do.
   - I have gone as far as I want to go with you.
   - I only want to touch with our clothes on.
   - I want to go slow.
   - Are you sure you are ready for this?
   - Do you really want to have sex?
   - We have been going out for a long time – I would love to have sex. What do you think?

   Role play if appropriate.

5. Teach that both men and women can give and receive sexual pleasure.

Stages of an Intimate Relationship

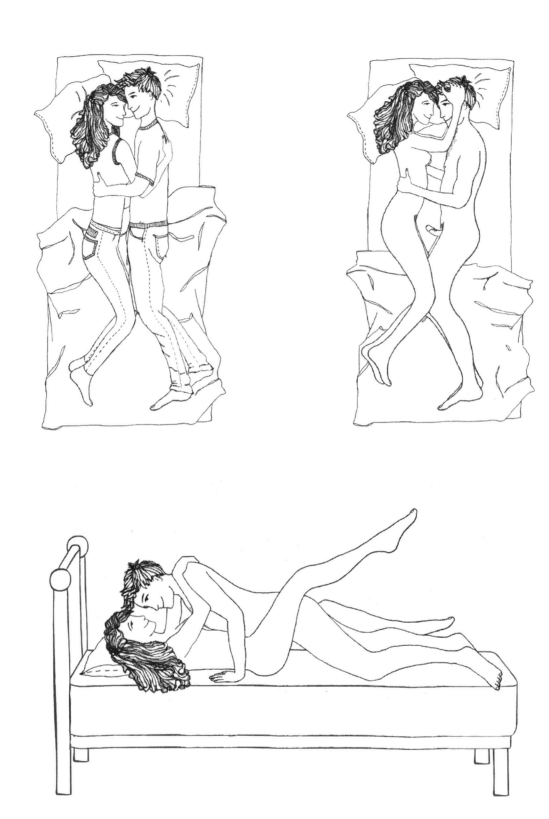

22

Teach a Sense of Self

Adolescence can be a confusing and frightening time of transition, a time when children typically start to think about and search for their own identity. It is also a time when children become acutely aware of any disability they may have and its impact on their life. They may start to question why they have their disability and why they don't attend the same school or receive the same privileges as their siblings. Life cycle events such as the first disco, learning to drive and leaving home can all be challenging. One of the developmental tasks of adolescence is making your own decisions and plans for the future. However, the reality for many children with ASD is that they may never become as independent as they would wish, leading to these developmental tasks being met only partially, or not at all.

Some parents believe that what is best for their child is to be surrounded by typically developing children and adults. However, this may have the effect of giving the child negative messages about disability, and therefore themselves, and does not support healthy identity development. It may also lead to a teenager or adult avoiding other people with 'special needs' and finding it difficult to find romantic partners as a result.

Today, high functioning adults with ASD are the first generation to receive their diagnoses, grow up with this identity and tell the rest of the world about what it means to be autistic. They also have a subculture, jargon and identity of their own. Many of these adults report unhappy and confusing childhoods, but also the benefits that came from learning about their diagnosis and therefore themselves, including more friendships, better relationships and increased self-acceptance. Many also reject the notion of ASD as a disability and call for societal changes in the way they are viewed and treated.

There are many ways in which it is difficult or impossible for me to meet standard definitions of normalcy. Some of these relate to impairments or deficits in functions that come easily to most people. Some relate to skills or strengths in functions that are difficult for most people. Some relate to ways of perceiving and responding that are neither better nor worse, but are qualitatively different from those of most people. Among my greatest strengths are my inner stability and my strong sense of who I am and what is important to me. Some of my greatest deficits involve my inability to learn and internalize social norms that appear meaningless to

197

me. There has been ample demonstration that I can function more effectively by starting from a position of strength rather than one of weakness: that is, by presenting myself as myself rather than trying to become something else. Given this foundation, is it possible for me to find – or create – a place in society that allows me to make maximum use of my strengths and to minimize the limitations of the things I can't do?... And the answer to that will be a lifelong adventure, for all of us. (Sinclair 1992)

Being different isn't bad, it's just different. Yes, there are some disadvantages to being autistic and gay. We will find it difficult to locate other individuals who will accept us for ourselves. Most of my friends tried to change me. Even my family tried to make both my ASD and my homosexuality go away. The best thing I did was stop believing that I was bad and recognize that other people are uncomfortable around us because they don't understand us. I keep company as much as possible with others who accept and encourage me to be myself... Bit by bit, as others come to know us they too might find that we are human beings with legitimate needs. In the meantime we need to look after ourselves and foster a belief system that supports who we are and does not attack us. (Lawson 2005, pp.85–86)

You've got to accept the fact that in certain ways you're always going to be fundamentally different than a lot of other people. Just accept it. Stop fighting it. It's just that way. But on the other hand, you have to keep yourself open to finding ways to negotiate through this world and arrive at a compromise between the way you'd like to be and the way that the workplace or your friends or whatever relationship you want, requires of you... You don't have to be normal. You have to be the best available version of you. (Jerry Newport, in Newport and Newport 2002, pp.207–208)

One of the most important elements of any SRE programme is to support the development of a positive, healthy and realistic sense of self, self-esteem and self-worth. This means understanding your own personal strengths and needs, your diagnosis and what it means to you, and includes teaching skills in self-advocacy, self-determination and disclosure about diagnosis. Children with ASD need to be taught that they matter and that they can have some kind of control over their lives. Understanding and respecting yourself is the basis of future successful relationships.

SELF-DETERMINATION

Often, the people who care for children with disabilities become so used to making decisions for them that they begin to do so automatically, further inhibiting children's ability to make decisions for themselves. Self-determination instead involves learning to problem solve and make their own decisions and life goals, thereby promoting independence and the ability to evaluate and manage themselves. Teaching self-determination skills involves giving children meaningful choices throughout the day. It also involves allowing them a wide range of experiences from which to learn.

SELF-ADVOCACY

Advocacy is realizing what a person needs in order to maximize his or her functioning in life and knowing how to arrange the environment or obtain the necessary accommodations to do so. Or put another way, it is being literal about a person's needs. (Shore 2003, p.173)

The road to advocacy includes discussions of disclosure, special interests, learning styles, learning accommodations, and even relationships. (Shore 2003, p.73)

If we want to be involved with the building of a better future for our children and for the human race in general, then we need to be involved with disclosure. (Lawson 2005, p.144)

Self advocacy may be the single most important change to service provision in years. (Hingsburger 2010, p.29)

The self-advocacy movement is one in which people with disabilities meet to discuss what is important in their lives and to learn how to speak up for themselves about their needs, rights and experiences. The motto of the Autism Self Advocacy Network (a non-profit organization run by and for people with ASD) is 'Nothing About Us Without Us', meaning that no decisions should be made or discussions held about an individual or group with ASD without their direct involvement. They too have a perspective on their own lives and know what is best for themselves. Self-advocacy can exist at an individual or international level to benefit people with ASD around the world.

Advocating for oneself can be particularly challenging for someone on the autism spectrum as they may be unaware of what they need or what changes need to be made to their environment for them to function optimally. Therefore, they need to be taught the *tools* of self-advocacy and taught them early. Learning these skills will be a lifelong process, should start from when the child first learns that they have a diagnosis, and should be included as part of every child's curriculum.

CASE EXAMPLE

Zane is a bright 18-year-old young man with a diagnosis of AS. Having received excellent grades in all of his exams, Zane was accepted to a top college to study engineering. Previously, Zane attended a special class within a mainstream school which has an excellent reputation and many years of experience educating children with ASD. Zane had the same SNA for many years, providing him with consistent support. Every day he sat at the same desk in the same room. His books and timetables were all colour coded for him. He received social skills classes. His peers understood his AS, watched out for him and talked to him about his special interests when they met him in the corridor. Zane had some idea that he had a thing called Asperger's and this meant that he was extremely intelligent and that he didn't care as much as other people about things such as football. Overall, Zane was happy, protected and safe in his school environment.

However, when Zane began college, he found himself lost in a scary, confusing and busy world. He didn't understand his timetables and so missed many of his classes.

His lecturers spoke quickly and left the lecture hall immediately after class. He couldn't find the lunch hall and was afraid to ask anyone for directions. He tried to talk to his classmates about computer programming (a special interest) but they began to avoid him and laugh when he walked by. He desperately wanted a girlfriend but had no idea how to go about this. His assignments were late and piling up because he was unused to writing by hand, and was finding it impossible to study in his bedroom because of the strip lighting flickering in from the hallway. Lonely, and finding it all too much to deal with, Zane took a bus home and told his mother that college wasn't for him.

Thankfully, Zane's mother was able to link him in with a college counsellor who was familiar with AS. There, Zane learned that if he understands and accepts his own needs and communicates these effectively to others, there are many strategies and supports available to him. Together, they made a list of the things that *Zane* needed to do to improve his college experience:

1. He needed to learn how to access Disability Services in college and other future environments.

2. He needed to find out the ways in which Disability Services could support him.

3. He needed to learn where to access information about his personal rights as a student and as an individual with ASD.

4. He needed to learn more about his diagnosis and how it was affecting his life.

5. He needed to learn how to disclose his diagnosis to appropriate people, so that he receives the support that he needs and deserves.

6. He needed to tell his lecturers about his diagnosis and request that he hand in assignments in a different format from the one requested (e.g. on PowerPoint and by email).

7. He needed to learn how to ask for extensions on assignments if required.

8. He needed to be able to locate and talk to the people who run his dormitory, and request that because of his AS and associated sensory sensitivities, he would need something done about the strip lighting, or else to move rooms.

9. Zane needed to explore college clubs in areas that he was interested in, e.g. the chess club.

10. He needed to link with other students with AS.

11. He needed to access some support in learning to approach and meet girls.

12. He needed to format his timetable in a way that he understood.

13. He needed to find or make a visual map of the college, which he could then keep in his wallet.

14. He needed to find ways to manage his anxiety, such as going to yoga classes or learning to meditate.

In the protected environment of his school, among the many things that Zane learned were valuable lessons in self-worth that he will carry with him for a lifetime. However, what he was not taught was a true understanding of his own personal strengths and needs, how to manage his own learning, how to advocate for himself, or how to develop new relationships (both friendships and intimate relationships) in an environment in which nobody knew him. Upon leaving school, children with ASD should be confident enough to communicate their needs to the people who matter, and use these skills to access the supports and strategies that they need to overcome them.

A Sense of Self: Teaching Activities and Recommendations

Work collaboratively with parents to promote independence. During the teenage years, parents need to stay supportive, teach responsibility for actions, give choices and allow their children to become separate while still connected to their family. Parents may also need reminding that pushing boundaries and limits is typical of this age group and may have little to do with their child's disability.

Teach Self-esteem

1. Provide achievable goals such as planning their own social lives, looking after a pet or volunteering in the community. Create experiences in which the child can experience success and constantly push slightly beyond these boundaries.

2. Emphasize the child's strengths and allow them to develop in those areas.

3. Be specific with praise and constructive criticism.

4. Encourage the child to share their achievements regularly.

5. Make posters with the child's achievements as a theme.

6. Encourage everyone around the child to treat them with respect, act pleased to see them, give them compliments and *tell them* they are happy to see them, that they like having them in their lives.

Teach Independence and Responsibility

1. Do not do anything for the child that they can do independently. There may need to be a review of the child's adaptive skills to assess the skills they are using independently in different environments.

2. Teach *why* it is important to be as independent as possible in life.

3. Develop worksheets that allow the child to analyse for themselves how independent they are and where they need to move towards, e.g.:

   - Do they make their own snacks?
   - Do they put their dirty clothes in the wash basket?
   - Do they do their homework without prompting by their mother?
   - Do they make sure that they get enough sleep or exercise?

4. Allow the child to make their own decisions and mistakes, which involves knowing their own personal likes and dislikes, taking responsibility for their decisions, making

realistic choices, asking for help and being able to compromise and negotiate. Teach these decision making skills.

5.   Talk to the child about their goals for the future. What are they? How do they plan on achieving them?

Teach Self-awareness

1.   Support the child in learning about themselves:
     - What do others like about me?
     - What am I good at?
     - What kind of a person am I?
     - Do I admire anyone/want to be like anyone?
     - What is it about them that I like?
     - What are the things I don't like about myself?

2.   Develop an 'All About Me' book or folder with the child. First, include pictures of things the child is good at, their family and friends, things they like and don't like, things they have done, achieved, accomplished, visited, what kind of a person they are (including personality traits). Then gradually add in things that the child finds challenging – perhaps football, socializing or eye contact. It is important that the child learns a positive but realistic sense of themselves. Remember that strengths should outweigh and 'sandwich' any needs.

3.   Start teaching early about individual differences and acceptance of difference in general.

4.   Teach about stereotypes and why they are bad.

Teach Self-advocacy

1.   Encourage everyone around the child to model good self-esteem.

2.   Provide positive role models who have a disability or difference.

3.   In conjunction with parents, support the child in learning about their diagnosis and what it means to them, providing positive, developmentally appropriate information.

4.   Make links with the self-advocacy movement.

5.   Provide the child with (vetted) reading material written by adults and teenagers with ASD.

6.   Teach the child how, why, when and with whom they may wish to disclose their diagnosis.

7.   Educate the child (and the people around them) about the positive, attractive qualities that many people with ASD possess, including being honest, kind, reliable and attentive and having clear moral beliefs and a strong sense of social justice.

8. Children should be involved in developing and leading their IEP process. Start small. The child could begin by reading a part of the plan, explaining their disability or sharing their strengths. However, the ultimate goal is a child-led IEP meeting. Information on teaching students to manage their own IEPs can be found on the National Information Centre for Children and Youth with Disabilities (NICHCY) website, www.nichcy.org.

Part IV
Responding

23

Responding to 'Inappropriate' Behaviours in the Area of Sexuality and Relationships

This chapter focuses on how best to *respond* to 'inappropriate' behaviours in the area of sexuality and relationships *if* they are already occurring. Responding to these behaviours will include selecting *reactive strategies* (i.e. what to do when a behaviour is actually occurring) as well as *intervention strategies* (i.e. strategies specific to the child and the behaviour). Following the **UPSR** Model, this **R**esponding stage is the last in a sequence of stages including **U**nderstanding (the child and their behaviour), **P**reventing (issues) and **S**upporting (sexuality and intimate relationships). Reactive behaviour management strategies in particular should never be used in isolation, but as part of a comprehensive plan including environmental changes, skills teaching and other preventative measures.

> *Behaviour programming at its best teaches people with disabilities new skills with which to control their own lives. Behaviour programming at its worst takes control of someone else's life. (Hingsburger 1996, p.10)*

In the past, for individuals with significant learning needs, the response to challenging behaviours in the area of sexuality was often institutionalization and treatment that focused on eliminating inappropriate behaviours by means of intrusive methods such as overcorrection and isolation. Today, best practice intervention approaches take a more holistic approach such as the Positive Behaviour Support model, where behaviours are not eliminated but instead replaced with appropriate behaviours that serve the same function. A staged approach is also now emphasized, with the least intrusive intervention methods always used first. While the ultimate aim of any behaviour management plan should be teaching the child insight and self-management skills, these can be difficult areas to teach even bright children with ASD, and often reward-based behavioural methods also need to be included in individualized planning.

One of the most important things that can be done in relation to behaviour management is to have a *written plan* in place for reacting and intervening, that is agreed by and followed through by all parties. It is also important to review, monitor and adapt the plan within agreed timeframes.

Reactive Strategies

As it is the only thing that we know we can truly change, the first and most important reactive strategy to plan is how *we* respond to the child. Sometimes we do not realize that the way we behave after a behaviour actually increases the likelihood of the behaviour happening again in the future. This is called 'accidental reinforcement' and can lead to problem behaviours being maintained. When dealing with challenging behaviours, feelings may arise of anger or weariness, affecting responses to the behaviour and leading to difficulties in responding positively. Behaviours can also be taken personally. It is important for adults around the child to remain calm, quiet and in control during challenging behaviours, using low arousal techniques. However, this is often difficult, and outside help in the form of supervision or counselling can be valuable.

Any reactive strategy should respond to the misbehaviour and not the child and should focus on what the child *can or should* do in a situation, *not* on what they should *stop* doing, that is, 'Focus on the dos not the don'ts'.

There are a number of different reactive strategies to choose from, and deciding on the most appropriate of these will depend on your understanding of the child and their behaviour following your in-depth FBA. It is possible that following environmental changes (say, to routines, exercise or activities) and skills teaching, the challenging behaviour will reduce significantly or even disappear. However, further intervention may still be needed.

There are typically a number of stages to a challenging behaviour, including early warning signs and an escalation stage. Any behaviour plan should detail exactly how people are to respond, step by step during each stage of the target behaviour, resulting in consistency in responding. Doing this also means that when the plan is reviewed, each individual step can be analysed to see what is working and what is not, and it places emphasis on preventing behaviours happening in the first place.

AN EXAMPLE OF STAGED REACTIVE STRATEGIES FROM A UPSR BEHAVIOUR MANAGEMENT PLAN

Stage 1: Mary stares at other women's breasts (early warning sign)

Reactive Strategies to Use

1. Remain calm.
2. Use a positive and upbeat voice.
3. Show Mary her 'Rules'.
4. Show Mary her star chart and what she is currently working for.
5. Distract.

Stage 2: Mary grabs other women's breasts (target behaviour)

Reactive Strategies to Use

1. Remain calm.
2. Use quiet voice.
3. Keep speech to a minimum.
4. Stop timer.
5. If in class, remove all other children.
6. If outside in the community, direct Mary away from other people.
7. Give Mary stress balls.
8. Wait three minutes before reminding Mary of her star chart. Start timer.

Some Examples of Reactive Strategies

1. Offer options.
2. Reduce language.
3. Reduce voice volume.
4. Distract.
5. Provide interaction.
6. Play calming music.
7. Dim the lighting.
8. Adopt non-threatening body posture.
9. Provide reminders (either visual or verbal).

10. Remind the child how they should behave, or in which ways they can avoid the problem behaviour.

11. Secure the environment and ensure the safety of the child and others, e.g. by removing any audience or items that could be dangerous.

12. Planned ignoring, as, for example, when a behaviour may be functioning to gain attention.

13. 'Quiet time' or 'Time out'. These will most likely be ineffective if the child is displaying a behaviour for self-stimulation purposes, as it just provides them with time alone.

14. Manage feelings (your own and the child's).

15. Follow through on consequences, which should be enforceable and consistent and relate directly to the behaviour.

IMPORTANT NOTE

Remember that more important than responding to any challenging behaviours is providing attention and positive responses to the positive, prosocial behaviours that the child displays. If this is being neglected (and it can be common in busy and stressful environments), it may be useful to create a schedule for the adults around the child, reminding them to acknowledge and reward positive behaviours. A discreet timer can help with this.

Intervention Strategies

Intervention strategies include specific interventions, such as reward and self-management systems that are individualized to the child and the specific challenging behaviour. Many intervention strategies have already been provided in Chapter 4, 'Teaching Tools and Recommendations' as well as subsequent chapters. Anger and anxiety management strategies (see Chapter 17, 'Teach Emotional Understanding and Regulation') are also particularly relevant here. Following are some more specific examples of intervention strategies that have been used and recommended by professionals working with children and adolescents with ASD (and other developmental disabilities) to target challenging behaviours in the area of sexuality and relationships:

1. *Reward systems* such as star charts. A child who is touching their genitals during class time could have a reward system whereby for every five minutes that they do not touch themselves, they earn a star towards the coveted reward of time in the library.

2. *Behaviour contracts*, i.e. a signed and agreed contract between the child and other relevant parties which details the child's goals, their rewards if they meet their goals and the consequences if they do not.

3. Individualized, colour coded *traffic light systems* to teach appropriate and inappropriate behaviours. For example, a certain child's *red* behaviours could include 'stealing', 'following girls' and 'touching a girl without permission'. Their *yellow* behaviours

could include 'standing too close' or 'staring at women in a sexual way', and their *green* behaviours could include 'saying "hello" to a girl' and 'being polite'. These can be made into highly visual posters or cards to be kept in the child's wallet.

4. *Rating scales* can be used to help the child understand appropriate and inappropriate behaviours (both their own and other people's). Using the previous example, a *1* could include 'saying "hello" to a girl and being polite'. A *3* could include 'staring at women in a sexual way' and a *5* could include 'following a girl' or 'touching a girl without permission' (Dunn Buron 2007). Also using rating scales, *worksheets* could be developed in which the child and another person independently rate a number of different behaviours before comparing and discussing their scores (Dunn Buron 2007). Rating scales should be highly visual, and ideally colour coded.

5. Worksheets or discussions to *develop insight and self-reflection skills* to use after the behaviour has occurred, including questions such as:

    - What bad choice did I make?
    - What happened because I made this bad choice?
    - How did it make people feel?
    - How did it make me feel?
    - What could I do different next time?
    - What will happen if I make a good choice next time?

6. *Thinking tools* and *coping strategies* that the child can use in specific situations, e.g. 'Stop and Think', 'Check Boundaries', 'Ask for Help' and 'Positive Self Talk' (Kisicki and Tedeschi 2001). These can be colour coded or made into visual representations, e.g. a 'stop' sign for 'Stop and Think'. They can also be taught as a sequence for the child to follow. These thinking tools should be taught during calm times but can also be laminated and kept near to the child, to be used as reminders when early warning signs of a behaviour are observed.

7. *Learning to check in and apologize*, e.g. by asking 'Did I say or do something wrong?' and if the answer is 'yes', saying 'I'm sorry'. This will help the child greatly with conflict resolution and maintaining relationships. It also helps them to learn that people may think differently from themselves (Dunn Buron 2007).

8. Creating *specific rules*, such as a 'Three Strikes and You are Out' dating plan, whereby adolescents can ask someone on a date only three times (of course, teach them also to pay close attention along the way to verbal and nonverbal signals). This information can be formatted into easy-to-read visual charts or worksheets (Dunn Buron 2007).

9. The '*old me/new me*' concept helps to teach children to become excited about change and growth in a de-personalized manner. Within this concept, any behavioural issue can be 'old me' and a battle can be created between the two, e.g. 'old me' would touch without thinking, 'new me' thinks first and goes for a walk. Create posters and success plans for the 'new me' (Kisicki and Tedeschi 2001).

24

Putting Together a Plan

So you have decided to implement an SRE programme for a child or a group of children. It is possible that along with this, you would like to work on specific behavioural issues that a child is displaying in relation to sexuality and relationships. This book enables you to individualize your programme in a number of ways, and some tools are provided to support you in this, including:

1. SRE Child Checklist

2. SRE Organization Checklist

3. SRE Individual Curriculum Plan

4. a Functional Behaviour Assessment

5. a UPSR SRE Individual Behaviour Plan

6. other supporting resources, including learning concepts lists, instructional stories and illustrations.

> *Our involvement in planning programmes for people with developmental disabilities gives us a position of power and control over the lives and behaviours of others. It behoves us then, to be thoughtful and non-judgemental in regard to this process and its results. (Dalrymple et al. 1991, p.17)*

The UPSR SRE Individual Behaviour Plan

How to use the UPSR Individual Behaviour Plan:

Look back at the information that you have read in this book and have learned about the child. Using positive language and in bullet points:

1. In the **Understanding** section, fill in what you have learned about the child and their behaviour.

2. In the **Preventing** section, fill in the skills the child needs to learn and the changes that need to be made to their environment.

3. In the **Supporting** section, fill in the ways that the child can be supported to develop a healthy sexuality and relationships, e.g. going on dates or having private time alone in their bedroom.

4. In the **Responding** section, fill in how people are to respond to the child's challenging behaviour in the moment. Specific interventions can also be included here, e.g. a 'traffic light system' for learning about inappropriate behaviours.

Table 24.1 at the end of the chapter shows an example of a UPSR Individual Behaviour Plan for Luke (the boy in the case example in Chapter 19). You will see that some points may be appropriate for more than one section. You will also see that it is designed to be quick to put together and easy to follow. This is by no means an example of a perfect plan, just a plan that is actually being worked on and implemented in a busy environment by busy professionals (i.e. it did not take days to prepare and write up yet has now been forgotten about and neglected until the next crisis).

Planning Steps

If you wish to put together a plan for a child (or a group of children) with *no* current behavioural concerns in this area, following are some steps that may help to guide the process:

1. Liaise with parents (at every step).
2. Analyse and update policies if necessary (using the Organization Checklist).
3. Get a baseline of skills (using the Child Checklist).
4. Decide on a curriculum and goals (using the Individual Curriculum Plan).
5. Decide on teaching methods.
6. Teach knowledge and skills.
7. Monitor and review.

If you wish to put together a plan for a child who *is* displaying behavioural concerns in this area, following are some steps that may help to guide the process:

1. Liaise with parents (at every step).
2. Analyse and update policies if necessary (using the Organization Checklist).
3. Get a baseline of skills (using the Child Checklist).
4. Decide on a curriculum and goals (using the Individual Curriculum Plan).
5. Do an FBA (a sample FBA is given in Appendix E).

6. Decide on:

- environmental changes
- preventative measures
- new skills
- replacement behaviours
- behaviour goals
- reactive strategies
- intervention strategies
- teaching methods.

7. Complete the UPSR Individual Behaviour Plan.

8. Make environmental changes.

9. Implement intervention and skills teaching.

10. Monitor and review.

IMPORTANT NOTE

Before implementing (or designing) any programme, it is important to think critically about your long-term goals for the child. Is it for them to 'fit in' to society? For all signs of autism to be concealed? That an inappropriate behaviour is eliminated, with no corresponding goal to increase positive social or sexual behaviours? In your goal setting, have you taken into account what the child themselves thinks and wants? Do you *know* what the child thinks and wants?

We need to be very careful in our work not to impose 'neurotypically' laden values on the clients we serve. While of course all members of a society need to abide by its laws, there is a strong advocacy movement which states that individuals with ASD should not have to conform to society's 'neurotypical' ways, and that what they need most is to be understood and accepted by others. Look at the child with whom you are working. Even if they are not able to articulate it themselves, how do you think *they* believe their quality of life could be improved? Do *they* care about fitting in or being different? What kind of relationships do *they* want? What does their preferred future look like? What will make them happy, now and into the future? Do they love and are they loved?

A truly successful SRE programme will support these person-centred goals above all else.

True, kind, meaningful support is the buoy that keeps Aspies from floating out to sea. (Holliday Willey 2012, p.48)

TABLE 24.1 UPSR SRE
INDIVIDUAL BEHAVIOUR PLAN FOR LUKE

UNDERSTANDING THE PERSON	PREVENTING ISSUES	SUPPORTING SEXUALITY AND INTIMATE RELATIONSHIPS	RESPONDING TO 'INAPPROPRIATE' BEHAVIOURS
• Gentle, no previous behavioural difficulties. • Special interests: cars and chocolate. • Likes active play and finger painting. • Responds well to praise. • Significant learning needs. • Needs visual supports to back up language. • Uses symbols to request food and TV programmes. • Experiencing typical sexual feelings. • Unaware how to masturbate to ejaculation – leading to agitation. • Unaware of social rules with regard to masturbation. • Using inappropriate objects to stimulate himself.	• Provide stimulating activities throughout the day. • Implement an individualized SRE programme. • Luke needs to learn public and private concepts and appropriate touching. • Create Circles of Intimacy poster using photos. • Teach public and private concepts using photos. • Teach 'private' and 'wait' symbols. • 'Private' sign to be put on Luke's door. • All staff to verbally label Luke's bedroom as 'private' regularly. • Teach 'touching rules' using visuals and photos.	• Ensure that Luke is given time alone – unrequested – in his bedroom throughout the day. • Create visual schedule for masturbation – line drawings. • Investigate whether *Hand Made Love* video is appropriate.	• Use calm tone of voice. • Say 'Private'. • Show Luke a photo of his bedroom. • Gently direct him to his bedroom. • Hand Luke his masturbation visual schedule. • Close bedroom door.

Date of plan: _____

Date for review: _____

Signed: Parent _____

Teacher _____

SNA _____

Appendices

APPENDIX A
Research Articles Related to Sexuality and ASD 1990–2012

Ballan, M. (2012) 'Parental perspectives of communication about sexuality in families of children with autism spectrum disorders.' *Journal of Autism and Developmental Disorders 42*, 5, 676–684.

Galluci, G., Hackerman, F. and Schmidt, C.W. (2005) 'Gender identity disorder in an adult male with Asperger Syndrome.' *Sexuality and Disability 23*, 1, 35–40.

Gilmour, L. Schalomon, P.M. and Smith, V. (2012) 'Sexuality in a community based sample of adults with autism spectrum disorder.' *Research in Autism Spectrum Disorders 6*, 1, 313–318.

Griffin-Shelley, E. (2010) 'An Asperger's adolescent sex addict, sex offender: A case study.' *Sexual Addiction and Compulsivity 17*, 46–64.

Haracopos, D. and Pedersen, L. (1992) *Sexuality and Autism, Danish Report.* United Kingdom: Society for the Autistically Handicapped. (Unpublished)

Hatton, S. and Tector, A. (2010) 'Sexuality and relationship education for young people with Autistic Spectrum Disorder: Curriculum change and staff support.' *British Journal of Special Education 37*, 2, 69–76.

Hellemans, H., Colson, K., Verbracken, C., Vermeiren, R. and Deboutte, D. (2007) 'Sexual behaviour in high-functioning male adolescents and young people with Autistic Spectrum Disorder.' *Journal of Autism and Developmental Disorders 37*, 260–269.

Hellemans, H., Roeyers, H., Leplae, W., Dewaele, T., and Deboutte, D. (2010) 'Sexual behaviour in male adolescents and young adults with Autism Spectrum Disorder and Mild/Borderline Mild Mental Retardation.' *Sexuality and Disability 28*, 93–104.

Kalyva, E. (2010) 'Teachers' perspectives of the sexuality of children with Autism Spectrum Disorder.' *Research in Autism Spectrum Disorders 4*, 433–437.

Konstantareas, M. and Lunsky, Y. (1997) 'Sociosexual knowledge, experience, attitudes and interests of individuals with autistic disorder and developmental delay.' *Journal of Autism and Developmental Disorders 27*, 397–413.

Mehzabin, P. and Stokes, M. (2011) 'Self-assessed sexuality in young adults with high functioning autism.' *Research in Autism Spectrum Disorders 5*, 614–621.

Nichols, S. and Blakeley-Smith, A. (2010) 'I'm not sure we're ready for this…: Working with families towards facilitating healthy sexuality for individuals with autism spectrum disorders.' *Social Work in Mental Health 8*, 72–91.

Ousley, O.Y. and Mesibov, G.B. (1991) 'Sexual attitudes and knowledge of high functioning adolescents and adults with autism.' *Journal of Autism and Developmental Disorders 21*, 471–481.

Ray, F., Marks, C. and Bray-Garretson, H. (2004) 'Challenges to treating adolescents with Asperger's syndrome who are sexually abusive.' *Sexual Addiction and Compulsivity 11*, 265–285.

Realmuto, G.M. and Ruble, L.A. (1999) 'Sexual behaviours in autism: Problems in definition and management.' *Journal of Autism and Developmental Disorders 29*, 2, 121–127.

Ruble, L.A. and Dalrymple, N.J. (1993) 'Social/sexual awareness of persons with autism: A parental perspective.' *Archives of Sexual Behaviour 22*, 3, 229–240.

Stokes, M. and Kaur, A. (2005) 'High-functioning autism and sexuality: A parental perspective.' *Autism 9*, 3, 266–289.

Stokes, M., Newton, N. and Kaur, A. (2007) 'Stalking, and social and romantic functioning among adolescents and adults with Autism Spectrum Disorder.' *Journal of Autism and Developmental Disorders 37*, 1969–1986.

Tissot, C. (2009) 'Establishing a sexual identity: Case studies of learners with autism and learning difficulties.' *Autism 13*, 6, 551–556.

van Bourgondien, M., Reichle, N. and Palmer, A. (1997) 'Sexual behaviour in adults with autism.' *Journal of Autism and Developmental Disorders 27*, 113–125.

Research Articles which Reference Sex Education and ASD, 1990–2012

Ballan, M. (2012) 'Parental perspectives of communication about sexuality in families of children with autism spectrum disorders.' *Journal of Autism and Developmental Disorders 42*, 5, 676–684.

Griffin-Shelley, E. (2010) 'An Asperger's adolescent sex addict, sex offender: A case study.' *Sexual Addiction and Compulsivity 17*, 46–64.

Hatton, S. and Tector, A. (2010) 'Sexuality and Relationship Education for young people with Autistic Spectrum Disorder: Curriculum change and staff support.' *British Journal of Special Education 37*, 2, 69–76.

Nichols, S. and Blakeley-Smith, A. (2010) 'I'm not sure we're ready for this…: Working with families towards facilitating healthy sexuality for individuals with autism spectrum disorders.' *Social Work in Mental Health 8*, 72–91.

Ray, F., Marks, C. and Bray-Garretson, H. (2004) 'Challenges to treating adolescents with Asperger's syndrome who are sexually abusive.' *Sexual Addiction and Compulsivity 11*, 265–285.

Realmuto, G.M. and Ruble, L.A. (1999) 'Sexual behaviours in autism: Problems in definition and management.' *Journal of Autism and Developmental Disorders 29*, 2, 121–127.

Ruble, L.A. and Dalrymple, N.J. (1993) 'Social/sexual awareness of persons with autism: A parental perspective.' *Archives of Sexual Behaviour 22*, 3, 229–240.

Stokes, M. and Kaur, A. (2005) 'High-functioning autism and sexuality: A parental perspective.' *Autism 9*, 3, 266–289.

Tissot, C. (2009). 'Establishing a sexual identity: Case studies of learners with autism and learning difficulties.' *Autism 13*, 6, 551–556.

van Bourgondien, M., Reichle, N. and Palmer, A. (1997) 'Sexual behaviour in adults with autism.' *Journal of Autism and Developmental Disorders 27*, 113–125.

Notes on the Child Checklist

1. The following checklist aims to cover the priority learning concepts within each SRE teaching concept. There will most likely be additional areas just as important as the ones listed, which will be specific to individual children.

2. Not all areas listed will be developmentally appropriate for all children. In addition, how a child shows that they understand a concept, or carries out a skill, will depend on the individual child. For example, one child with little language may show that he knows his own gender by correctly pointing to pictures of boys, while another may be able to answer verbally. In addition, the degree of independence expected of the child in carrying out these skills also needs to be individualized, as some children may always need some support, e.g. prompting. Criteria for success need to be decided by the child's parents and professional team.

PRIORITY LEARNING CONCEPT	YES	NO
Gender		
Does the child know their own gender?	☐	☐
Do they know other people's genders?	☐	☐
Body Parts and Fluids		
Does the child know the basic body parts?	☐	☐
Can they label sexual anatomy?	☐	☐
Can they label internal body parts?	☐	☐
Can they label body fluids?	☐	☐
Do they have an understanding of the function of the body parts?	☐	☐
Do they have an understanding of the function of the body fluids?	☐	☐
Growing and Changing		
Does the child understand that their body will change?	☐	☐
Do they understand about change and growth in general, e.g. aging and future changes in circumstances?	☐	☐
Do they understand where they fit into the life cycle?	☐	☐

PRIORITY LEARNING CONCEPT	YES	NO

Puberty – Girls

Is the girl aware of the changes that will occur (or have occurred) to her during puberty? ☐ ☐

Does she understand menstruation? ☐ ☐

Can she understand and use a calendar? ☐ ☐

Can she carry out the steps to changing a sanitary pad or tampon? ☐ ☐

Can she put on and accept wearing a bra? ☐ ☐

Puberty – Boys

Is the boy aware of the changes that will occur (or have occurred) to him during puberty? ☐ ☐

Is he prepared for wet dreams? ☐ ☐

Is he prepared for his voice breaking? ☐ ☐

Is he prepared for unexpected erections? ☐ ☐

Appearance and Hygiene

Is the child doing the following self-care tasks as independently as possible?

Brushing teeth ☐ ☐

Washing and brushing hair ☐ ☐

Showering or bathing ☐ ☐

Washing hands ☐ ☐

Washing face ☐ ☐

Wearing deodorant ☐ ☐

Caring for nails ☐ ☐

Caring for nose ☐ ☐

Shaving or waxing ☐ ☐

Caring for body (e.g. through diet or exercise) ☐ ☐

Looking after skin ☐ ☐

Wearing appropriate make-up ☐ ☐

Wearing clean clothes ☐ ☐

Washing and drying own clothes ☐ ☐

Buying new clothes ☐ ☐

Dressing appropriately for occasions ☐ ☐

PRIORITY LEARNING CONCEPT	YES	NO

Public and Private

Can the child differentiate between public and private places? ☐ ☐

Can they differentiate between public and private behaviours? ☐ ☐

Can they differentiate between public and private conversation topics? ☐ ☐

Do they display an understanding of public and private concepts through their behaviours? ☐ ☐

Can they label male and female private body parts? ☐ ☐

Safety Skills

Can the child say 'No' assertively and at appropriate times? ☐ ☐

Do they display non-compliance at appropriate times? ☐ ☐

Do they know the characteristics of healthy and unhealthy relationships? ☐ ☐

Can they recognize and respond appropriately to bullying, including cyber-bullying? ☐ ☐

Do they know the difference between surprises, privacy and secrets? ☐ ☐

Do they know the ways in which people may try to control them? ☐ ☐

Do they understand concepts such as sexual harassment, sexual abuse, rape, abuse within relationships, consent, pornography and prostitution? ☐ ☐

Do they display safety skills when answering the door and the phone? ☐ ☐

Do they display internet safety skills? ☐ ☐

Do they have an understanding of dating safety skills? ☐ ☐

Can they recognize abuse? ☐ ☐

Do they have skills in reporting abuse? ☐ ☐

Do they know the difference between appropriate and inappropriate touch? ☐ ☐

Can they name trusted people to talk to about any topic? ☐ ☐

Do they know the different types of touch? ☐ ☐

Are they aware of 'touching rules'? ☐ ☐

Emotional Understanding and Regulation

Is the child aware of their own feelings? ☐ ☐

Do they understand their own feelings? ☐ ☐

Are they aware of other people's feelings? ☐ ☐

Do they understand other people's feelings? ☐ ☐

Can they label a range of emotions? ☐ ☐

PRIORITY LEARNING CONCEPT	YES	NO
Do they express a range of emotions?	☐	☐
Do they express strong emotions appropriately?	☐	☐
Do they possess anger and anxiety management skills?	☐	☐
Are they able to express their needs and wishes appropriately?	☐	☐
Do they understand love and how it is expressed differently with different people?	☐	☐
Do they understand sexual feelings?	☐	☐
Do they express their sexuality in socially appropriate ways?	☐	☐

Relationships

	YES	NO
Can the child define different types of relationships (e.g. friendship, family and marriage)?	☐	☐
Do they know how the people in their lives fit into different relationship categories, and why?	☐	☐
Do they understand homosexual relationships?	☐	☐
Do they have skills in making relationships?	☐	☐
Do they have skills in maintaining relationships?	☐	☐

A Sense of Self

	YES	NO
Is the child aware of their own strengths and weaknesses?	☐	☐
Are they aware of their diagnosis?	☐	☐
Are they aware of what their diagnosis means for them?	☐	☐
Are they able to advocate for themselves (e.g. are they able to communicate their needs and wants)?	☐	☐
Are they involved in their own IEP planning?	☐	☐
Are they involved in their own decision making?	☐	☐
Do they value themselves?	☐	☐
Are they aware of their rights within the systems in which they operate?	☐	☐
Do they respect other people's viewpoints?	☐	☐
Do they respect difference?	☐	☐
Do they strive for independence?	☐	☐
Are they aware of the Autism Advocacy Movement?	☐	☐

PRIORITY LEARNING CONCEPT	YES	NO

Sensory Sensitivities

	YES	NO
Is the child aware of, and do they understand, their own sensory profile?	☐	☐
Are they able to advocate for their own sensory needs?	☐	☐
Are they able to take preventative measures to regulate their sensory sensitivities?	☐	☐

Sexual Health

	YES	NO
Is the adolescent aware of their own sexual health needs?	☐	☐
Are they aware of sexual health services available to them in their community?	☐	☐
Are they able to access sexual health services?	☐	☐
Can they access sexual health *information* from appropriate sources?	☐	☐
Are they able to advocate for their own sexual health needs?	☐	☐
Can they choose, buy and use contraception appropriately?	☐	☐
Are they aware of what a healthy body should feel and look like?	☐	☐
Are they able to do self-examinations (i.e. breast or testicular exams)?	☐	☐
Do they display personal hygiene and cleanliness?	☐	☐
Can they recognize the signs of STIs?	☐	☐
Do they know how to prevent STIs?	☐	☐
Are they involved in managing their own medical appointments?	☐	☐
Are they aware of any medication they may be on (including why they are on it and any potential side effects)?	☐	☐
Are they able to locate and rate pain?	☐	☐

Conception, Pregnancy and Birth

Does the child understand the following concepts?

	YES	NO
Fertilization and conception	☐	☐
The development from a zygote to a baby	☐	☐
Staying healthy (and keeping a baby healthy) during pregnancy	☐	☐
Signs of pregnancy	☐	☐
Labour and Caesareans	☐	☐
Body parts related to birth (e.g. placenta)	☐	☐
Breastfeeding and bottle-feeding	☐	☐
Miscarriage	☐	☐

✓

PRIORITY LEARNING CONCEPT	YES	NO
Fertility	☐	☐
Abortion	☐	☐
IVF	☐	☐
Surrogacy	☐	☐
Menopause	☐	☐
Adoption	☐	☐
Sterilization	☐	☐
Genes, chromosomes and how these are passed down	☐	☐
Do they know the steps to take if they suspect that they (or partner) are pregnant?	☐	☐

SRE in a Modern Age

	YES	NO
Does the child display online safety skills?	☐	☐
Can they recognize and respond appropriately to cyber-bullying?	☐	☐
Do they display good texting and emailing skills?	☐	☐
Do they display appropriate online behaviour (e.g. not sending the same email repeatedly)?	☐	☐
Can they recognize credible websites?	☐	☐
Do they avoid unsuitable websites (e.g. pro-anorexia sites)?	☐	☐
Do they display an understanding of the importance of privacy online?	☐	☐
Do they know how to block people or content?	☐	☐
Do they know the steps to take if they see something online that makes them uncomfortable or is illegal?	☐	☐
Do they understand the nature of online friendships?	☐	☐
Do they understand that people may not be who they say they are online?	☐	☐
Do they know the steps to take if someone online asks to meet them in person?	☐	☐
Do they know not to upload or send anyone photos of their bodies?	☐	☐

Dating, Intimate Relationships and Sex

	YES	NO
Does the adolescent understand attraction?	☐	☐
Do they understand flirting and can they display any flirting skills?	☐	☐
Can they label positive qualities that they would like in a partner?	☐	☐
Are they able to plan for a date?	☐	☐
Do they display an awareness of the skills that may be needed on a date (e.g. conversation skills)?	☐	☐

PRIORITY LEARNING CONCEPT	YES	NO
Do they display relationship skills, e.g. listening, sharing and compromising?	☐	☐
Can they label categories of intimate relationships?	☐	☐
Are they aware of the different relationship stages?	☐	☐
Are they able to match their behaviour to appropriate levels of intimacy?	☐	☐
Do they understand and show acceptance of homosexual relationships?	☐	☐
Do they know the characteristics of healthy and unhealthy intimate relationships?	☐	☐
Do they understand concepts related to abuse within relationships?	☐	☐
Do they have skills to deal with rejection and cope with unrequited feelings?	☐	☐
Do they know how to end relationships appropriately?	☐	☐
Have they considered disclosure about their diagnosis within relationships?	☐	☐
Do they understand consent?	☐	☐
Are they able to recognize when they are ready for a sexual relationship?	☐	☐
Are they aware of the 'mechanics' of sexual intercourse?	☐	☐
Are they aware that media portrayals of intimate relationships and sex are unrealistic?	☐	☐
Are they aware of concepts related to sex and religion?	☐	☐
Do they understand the law as it relates to themselves and sex?	☐	☐
Do they have skills in making their own sexual decisions?	☐	☐
Are they aware of the sexual choices available to them?	☐	☐
Are they aware of the consequences of their actions in relation to sex?	☐	☐
Are they able to recognize and respond appropriately to peer pressure with regard to sex?	☐	☐

Additional Notes

Date: _____

Date for review: _____

Signed: _____

✓

PRIORITY POLICY AND PROCEDURES AREAS	YES	NO

SRE Programmes

Is SRE being taught in a planned and consistent manner to all children within the organization? ☐ ☐

Are SRE goals included in IEPs? ☐ ☐

Are programmes individualized? ☐ ☐

Are programmes developmentally appropriate? ☐ ☐

Do programmes include person-centred goals relating to a healthy sexuality and the development of intimate relationships? ☐ ☐

Are children receiving a concurrent, comprehensive social skills programme? ☐ ☐

Are programmes taking into account up-to-date research into best practice interventions and teaching tools with regard to ASD? ☐ ☐

Do staff feel confident in providing SRE? ☐ ☐

Are staff being provided with support (e.g. supervision, training, mentoring or shadowing) in the area of SRE? ☐ ☐

Are all staff (including frontline staff) involved in all steps of the child's SRE programme? ☐ ☐

Child Protection

Are staff regularly trained in child protection issues (e.g. identifying and reporting abuse, and managing disclosure)? ☐ ☐

Are children also trained in recognizing and reporting abuse, as is developmentally appropriate? ☐ ☐

Behaviour

Are staff aware of the typical sexual behaviours displayed by children? ☐ ☐

Are staff aware of the reasons why a child with ASD may be displaying sexual behaviours? ☐ ☐

Are staff trained in positive behaviour management strategies, including low arousal techniques? ☐ ☐

Are staff proficient in undertaking and analysing FBAs? ☐ ☐

Are *all* staff responding to challenging behaviours consistently? ☐ ☐

PRIORITY POLICY AND PROCEDURES AREAS	YES	NO
Are there clear procedures for staff to follow when a child displays inappropriate sexual behaviours?	☐	☐

Policies

	YES	NO
Are child protection policies up to date?	☐	☐
Are SRE policies up to date?	☐	☐
Are the aims, objectives and goals of SRE programmes clearly stated within policies?	☐	☐
Have all stakeholders (including children) been included in developing the SRE policies and procedures?	☐	☐
Are behaviour management policies up to date?	☐	☐
Are policies relating to children's privacy and personal space up to date?	☐	☐
Is what is considered acceptable sexual expression within the organization clearly stated within policies?	☐	☐
Are policies linked to a national approach?	☐	☐
Are policies in place for when disagreements occur (e.g. if a parent does not wish for their child to take part in SRE)?	☐	☐
Are staff aware that these policies exist?	☐	☐
Are staff following policy on a daily basis?	☐	☐
Do policies need to be re-evaluated?	☐	☐

Parents

	YES	NO
Are staff aware of the potential barriers to parental involvement for their particular client group?	☐	☐
Have parent committees been involved in the development of the SRE programmes within the organization?	☐	☐
Have *all* parents been asked for their views and opinions?	☐	☐
Are lines of communication open with parents?	☐	☐
Does the organization have relevant and accessible information and resources to provide or recommend to parents?	☐	☐

Resources

	YES	NO
Do staff have access to appropriate, best practice SRE resources?	☐	☐
Are resources being shared across the organization?	☐	☐

Community Links

	YES	NO
Is the organization committed to the inclusion of individuals with ASD in the communities in which they live?	☐	☐

PRIORITY POLICY AND PROCEDURES AREAS	YES	NO
Have formal community links been made (e.g. to social work services, local health clinics and youth clubs)?	☐	☐
Are staff aware of the services (e.g. sexual health clinics) available to their clients in their locality?	☐	☐

Additional Notes

Date: _____

Date for review: _____

Signed: _____

SRE CURRICULUM PLAN FOR _____

CURRICULUM CONCEPT	GOALS FOR THE CHILD IN THIS AREA
Gender	
Body Parts and Fluids	
Growing and Changing	
Puberty	
Appearance and Hygiene	

✓

CURRICULUM CONCEPT	GOALS FOR THE CHILD IN THIS AREA
Public and Private	
Safety Skills	
Emotional Understanding and Regulation	
Relationships	
Sense of Self	
Sensory Sensitivities	
Sexual Health	

CURRICULUM CONCEPT	GOALS FOR THE CHILD IN THIS AREA
Conception, Pregnancy and Birth	
Sex Education in a Modern Age	
Dating, Intimate Relationships and Sex	
Other	

Additional Notes

Date of plan: _____

Date for review: _____

Signed: _____

PERSONAL DETAILS	
Name of child:	Date of birth:
Date of assessment:	Chronological age:
Person/s completing the assessment:	

STEP 1: DEFINE THE BEHAVIOUR

Define the behaviour.

Establish a baseline.
1. How often is the behaviour occurring?
2. How long does it last?
3. At what intensity? (*Try to be as objective and descriptive as possible.*)

STEP 2: ASK THE CHILD

What do you think is the child's understanding of their behaviour?

STEP 2: ASK THE CHILD
What attempts have been made to elicit information from the child about the behaviour (either verbally or nonverbally)? *(If there have been no attempts, please do so at this stage.)*
Is the child aware that a behavioural investigation is underway? *(If not, you may consider informing them.)*

STEP 3: INVESTIGATE
Communication
Describe the child's receptive language skills.
How do they communicate? *(Include positive and negative communications.)*
Are there things that the child is unable to communicate?

STEP 3: INVESTIGATE

Are efficient, effective communication strategies being taught to the child on a daily basis?

Are visual supports being used by adults to aid communication with the child?

Are positive communication efforts being rewarded throughout the day?

STRENGTHS

List the child's strengths.

List the positive social behaviours the child displays.

STRENGTHS

List the interventions that have been successful in the past.

List things that the child likes and finds reinforcing (including food, toys, settings, activities and people).

HEALTH/MEDICAL

Have medical causes been ruled out?

Is the child on any medication which could be affecting their behaviour? If yes, describe how and why.

Has the behaviour come out of the blue? *(If the answer is yes, it needs to be taken into serious consideration as to why.)*

HEALTH/MEDICAL
Have there been recent changes in the child's eating, sleeping or diet?
Describe their current sleeping pattern.
Describe their current diet.
Have there been any recent stresses or changes in the child's home or school life?
Have there been any recent changes to routine?

HEALTH/MEDICAL

List the child's sensory sensitivities. Could these be impacting on the behaviour?

ENVIRONMENT AND SOCIAL SETTING

Are there opportunities for fun in the child's day?

Does their environment provide interesting, age-appropriate items and activities?

Is the child's curriculum achievable and interesting?

Are activities varied?

ENVIRONMENT AND SOCIAL SETTING

Is work individualized to meet the child's specific learning needs?

Look at the child's timetable:

- Are activities predictable?

- Do they know what comes next in their day?

- Do they struggle between activities?

- Does the child have visual schedules (easily viewed and understood by the child) to support timetable transitions throughout the day?

Is the support provider ration adequate/too high? How many adults are usually around the child?

Does the child experience positive rapport and relationships with their care providers?

ENVIRONMENT AND SOCIAL SETTING

Do they experience choice throughout the day in terms of what he/she will do, when, with whom, and what rewards they will receive?

SKILLS

How does the child react...?

When they are given a difficult task.

When a highly preferred activity ends.

To sudden and unexpected changes to their routine.

When they are left alone.

SKILLS
How does the child react…?

When they are ignored

When they can see a preferred item but cannot have it

Can the child…?

Wait

Ask for something

Express anger

SKILLS
Can the child...?
Control their temper
Relax
Identify their feelings

STEP 4: IDENTIFY INITIAL CHANGES
Now go back over everything and highlight answers you think might play a part in the problem. List the changes that can be made already.

✓

STEP 5: COMPLETE ABCS (ANTECEDENTS, BEHAVIOURS, CONSEQUENCES)

Focus on the target behaviour across settings

ANTECEDENT	BEHAVIOUR	CONSEQUENCE

STEP 6: ANALYSE THE INFORMATION

The behaviour is *least likely* to occur:

Setting

| Time |

| Activity |

| With this person(s) |

The behaviour is *most likely* to occur:

Setting

| Time |

| Activity |

| With this person(s) |

Most common antecedents?

What are the triggers to the behaviour?

Most common consequences?

What is the child gaining, feeling, escaping or avoiding by displaying the behaviour?

STEP 7: COME UP WITH A HYPOTHESIS

What is causing and maintaining the behaviour? After all of your observation and analysis, why do you think the child is displaying it? (Remember that your hypothesis can be changed after a period of intervention or if new information comes to light.)

UPSR SRE INDIVIDUAL BEHAVIOUR PLAN FOR: _____

UNDERSTANDING THE PERSON	PREVENTING ISSUES	SUPPORTING SEXUALITY AND INTIMATE RELATIONSHIPS	RESPONDING TO 'INAPPROPRIATE' BEHAVIOURS

Date of plan _____ Date for review _____ Signed _____

✓

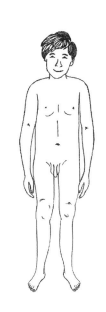

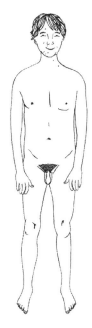

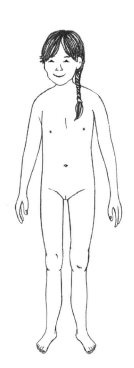

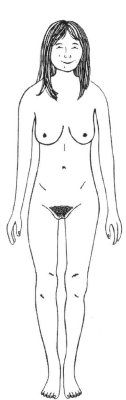

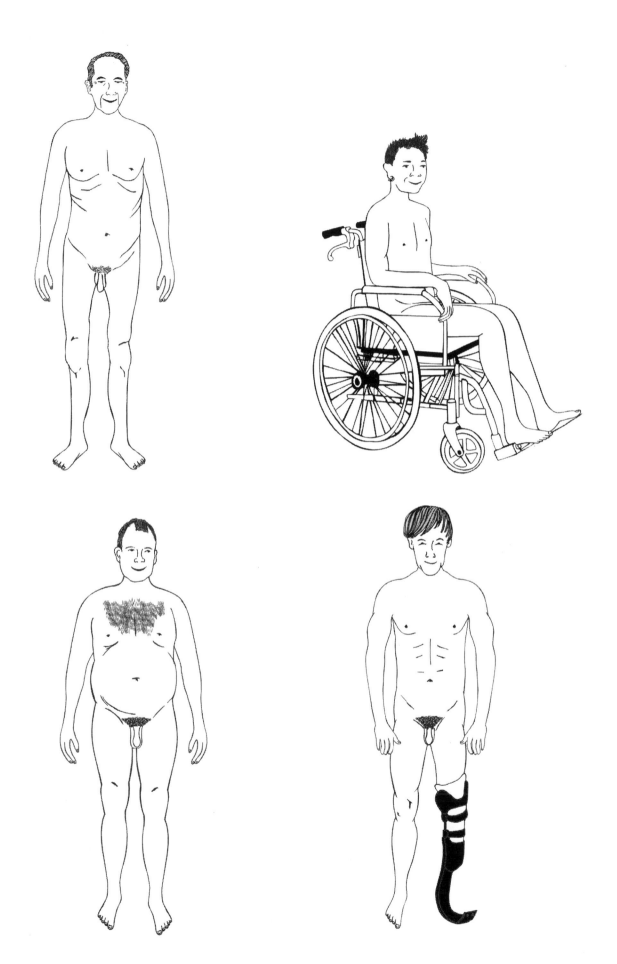

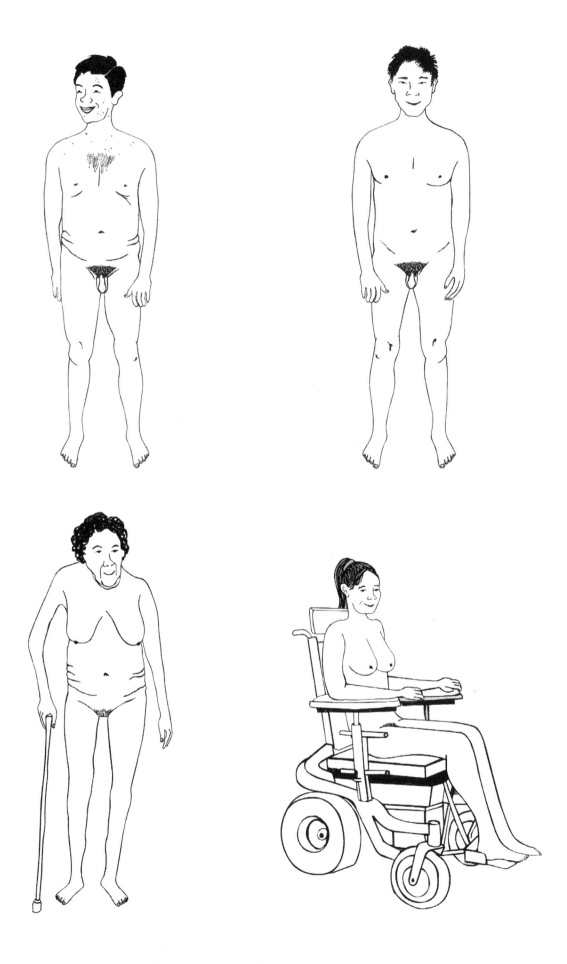

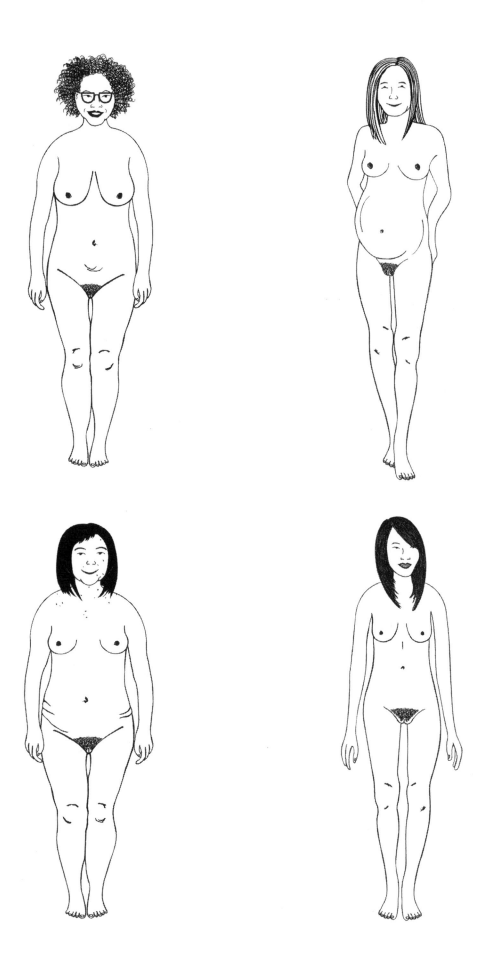

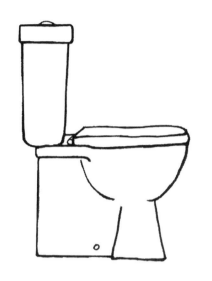

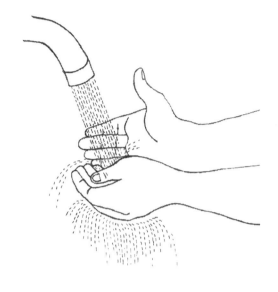

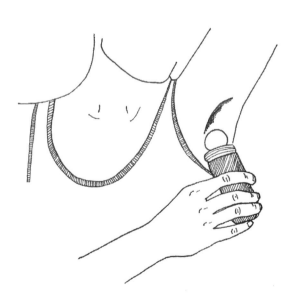

✓

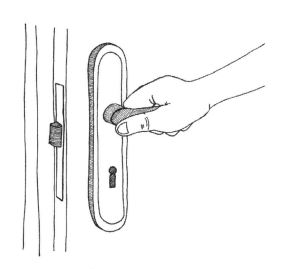

✓

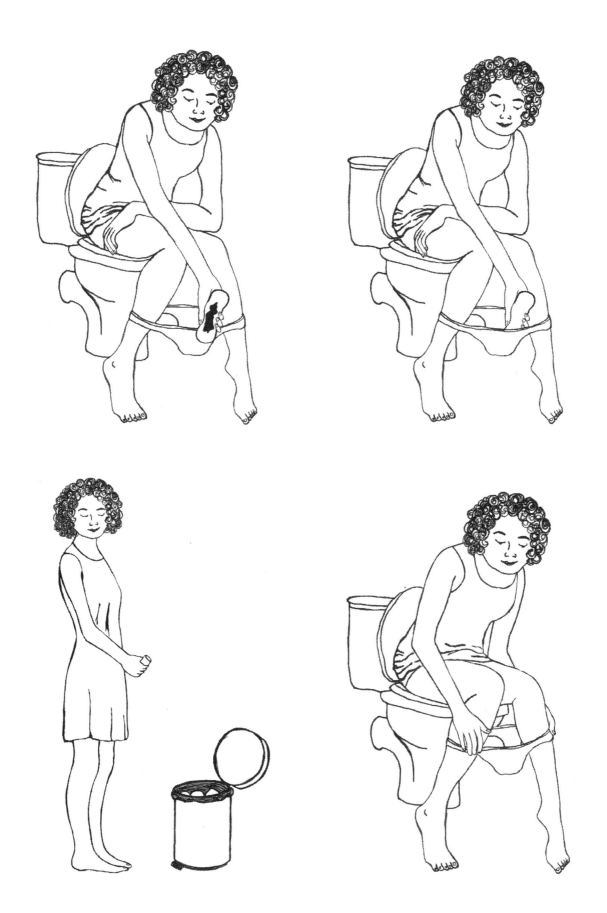

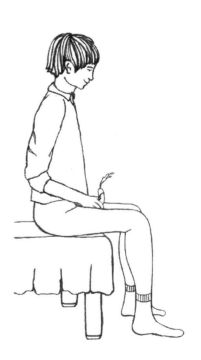

✓

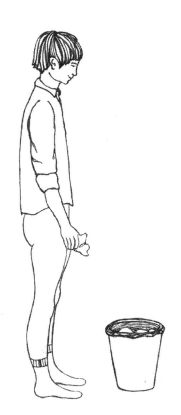

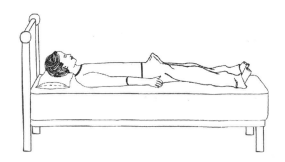

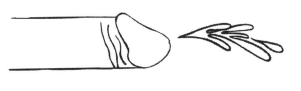

✓

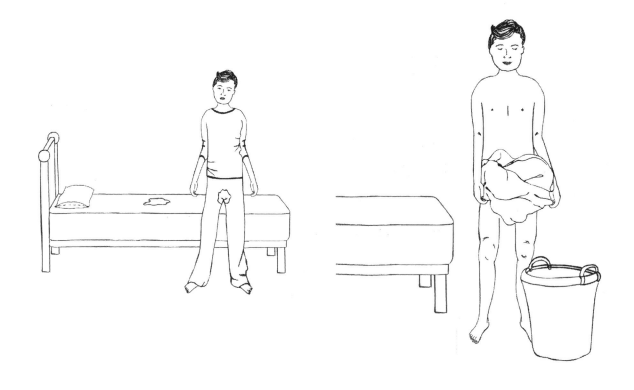
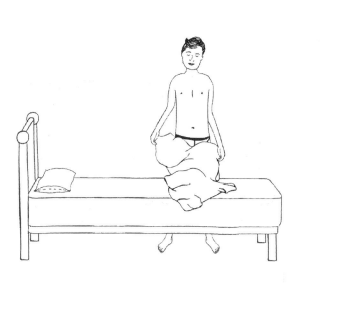

✓

Alford, S. (2008) *Science and Success: Sex Education and Other Programmes that Work to Prevent Teen Pregnancy, HIV and Sexually Transmitted Infections.* Washington, DC: Advocates for Youth.

American Psychiatric Association (1987) *Diagnostic and Statistical Manual of Mental Disorders* (3rd edition, revised). Washington, DC: American Psychiatric Association.

American Psychological Association (2012) 'Child sexual abuse: What parents should know.' Available at at www.apa.org/pi/families/resources/child-sexual-abuse.aspx, accessed on 13 December 2012.

Ashkenazy, E. and Yergeau, M. (eds) (2013) *Relationships and Sexuality.* Washington, DC: Autistic Self Advocacy Network.

Ballan, M. (2012) 'Parental perspectives of communication about sexuality in families of children with autism spectrum disorders.' *Journal of Autism and Developmental Disorders 42,* 5, 676–684.

Bauminger, N., Shulman, C. and Agam, G. (2003) 'Peer interactions and loneliness in high functioning children with autism.' *Journal of Autism and Developmental Disorders 33,* 489–507.

Bellini, S. (2006) 'The development of social anxiety in adolescents with autism spectrum disorders.' *Focus on Autism and Other Developmental Disabilities 19,* 78–86.

Cambridge, P., Carnaby, S. and McCarthy, M. (2003) 'Responding to masturbation in supporting sexuality and challenging behaviour in services for people with learning disabilities: A practice and research overview.' *Journal of Learning Disabilities 7,* 251–266.

Cavanagh Johnson, T. (2002) 'Some considerations about sexual abuse and children with sexual behaviour problems.' *Journal of Trauma and Dissociation 3,* 83–105.

Chivers, J. and Mathieson, S. (2000) 'Training in sexuality and relationships: An Australian model.' *Sexuality and Disability 18,* 1, 73–80.

Dalrymple, N., Gray, S. and Ruble, L. (1991) 'Sex Education: Issues for the Person with Autism.' (Revised.) In *Functional Programming for People with Autism: A Series.* Indiana Resource Centre for Autism. Indiana University. (Original edition published 1987.)

Davies, C. and Dubie, M. (2012) *Intimate Relationships and Sexual Health: A Curriculum for Teaching Adolescents/Adults with High-Functioning Autism Spectrum Disorders and Other Social Challenges.* Overland Park, KS: Autism Asperger Publishing Company.

Department of Justice (1993) Criminal Law (Sexual Offences) Act. Dublin: The Stationery Office.

Dunn Buron, K. (2007) *A 5 is Against the Law! Social Boundaries: Straight Up!* Overland Park, KS: Autism Asperger Publishing Company.

Edelson, M.G. (2010) 'Sexual abuse of children with autism: Factors that increase risk and interfere with recognition of abuse.' *Disabilities Studies Quarterly 30,* 1. Special Issue: Autism and Neurodiversity.

Farrugia, S. and Hudson, C. (2006) 'Anxiety in adolescents with Asperger syndrome: Negative thoughts, behavioural problems, and life interference.' *Focus on Autism and other Developmental Disabilities 21,* 25–35.

Friedrich, W.N., Fisher, J., Broughton, D., Houston, M. and Shafran, C.R. (1998) 'Normative sexual behaviour in children: A contemporary sample.' *Pediatrics 101,* 4, 9–14.

Galluci, G., Hackerman, F. and Schmidt, C.W. (2005) 'Gender identity disorder in an adult male with Asperger Syndrome.' *Sexuality and Disability 23,* 1, 35–40.

Gilberg, C. (1984) 'Autistic children growing up: Problems during puberty and adolescence.' *Developmental Medicine and Child Neurology 26,* 125–129.

Goldacre, B. (2008) *Bad Science.* London: Harper Perennial.

Golubock, S. (2009) 'What we don't know (about relationships) CAN hurt us: The hazards of not understanding, relating to and communicating with others.' *Autism Advocate 1,* 55–58.

Gougeon, N.A. (2010) 'Sexuality and autism: A critical review of selected literature using a social-relational model of disability.' *American Journal of Sexual Education, 5,* 328–361.

Grandin, T. (2006) *Thinking in Pictures.* New York, NY: Bloomsbury Publishing plc.

Griffin-Shelley, E. (2010) 'An Asperger's adolescent sex addict, sex offender: A case study.' *Sexual Addiction and Compulsivity 17,* 46–64.

Haracopos, D. and Pedersen, L. (1992) 'Sexuality and autism. Danish report.' United Kingdom. Society for the Autistically Handicapped. Available at www.autismuk.com/?page_id=1293, accessed on 13 January 2013.

Harris, R.H. and Emberley, M. (2009) *Let's Talk About Sex: Changing Bodies, Growing Up, Sex and Sexual Health.* London: Walker Books.

Hatton, S. and Tector, A. (2010) 'Sexuality and Relationship Education for young people with Autistic Spectrum Disorder: Curriculum change and staff support.' *British Journal of Special Education 37*, 2, 69–76.

Hellemans, H., Colson, K., Verbracken, C., Vermeiren, R. and Deboutte, D. (2007) 'Sexual behaviour in high-functioning male adolescents and young people with Autistic Spectrum Disorder.' *Journal of Autism and Developmental Disorders 37*, 260–269.

Hellemans, H., Roeyers, H., Leplae, W., Dewaele, T., and Deboutte, D. (2010) 'Sexual behaviour in male adolescents and young adults with Autism Spectrum Disorder and Mild/Borderline Mild Mental Retardation.' *Sexuality and Disability 28*, 93–104.

Hingsburger, D. (1994) 'The Ring of Safety: Teaching people with disabilities to be their own first line of defence.' *Developmental Disabilities Bulletin 22*, 2, 72–79.

Hingsburger, D. (1995) *Just Say Know! Understanding and Reducing the Risk of Sexual Victimization of People with Developmental Disabilities.* Barrie, Ontario: Diverse City Press Inc.

Hingsburger, D. (1996) *Behaviour Self!* Barrie, Ontario: Diverse City Press Inc.

Hingsburger, D. (1998) *Hand Made Love: A Guide for Teaching Male Masturbation.* Barrie, Ontario: Diverse City Press Inc.

Hingsburger, D. (2010) *Home Safe: A Manual about Abuse: Preventing and Reporting in Community Services.* Barrie, Ontario: Diverse City Press Inc.

Hingsburger, D. and Haar, S. (2003) *Finger Tips: A Guide for Teaching about Female Masturbation.* Barrie, Ontario: Diverse City Press Inc.

Holliday Willey, L. (2012) *Safety Skills for Asperger Women: How to Save a Perfectly Good Female Life.* London: Jessica Kingsley Publishers.

Howlin, P. and Moss, P. (2012) 'Adults with Autism Spectrum Disorders.' *The Canadian Journal of Psychiatry 57*, 5, 275–283.

Hutton, J., Goode, S., Murphy, M., Le Couteur, A. and Rutter, M. (2008) 'New-onset psychiatric disorders in individuals with autism.' *Autism 12*, 373–390.

Jackson, L. (2002) *Freaks, Geeks and Asperger Syndrome: A User Guide to Adolescence.* London: Jessica Kingsley Publishers.

Kaeser, F. and O'Neil, J. (1987) 'Task analysed masturbation instruction for a profoundly mentally retarded adult male: A data based case study.' *Sexuality and Disability 8*, 17–24.

Kalyva, E. (2010) 'Teachers' perspectives of the sexuality of children with Autism Spectrum Disorder.' *Research in Autism Spectrum Disorders 4*, 433–437.

Kellogg, N.D. (2009) 'Clinical report – the evaluation of sexual behaviours in children.' *Pediatrics 124*, 992–998.

Kisicki, J. and Tedeschi, P. (2001) 'Healthy sexuality in special needs populations.' *Quarterly 7*, 1, 12–14.

Knickmeyer, R.C., Wheelright, S., Hoekstra, R. and Baron-Cohen, S. (2006) 'Age of menarche in females with autism spectrum conditions.' *Developmental Medicine and Child Neurology 28*, 1007–1008.

Konstantareas, M. and Lunsky, Y. (1997) 'Sociosexual knowledge, experience, attitudes and interests of individuals with autistic disorder and developmental delay.' *Journal of Autism and Developmental Disorders 27*, 397–413.

Lang, R., O'Reilly, M., Healy, O., Rispoli, M. *et al.* (2012) 'Sensory integration therapy for autism spectrum disorders: A systematic review.' *Research in Autism Spectrum Disorders 6*, 3, 1004–1018.

Lawson, W. (2005) *Sex, Sexuality and the Autism Spectrum.* London: Jessica Kingsley Publishers.

Lee, D.O. (2004) 'Menstrually related self-injurious behaviour in adolescents with autism.' *Journal of the American Academy of Child and Adolescent Psychiatry 43*, 1193.

Litwiller, B.J. and Brausch, A.M. (2013) 'Cyber bullying and physical bullying in adolescent suicide: The role of violent behavior and substance abuse.' *Journal of Youth and Adolescence 42*, 675–684.

Mansell, S., Sobsey, D. and Moskal, R. (1998) 'Clinical findings among sexually abused children with and without developmental disabilities.' *Mental Retardation 36*, 12–22.

McCall, D.S. (2012) 'Teaching sexual health education: A primer for new teachers, a refresher for experienced teachers.' Available at www.sexualityandu.ca/uploads/files/TeachingSexEdManual.pdf, accessed on 28 September 2012.

McGovern, C.W. and Sigman, M. (2005) 'Continuity and change from early childhood to adolescence in autism.' *Journal of Child Psychology and Psychiatry 46*, 4, 401–408.

Mehzabin, P. and Stokes, M. (2011) 'Self-assessed sexuality in young adults with high functioning autism.' *Research in Autism Spectrum Disorders 5*, 614–621.

Molloy, H. and Vasil, L. (2004) *Asperger Syndrome, Adolescence, and Identity: Looking Beyond the Label.* London: Jessica Kingsley Publishers.

Murphy, N.A. and Elias, E.R. (2006) 'Sexuality of children and adolescents with developmental disabilities.' *Pediatrics 118*, 398–403.

Newport, J. and Newport, M. (2002) *Autism-Asperger's and Sexuality: Puberty and Beyond.* Arlington, TX: Future Horizons.

Nichols, S. and Blakeley-Smith, A. (2010) 'I'm not sure we're ready for this…: Working with families towards facilitating healthy sexuality for individuals with autism spectrum disorders.' *Social Work in Mental Health 8*, 72–91.

Nichols, S., Moravcik, G.M. and Tetenbaum, S.P. (2009) *Girls Growing Up on the Autism Spectrum: What Parents and Professionals Should Know about the Pre-Teen and Teenage Years.* London: Jessica Kingsley Publishers.

Orsmond, G., Krauss, M.W. and Seltzer, M.M. (2004) 'Peer relationships and social and recreational activities among adolescents and adults with autism.' *Journal of Autism and Developmental Disorders 34*, 245–256.

Ousley, O.Y. and Mesibov, G.B. (1991) 'Sexual attitudes and knowledge of high functioning adolescents and adults with autism.' *Journal of Autism and Developmental Disorders 21*, 471–481.

Ray, F., Marks, C. and Bray-Garretson, H. (2004) 'Challenges to treating adolescents with Asperger's syndrome who are sexually abusive.' *Sexual Addiction and Compulsivity 11*, 265–285.

Rayner, C.S. (2010) 'Video modelling to improve task completion in a child with autism.' *Developmental Neurorehabilitation 13*, 3, 225–230.

Realmuto, G.M. and Ruble, L.A. (1999) 'Sexual behaviours in autism: Problems in definition and management.' *Journal of Autism and Developmental Disorders 29*, 2, 121–127.

Robinson, S.J. (2012) 'Childhood epilepsy and autism spectrum disorders: Psychiatric problems, phenotype expression, and anti-convulsants.' *Neuropsychology Review 22*, 3, 271–279.

Ruble, L.A. and Dalrymple, N.J. (1993) 'Social/sexual awareness of persons with autism: A parental perspective.' *Archives of Sexual Behaviour 22*, 3, 229–240.

Seltzer, M., Krauss, M.W., Shattuck, P.T., Orsmond, G. *et al.* (2003) 'The symptoms of autism spectrum disorders in adolescence and adulthood.' *Journal of Autism and Developmental Disorders 33*, 565–581.

Seltzer, M.M., Shattuck, P., Abbeduto, L. and Greenberg, J.S. (2004) 'Trajectory of development in adolescents and adults with autism.' *Mental Retardation and Developmental Disabilities Research Reviews 10*, 234–247.

Schopler, E. (1997) 'Implementation of TEACCH Philosophy.' In D.J. Cohen and F. R. Volkmar (eds) *Handbook of Autism and Pervasive Developmental Disorders*, 767–795. New York, NY: John Wiley.

Shattuck, P.T., Seltzer, M.M., Greenberg, J.S., Orsmond, G.I. *et al.* (2007) 'Change in autism symptoms and maladaptive behaviours in adolescents and adults with an autism spectrum disorder.' *Journal of Autism and Developmental Disorders 37*, 1735–1747.

Shore, S. (2003) *Beyond the Wall: Personal Experiences with Autism and Asperger Syndrome.* Overland Park, KS: Autism Asperger Publishing Company.

Sinclair, J. (1992) 'What does being different mean?' Our Voice 1, 1. Available at www.autism-help.org/story-adult-being-different.htm, accessed on 13 March 2013.

South Eastern CASA (South Eastern Centre Against Sexual Assault) (2013) 'Age appropriate sexual behaviour guide.' Available at www.secasa.com.au/pages/age-appropriate-sexual-behaviour-guide, accessed on 20 June 2013.

Stewart, M.E., Barnard, L., Pearson, J., Hasan, R. and O'Brien, G. (2006) 'Presentation of depression in autism and Asperger syndrome.' *Autism 10*, 103–116.

Stokes, M. and Kaur, A. (2005) 'High-functioning autism and sexuality: A parental perspective.' *Autism 9*, 3, 266–289.

Stokes, M., Newton, N. and Kaur, A. (2007) 'Stalking, and social and romantic functioning among adolescents and adults with Autism Spectrum Disorder.' *Journal of Autism and Developmental Disorders 37*, 1969–1986.

Sullivan, P.M. and Knuton, J.F. (2000) 'Maltreatment and disabilities: A population based epidemiology study.' *Child Abuse and Neglect 24*, 10, 1257–1273.

Tarnai, B. (2006) 'Review of effective interventions for socially inappropriate masturbation in persons with cognitive disabilities.' *Sexuality and Disability 24*, 151–168.

Tissot, C. (2009) 'Establishing a sexual identity: Case studies of learners with autism and learning difficulties.' *Autism 13*, 6, 551–556.

United Nations Enable (2012) 'Conventional and optional protocol signatures and ratifications.' Available at www.un.org/disabilities/countries.asp?navid=12&pid=166, accessed on 7 September 2012.

Urbano, M.R., Hartmann, K., Deutsch, S.I., Bondi Polychronopoulos, G.M. and Dorbin, V. (2013) 'Relationships, Sexuality and Intimacy in Autism Spectrum Disorders.' In M. Fitzgerald (ed.) *Recent Advances in Autism Spectrum Disorders. Volume 1.* Rijeka: In Tech.

van Bourgondien, M., Reichle, N. and Palmer, A. (1997) 'Sexual behaviour in adults with autism.' *Journal of Autism and Developmental Disorders 27*, 113–125.

Volkmar, F.R. and Klin, A. (1995) 'Social Development in Autism: Historical and Clinical Perspectives.' In S. Baron-Cohen, H. Tager-Flusberg and D.J. Cohen (eds) *Understanding Other Minds: Perspectives from Autism.* New York, NY: Oxford University Press.

Williams, D. (1992) *Nobody Nowhere: The Remarkable Autobiography of an Autistic Girl.* London: Jessica Kingsley Publishers.

World Health Organization (2012) 'Sexual and reproductive health: Gender and human rights.' Available at www.who.int/reproductivehealth/topics/gender_rights/sexual_health/en, accessed on 14 September 2012.

Recommended Reading and Resources

See my website www.autismsexeducation.com for a constantly updating blog and list of resources (including books, academic articles, blogs, information resources and multimedia links) in relation to sexuality, SRE and ASD. Following is a select list of resources from this website which are particularly recommended:

American Girl (1998) *The Care and Keeping of You: The Body Book for Girls.*
This is a beautiful colour-illustrated book written for typically developing pre-teens and teens. It includes information for girls on topics such as hair care, braces, acne, bras, the use of tampons and body image, and is recommended for girls with good reading skills.

Ashkenazy, E. and Yergeau, M. (eds) (2013) 'Relationships and sexuality.' Autistic Self Advocacy Network. Available to download for free at: www.autismnow.org/wp-content/uploads/2013/02/Relationships-and-Sexuality-Tool.pdf.
Produced by Autism NOW, a national initiative of The Arc and the Autistic Self-Advocacy Network, this manuscript, described as an 'anthology of autistic relationships', is written by and for adults with ASD and covers a number of topics, including moving in together, complex and atypical relationships, orgasms, asexuality, abuse and debunking myths and stereotypes, all through the eyes of self-advocates with ASD. Highly recommended for professionals and parents looking for insights into ASD and sexuality.

Atwood, S. (2008) *Making Sense of Sex: A Forthright Guide to Puberty, Sex and Relationships for People with Asperger's Syndrome.* London: Jessica Kingsley Publishers.
This comprehensive book, which includes illustrations, is aimed at both males and females with AS. It is beneficial in that it is more factually based than most other sex education books. Topics include puberty, caring for your body, understanding emotions and sexual health. It is recommended for those with good literacy skills. As it covers sex and sexual relationships, it would need to be read and approved before being given to children.

Davies, C. and Dubie, M. (2012) *Intimate Relationships and Sexual Health: A Curriculum for Teaching Adolescents/Adults with High Functioning Autism and Other Social Challenges.* Overland Park, KS: Autism Asperger Publishing Company.
This curriculum is divided into an 11-week workshop programme. It is extremely comprehensive, easy to follow and includes everything you need to run a group, including a range of activities for each workshop. Activities are up to date and interesting, including the use of specific online video clips. Resources are provided in the book as well as on an accompanying CD. It also includes tips on how to adapt the programme to work with individual students. The programme is geared towards older teenagers and adults with good language skills, but some activities could be adapted for younger children.

Dunn Buron, K. (2007) *A 5 is Against the Law! Social Boundaries: Straight Up! An Honest Guide for Teens and Young Adults.* Overland Park, KS: Autism Asperger Publishing Company.
This thin workbook is highly recommended. It is aimed at teens and young adults who are experiencing difficulties with appropriate behaviours in the areas of social boundaries and

relationships and aims to help them understand other people's perspectives in order to keep themselves safe. Relatively good reading skills are needed to complete the workbook, but it could be adapted and is designed to be worked through with an adult anyway. Scaling is used within the workbook to classify behaviours.

Harris, R. (2009) *Let's Talk about Sex! Changing Bodies, Growing Up, Sex and Sexual Health.* London: Walker Books.

This is a popular sex education book for typically developing children aged ten and over, which includes attractive colour illustrations on every page depicting a range of body shapes. It has a positive, upbeat tone and is recommended for both girls and boys with good language skills. The author has also written two other sex education books for younger children which are also recommended.

Hingsburger, D. (1995) *Just Say Know! Understanding and Reducing the Risk of Sexual Victimization of People with Developmental Disabilities.* Barrie, Ontario: Diverse City Press.

This thought-provoking, engaging and moving book should be required reading for anyone working with people with disabilities.

Hingsburger, D. (1998) *Hand Made Love: A Guide for Teaching Male Masturbation.* Barrie, Ontario: Diverse City Press.

Hingsburger, D. and Haar, S. (2003) *Finger Tips: A Guide for Teaching about Female Masturbation.* Barrie, Ontario: Diverse City Press.

Finger Tips and *Hand Made Love* are videos with accompanying 'photographic essays' to teach women and men with disabilities how to masturbate. The content is, naturally, sexually explicit and would need to be approved before use with children. Other books and DVD guides from Diverse City Press include *Under Cover Dick*, which teaches men with disabilities to use condoms (see www.diverse-city.com).

Holliday Willey, L. (2012) *Safety Skills for Asperger Women: How to Save a Perfectly Good Life.* London: Jessica Kingsley Publishers.

Liane Holliday Willey, an insightful author with AS, provided many of the quotes contained within this book. Her book includes information on the daily issues that women on the spectrum face and how to overcome them. Advice is given about staying safe when out and about, developing social skills and looking after your appearance. This book is recommended for older female teenagers and adults with AS to read, as well as parents and professionals looking for insights.

Jackson, L. (2002) *Freaks, Geeks and Asperger Syndrome: A User's Guide to Adolescence.* London: Jessica Kingsley Publishers.

Luke Jackson wrote this book when he was 13 years old. It is an easy-to-read and humorous book which contains information on friendship, dating and the importance of hygiene. Insights are also provided into special interests, bullying, sleep and school issues. Recommended for children and adults with ASD as well as parents or professionals looking for insights.

Koegel, L.K. and LeZebnik, C. (2009) *Growing Up on the Spectrum: A Guide to Life, Love and Learning for Teens Adults with Autism and Asperger's Syndrome.* New York, NY: Viking Adult.

This is a nice, easy-to-read book to recommend to parents as an introduction to this area. It is co-written by a parent and a professional, giving a good balance of perspectives. It also includes lots of practical, good quality advice and a good chapter on developing conversation skills. This book is geared more towards individuals with ASD who have good language skills – for example, giving information about transitioning to college.

National Guidelines Task Force: Sexuality Information and Education Council of the US (2004) 'Guidelines for comprehensive sexuality education – kindergarten through 12th grade.' (3rd edition.)
These guidelines are produced by SIECUS (the Sexuality Information and Education Council of the United States) and are available to download for free at: www2.gsu.edu/~wwwche/Sex%20 ed%20class/guidelines.pdf

They are designed to help educators create new sexuality education programmes and evaluate already existing curricula, and are one of the most influential publications in the field of sex education. Written specifically for typically developing children, the majority of the information is relevant for children with disabilities. Recommended for professionals.

Nichols, S. (2009) *Girls Growing Up on the Autism Spectrum: What Parents and Professionals Should Know about the Pre-teen and Teenage Years.* London: Jessica Kingsley Publishers.
This important book is a genuine must for any parent of, or professional working with, a girl on the spectrum. It is comprehensive, covers many topics related to girls that are neglected in other books and contains practical advice, up-to-date research and good resource recommendations.

Wrobel, M. (2003) *Taking Care of Myself: A Hygiene, Puberty and Personal Curriculum for Young People with Autism.* Arlington, TX: Future Horizons.
This practical book is essentially a collection of instructional stories related to hygiene and appropriate sexual behaviour. It provides some good examples of the use of visuals. However, parents and professionals should note that these instructional stories will most likely need to be adapted according to the particular language skills and needs of individual children.

www.autisticadvocacy.org
A powerful voice in the community, the Autistic Self Advocacy Network (the ASAN) is a non-profit organization run by and for people with ASD, whose motto is 'Nothing About Us Without Us'. The ASAN was created to provide support and services to individuals on the autism spectrum while working to educate communities and improve public perceptions of ASD.

www.visualaidsforlearning.com
This is an excellent website containing free-to-download colour visual supports and instructional stories. Recommended for parents and professionals. Contained in the website is an 'Adolescence Pack' of illustrations, including visual supports for topics such as wet dreams, menstruation and appropriate touching.

www.sexedlibrary.com
Aimed at professionals working with typically developing children, the Sex Education Library is a comprehensive resource also brought to you by SIECUS. It contains links to a wide range of sex education lesson plans, resources and curricula, which could be adapted for use with children with ASD.

www.autism.org.uk

This is the website of the National Autistic Society, a leading UK charity. The NAS consistently provides reliable, good quality information, services and support for parents, professionals and individuals with ASD. A good website to recommend to parents.

www.disabilityscoop.com

Founded in 2008, Disability Scoop is a news website covering only developmental disability news, offering a timely take on the issues that matter most to the developmental disability community. The site contains a specific section for 'Autism' news.

Index

Printed in Great Britain
by Amazon